The Class of '58 Writes a Book

A collection of original stories By the Class of 1958
Wheat Ridge High School — Wheat Ridge, Colorado

Edited by Don Shepperd

authorHOUSE®

AuthorHouse™
1663 Liberty Drive, Suite 200
Bloomington, IN 47403
www.authorhouse.com
Phone: 1-800-839-8640

First published by AuthorHouse 7/30/2008

ISBN: 978-1-4343-9727-0 (sc)
Library of Congress Control Number: 2008906284

Printed in the United States of America
Bloomington, Indiana

This book is printed on acid-free paper.

The Shepperd Group, Inc.
4087 E. Playa de Coronado
Tucson, AZ 85718-1530
shepdonald@aol.com

Other books by Don Shepperd

Misty – First person Stories of the Misty F-100 Fast FACs in the Vietnam War - ed. – 2002,
1stBooks, Bloomington IN

Bury Us Upside Down – the Misty Pilots and the Secret Battle for the Ho Chi Minh Trail
– with Rick Newman, foreword by Sen. John McCain – 2006, Ballantine Books, New
York, Presidio Press, a division of Random House, Inc. New York

For a CD containing original pictures of the authors in school and later life contact
shepdonald@aol.com

Dedication

Original stories - stories of schooldays and later in life

These are stories about growing up in the 1940s and 50s, written by class members in their late 60s. They are stories of our early years and stories from later in life. They are stories of things seen through our eyes and those of our friends. They are funny and they are sad. They are full of joy and glory, sadness and tragedy. They are our lives. The stories are published in the order received and alternate between men and women.

To our classmates, families, friends and teachers...

Thanks for getting us started and sharing our lives...it wasn't always easy...it wasn't always fun...but, it was always Wheat Ridge.

...the WRHS class of '58

Quotes

We were children who grew up in the 1940s and reached adulthood in the 1950s. They were wonderful times. As children we lay in our beds and dreamed of the joy, wonder and excitement to come in our lives...not realizing that we were already near them...

Life is what happens to us while we are waiting for fame, fortune, happiness and success...

We are all thousands of stories surrounded by friends and family

Stories are the way we vicariously participate in the secret lives of others...

...Don Shepperd, WRHS '58

In Memoriam

To our departed classmates who have "slipped the surly bonds of earth" – we hope you are "dancing the skies on laughter-silvered wings" above crystalline, snow-capped Colorado mountains.

Mary Albrighton Coonrod
Bill Bailey
Jack Beye
Carol Butler Cozier
Sue Engstrom Balston
Jim Ewart
Beth Fenwick Nolte
Daniel Fletcher
Sandra Gaither Clark
Donna Ghigliano Johnson
Larry Gregg
Linda Henderson Carlson
Eugene Hollenbaugh
Ed Kessinger
Kathie Krebs Gonzalez
Gaynel Long Nolte
Charles Lyons
Ed Mulling
Dick Norwood
Sharon Parson Hobbs
Don Payne
Jim Ryall
Katie Smith
William Perry Smith

Bill Stuerke
Pat Sullivan Williams
David Sutcliffe
Dr. Gary Taylor
Sue Wiltsie Fletcher

* words in quotes adapted from *High Flight by John Gillespie Magee*

Table of Contents

Introduction

When we moved to Wheat Ridge, Colorado, in 1949, it was little more than a farming community. I lived in the furthest north house in town. Well, it really wasn't a town. We weren't incorporated. In fact I'm not really sure what we were. We had an identity. Our high school nickname was, "the Farmers," but beyond that dubious distinction we had little going for us – little, that is, except the chance to grow up in a wonderful place at an interesting time in history – a time of transition; a time of innocence; a time of hope.

The 50's were an "in-between" generation. The 40's had their World War II. The early 50's had its Korea. We had…well, we had Elvis Presley and cars with long tail fins, Coors beer and clean air cooled by mountains to the west where we could escape for hunting, fishing and skiing. Denver was still a cow town. It was small enough, and yet big enough. It was our town.

We were the generation that grew up hiding under our school desks to avoid the nuclear flash. Our teachers helped us practice. We saw V-E Day and V-J Day with people dancing in the streets at the end of World War II, but at five years old it didn't mean much to us. We lived through the polio scares and later saw the vaccine virtually eliminate the dreaded disease. We saw Korea and the first hints that there were limitations to U.S. power. Although Elvis was King, we also saw the Beatles make their first appearance on Ed Sullivan, and our parents laughed and shook their heads in disgust at the long-haired coiffeurs we were later to adopt. We ate our dinners on TV trays in front of the television while our parents watched Lawrence Welk. We came before drugs. I often wonder how we would have handled the temptations to which modern kids are exposed. We also saw the first Sputnik orbit, an event that triggered the space race. We saw President Kennedy announce we would, "...go to the moon," and we did. Then, we saw him shot. We also saw his brother, Bobby, shot as well as, Martin Luther King. Our government sent us to the jungles of Vietnam to give our lives for meaningless hilltops. We lost our innocence there. We watched the nation come apart over Vietnam, and as we watched the last helicopter depart from the Saigon embassy roof, we realized we had lost the war. We witnessed the Freedom Marches and Sheriff Bull Connor's dogs attack brave black people over race relations. We saw Haight-Ashbury and Woodstock. We saw the first president resign from office. We watched the Berlin Wall go up, and then, come down. We watched the Gulf War, in fact two of them, and we saw the airliners impact the World Trade Center on 9-11. Indeed, our generation occupied an interesting time in history.

These stories are personal stories written by members of the class of 1958 Wheat Ridge High School, Wheat Ridge, Colorado. They are not intended to be a chronicle of events, nor a history. We hope they give the reader a flavor for the times. They would make a good TV series, like Fred Savage in *"The Wonder Years,"* or they could be read like Bailey White, or Baxter Black, on National Public Radio. These stories will be good for our grandchildren. Maybe it will give them a flavor of what it was like growing up in Wheat Ridge, Colorado in the 1940s and 50s – a wonderful place full of wonderful people - our families and friends.

*Editor's note
Any resemblance to any person, living or dead is purely intentional. These are real people and these things really did happen.

Hindu, Shep and the Fish
By Don Shepperd

We were sixteen. It was the summer before we were to enter our senior year of high school, and it was to be the fishing trip to end all fishing trips. We were to use Frank Fishman's (the Fish's) car, my fishing location on the Frying Pan River near Basalt, Colorado, and Bill Henderson's (the Hindu's) good looks and affable personality to get us beer. And so it was, as we set off on our high adventure in August of 1957.

Frank had an old, brown 1946 Chevrolet. Hindu said the car was simply a collection of random parts, but he thought it would get us there. We pooled our money, garnered from summer jobs, to buy gas and groceries. My mother signed on the dotted line to make reservations for us at the cabins at, "Bud and Ellen Williams' Resort" (a loose description meaning a collection of eight unimproved cabins with electricity, but no running water, an iron stove and communal toilets) near Thomasville on the upper Frying Pan River.

To get Ellen Williams to allow three teenage boys to stay alone in the cabins, my mother had to assure her we would not drink alcohol, would not make disturbances bothering the other guests and would not tear-up the cabin. We also had to promise my mother we would not do any of the above, which we did with honest and straight faces, and I'm sure we did not intend to do any of those things - at least for about 10 seconds – then, the planning to acquire beer began in earnest.

We tried to go about our alcohol search logically. That meant we first tried to bribe Doug Buffum, who worked in a drug store that sold liquor, to acquire booze for us on the black market. We found Doug was out of state on vacation. So, our backup was a straight-forward, honest approach – we would stop in Idaho Springs and lie about our age. A great debate occurred over who looked the oldest. We voted on Hindu, who strode into the first liquor store on the right side of the road in Idaho Springs, lowered his voice and demanded of the storekeeper, "Gimme' a case of Coors and a fifth of Hiram Walker."

"How old are you, son?" asked the old man running the store.

"Just turned 18," replied Hindu, lowering his voice even more, "And I sure do like that whiskey. Yessir. Now gimme' that stuff. I gotta be on my way. Lot's of fishing to be done, ya know?"

"How much do you drink?" asked the old man.

"Oh, I don't know, about a case and a quart a week," Hindu replied. "Yessir, startin to worry about my liver."

"Well, son. If you drink that much then you must know that at 18 you can't buy whiskey. And, if you were 18 you could only get 3.2 beer. So why don't you haul your little under-aged ass out of my store before I call the cops!"

Frank and I had moved to the other side of the store to listen to the dialogue. Upon hearing the threat to call the police, we all headed for the door. Watching three 16 year old boys try to squeeze through at the same time must have given the old man extra impetus because he yelled, "And I think I'll take your license plate number and call the State Poleece! You little punks better get the hell outta town, RIGHT NOW! YOU HEAR?" Frank put the car in gear, popped the clutch, and we laid rubber out of the parking lot in a cloud of dust as Hindu flipped the man the bird.

"Jesus Christ, Hindu! You're going to get us all put in jail. 'A case and a quart a week???...and worried about your liver???' Talk about overplaying your hand," Frank and I howled. "And then you flip him off? Good thinking - Smooth!"

"OK, well let's see you jerks get beer," retorted Hindu. "I thought I was pretty cool...at least until he said he was going to call the cops... then, I almost pooped my pants."

We debated "getting out of town" as instructed by the store owner, but the lure of illegal liquor was too strong. We passed another liquor store, did a quick 180-degree turn, almost rolling the heavily loaded vehicle, and decided the Fish would be number two on the firing line. "OK," Hindu and I instructed, "Now, Frank, your strength is sincerity. So, don't blow it. Go in there and fake sincerity! We'll be there to back you up…and no talk about your liver!"

Our plan was carefully constructed. We would all go in together. Hindu and I would pick up a big pile of snacks, while the Fish picked up the liquor. Then, we would all go to the counter and dump the entire cache on the counter in a big pile. It was certain that no reputable Idaho Springs liquor store would risk losing a big dollar sale by refusing to sell a paltry case of beer. If the salesperson asked for a driver's license, Frank was to claim he inadvertently left it at home. This strategy was a sure-fire winner, and we would be downing "brew-skis" shortly!

We entered the store bantering loudly about our fishing trip and party plans for the evening. We wanted to make it clear to the clerk that we were big spenders, who just might be back later in the evening. Hindu and I scooped up loads of potato chips, cheeses and crackers and dumped them by the cash register, while Frank hefted two cases of Coors onto the counter. The clerk barely looked at us and began to sort the snacks.

"Do you think we should get four cases now, or come back later this evening?" Frank questioned Hindu and me. He was playing his role perfectly.

"Naw, let's just do the two cases right now. We'll send the other guys to get more later today. And, I think we'll need at least two, maybe four more cases," Hindu emphasized, furrowing his brow in faked concern.

"Big party tonight, boys?" the clerk asked.

"Oh yes, big, very big," Hindu answered. "We're expecting about 30 people, but you never know, it could go to 50, maybe even reach 100, so stay stocked up for us, will you? I always hate to run short," Hindu was beginning to push it again.

The clerk began ring up the goods. "We are in!!!" I thought. "The Fish is my hero. Beer city, here we come!" I could already taste the cool Coors sliding down my throat.

"I have to ring this up separate," the clerk offered. We began to get nervous.

"Oh sure, no problem," Hindu replied. "We're used to that. We do a lot of partying. Go ahead, no problem. No sir, no problem at all."

As the clerk began to ring up the goods, I kicked Hindu's shin and whispered through pursed lips, "Shut up!"

"That will be $20.46," said the clerk.

"Yes! Oh yes!" I thought. "We did it!" We paid and began to pick up the goods

"Now, we have to ring up the beer," offered the clerk, "and I'll need some ID."

"Shit! Damn! Hate! – Busted!" I thought.

We climbed back into the car, three abject failures. Hindu grumbled, "That guy knew exactly what he was doing all along. He got our 20 bucks – He stole it!!! – knowing full well he had no intention of selling us booze. What a dishonest bastard! We ought to go to the police."

"Oh, great idea," offered the Fish. "Yeah, let's go to the cops and tell them we were trying to buy liquor illegally and the old bastard wouldn't sell it to us. That would be a great idea. He'd get a good citizen's award and we'd spend the night in jail. Yeah, let's pull right into the police station. You got good ideas, Hindu!" And, we continued on through town.

"Well, I guess it's my turn," I offered. "Let me try it alone. I work best on my own…and God knows your techniques haven't worked so far." Hindu and the Fish grumbled reluctant agreement.

We pulled into the last liquor store at the far end of town. I screwed up my courage and entered confidently through the door. The clerk, a large, rough-looking, bearded man, accosted me immediately. "What you want, Sonny?" he asked belligerently. I made an immediate mental note that this was not going well.

"Beer," I replied.

"Sonny boy, you don't look old enough to drive, much less buy beer. Get your skinny little ass outta' my store fore I kick it!!!" he threatened.

I strode rapidly back to the car, "Guess we drink cokes tonight, guys," I reported in failure. My whole attempt had taken less than 20 seconds. "I'd rather fish than drink anyway."

"What'd he say? What'd he say?" demanded Hindu and the Fish.

"Not much," I replied demurely.

"Come on. What'd he say? Tell us!" they probed.

"He said he was out of beer," I smirked.

"Out of beer?" demanded Hindu.

"Yeah, out of beer!" I laughed. "He said, if I could show him an ID he might be able to scrounge some from the back room."

"In your dreams, stud," replied Hindu. "He saw you were a skinny little wimp and threw you out just like me. Outta beer, my Scandinavian butt."

"I didn't want to drink tonight anyway," Frank offered. "Probably give us a hangover."

"Bullshit!" argued Hindu. "We just gotta figure out how to get us some beer, or this whole trip's gonna be wasted." Hindu continued to pout and plan as we proceeded west out of Idaho Springs, three complete failures.

Our next serious challenge was to get Frank's badly overloaded car past Loveland and Vail Passes, no small feat, and to make matters worse, it had to be done without beer. Knowing the condition of Frank's car, we carefully calculated the supplies required to make it over the mountains and back. We had a case of Quaker State motor oil and a 10-gallon jerry can of water. Oil and water were even more important than beer since Frank's car leaked oil from every seal and gasket, and a slight plume of gray smoke emitted from the exhaust. We had no backup plan. If the car crumped we were toast. We had no money to have the car towed and we had no tools to fix it. Frank had spent his last dollar getting the car to work, when he bought it. He said, when he first purchased it for $50, it seldom ran, and after he got it in shape, it seldom broke. So, we prayed and continued west.

At the foot of Loveland Pass we stopped to give the old car a rest. We let the engine cool for about 30 minutes, while we chunked rocks at chipmunks, and soaked our feet in the roadside stream. Then, we carefully screwed-off the radiator cap and poured most of the 10 gallons of jerry can water into the radiator and added two quarts of oil. We refilled the jerry can from the stream and noted we were only 70 miles from home. We had already consumed two of our twelve cans of oil with two passes yet to go and we had to cross the same two passes coming home. This was an omen that did not bode well for the trip. Since we had spent $20 on unnecessary snacks in our abortive attempt to buy beer, we had just enough money left to buy gas, at 25 cents a gallon, for the roundtrip. Of course we also maintained an inviolate cache of $4.25 savings, just on the outside chance we could find a case of beer. Although we bought staples (tomatoes, lettuce, bread, cheese, eggs, potatoes and butter) from home, it was essential for us to catch fish, or we would starve.

No problem," I assured the group. "In August you can't miss on the Frying Pan River. We'll roll in fish."

After an ample rest, and having been replenished, the old car started the tough, switchback climb across Loveland Pass. This was long before the Eisenhower Tunnel had even been considered. We passed the Loveland Ski Basin, and the car began to wheeze and buck, but we maintained steady progress up the mountain. At the crest of the pass we stopped to let the gallant old lady cool, while we marveled at the mountain panorama before us, added another quart of oil to the crankcase and chunked more rocks at chipmunks and marmots.

"I'm gonna be a fighter pilot some day," I said, "and I'm gonna get in an airplane come back to these mountains and buzz through these valleys at a thousand miles an hour. I can't wait to get up there flying." Little did I know how prophetic those words were. During the ensuing years, in one of the role reversals in life, I crossed the mountains many times in civilian and military airplanes and found myself "up there flying," wishing I was "down there fishing." I guess we always want what we don't have. That's what life and dreams are all about.

We continued west and topped Vail Pass without incident stopping several times to rest, oil and water the old car. The car seemed to gain strength and enthusiasm as we got closer to fishing country. She seemed as eager to make it as we were. At Eagle we stopped for gas and inquired about the condition of the dirt road through the back range, over Cottonwood Pass, to the Frying Pan.

"Don't think I'd try it in this old car," offered the gas station attendant, who appeared to be about 20 years old. "It's rained a couple of times in the last week, and you never know what the road condition is like. The state don't maintain it very good, cuz there ain't much traffic, and if you get stuck up there you might just be there for the winter."

"Hey, we're underage. Any place to get beer around here?" questioned Hindu.

"Naw, they're pretty tight around here," replied the attendant. "And, the Sheriff's pretty nasty if you get caught."

"Well, you look like you're 3.2 age," pressed Hindu. "How bout if we paid you to get us a case of Coors?"

"Naw, I'm a Mormon," replied the young man. "I don't do that stuff."

"So, you're a Mormon," continued Hindu. "No kidding? Do you know Jerry Jensen from Wheat Ridge? He's a Mormon."

The young attendant laughed. "Nope. Don't know him. There's a few million of us ya know."

Two more cans of oil went into the crankcase and we were on our way. We followed the attendant's advice and decided to drive on to Glenwood Springs rather than take the back road, then cut south towards the Frying Pan. Things were looking up, except for beer.

Back in the car Hindu grumbled, "Just our luck…a durned Mormon, who doesn't even know Jerry Jensen!"

Approaching Glenwood Springs, we stopped to swim in the hot springs mineral pool and let the car cool and rest. We swam back and forth between the cold and warm sections of the giant pool, reveling at the contrast. Hindu struck up a conversation with some young, good-looking girls, who appeared to be our age, and who were diving off the deep end board.

"Where ya from?" he questioned.

"Locals. We're Glenwoodies," the girls replied.

"Well, we're Wheatridgies. How'd you like to go fishing?" Hindu continued.

"Hey!" Frank objected. "We're here to fish, not chase women."

"Shut the hell up," Hindu whispered from the side of his mouth. "I know what I'm doin."

Hindu continued with the girls, "Seriously…we're going up on the Frying Pan to fish. Would you girls like to go? We could show you the time of your life complete with fresh-caught trout dinner, cooked by us!"

"This Hindu is one cocksman," I thought.

The girls giggled. "Well, sure. Will you bring us back this afternoon?"

"Hindu," I hissed. "We barely have enough gas money to get there and get back home. If we have to make a roundtrip with these girls, we won't be able to go back to fish."

"Stay with me," Hindu whispered. "I know what I'm doin. I've got a way with women."

"Well, Frank and I don't care about women this weekend," I argued. "We want to fish!"

I could see the girls giggling and discussing who would "go" with who. I had the distinct feeling the loser would get me if this ploy worked; however, from our standpoint there were no losers. The girls were all cute and had ample accoutrements.

"OK," Hindu continued, "Here's the deal - you girls get to go with us for a day of fishing and dinner. We supply the gas up the river and the fish. In return you have to go home and steal your old man's booze. You get the beer, OK? Oh, and by the way, when we bring you back, you have to fill up our tank with gas, so we can get back up-river."

Frank and I looked at each other incredulously. We were both thinking, "This guy has cojones the size of Dallas."

"EAT DIRT!!! YOU LOSER!!!" yelled the good-looking blonde leader of the group.

"Yeah, EAT DIRT!" I exclaimed less forcefully to Hindu. "Geez I really apologize, girls. He's had mental problems and we were just taking him out of the home for a weekend trying to get him some fresh air."

"Yeah, well he's crazy all right. You guys better get outta town or we'll go get some of our homegrown cowboys to kick your butts," snarled the blonde. "Go get a bum to buy your booze, city boys!"

Hindu's face brightened. "What a great idea. Never thought of it," he beamed. "Where do your bums hang out in this town?"

Frank and I literally dragged Hindu out of the water backwards. "I guess a kiss is out of the question?" he yelled at the girls, smacking his lips loudly.

"Hindu, you are a certified asshole!" charged Frank. "You are going to get us killed, or jailed, before this trip is over." Hindu was not only a certified asshole, he was a persistent one as well. We soon found ourselves cruising the downtown streets looking for bums to buy us beer.

"Quick, pull over! There's a bum!" exclaimed Hindu. Sure enough on the side of the street was a bearded old man with his head in his hands sitting on the curb just three doors down the street from a liquor store. At his feet was a paper sack with an empty wine bottle inside. "Bonanza!" smiled Hindu coyly. "Not just a bum, but a real live wino! We hit the mother lode!"

All three of us got out of the car and walked past the man, being careful not to appear as though we were staring at him. At the end of the block we turned around and proceeded back to the old derelict's side. "Excuse me, sir. Are you a wino?" questioned Frank.

"Jesus, Fish!" Hindu grabbed Frank's arm, pulled him back and spoke softly to the old man. "Sir, we were just wondering…if we gave you the money and bought you a bottle of wine…would you go buy us a case of beer?"

The old man's eyes brightened. "Sure, Sonny," he replied. "Glad to."

Hindu opened his wallet and picked out a crisp $10 bill. "Here you go, Sir," he smiled sweetly (Hindu had a cherubic face and a toothy smile). Get us a case of Coors, – real Coors, not that 3.2 junk! And get yourself a bottle of wine and keep the change," encouraged Hindu.

"You bet I will," said the old man. "Now you kids get outta sight in case the cops come by."

We all piled into the car and circled the block. We passed the liquor store window and peered inside. The store was fairly large, and we couldn't see all the way to the back of the store where the cash register appeared to be. Reaching the corner, we decided to open the trunk and leave it ajar, so that we could grab the case of beer, shove it quickly into the trunk and peel out for the Frying Pan. We circled the block again and pulled slowly by the store; still no sign of the old man. By the eighth circle of the block it should have been obvious to us that we were never going to see the old bum again. Not to be deterred, we pulled to a stop against the curb and Hindu raced into the store.

"Seen an old bum in here?" inquired Hindu.

"A what?"

"A bum…an old bum!" shouted Hindu. "The sonofabitch stole our money! We told him to come in here and buy us a case of Coors and a bottle of wine for himself and the bastard's disappeared!"

The clerk laughed a hearty laugh. "Well, if he comes in we'll be sure to tell him you're looking for him," he said.

Frank and I wanted to blame Hindu, but the harsh fact was, we all had a hand in this one. God had punished us for trying to take advantage of a poor old derelict and we were now destined to spend the rest of the trip without beer. The problem was we had blown $20 on snacks, and now $10 more, with nothing to show for it. The real question was – did we have enough money to get home? Frank pulled the car to the side of the road and took out his slide rule. It was a log-log, deci-trig, the latest model recommended by Mr. Marvin in advanced geometry class. Frank slipped the rule back and forth. "OK, guys. We got 13.1 miles to the gallon coming over here. It's been 230 miles. We have another 50 miles to go to Basalt and up the Frying Pan. Add another 50 miles for screwing around up and down the river fishing. Then, we got 230 plus 50, for 280 home, plus the 100 to Basalt and fishing. We're at higher altitude up here so we'll get less gas mileage. Let's assume we'll average 12 miles per gallon, so 380 divided by 12 is 31.66 gallons times 25 cents equals…(he slipped the rule expertly back and forth)…$7.92 cents for gas. Write that down, Shep, and don't let Hindu touch that pencil. He's already got us in enough trouble."

"Now wait a minute!" exclaimed Hindu. "If you guys would have just let me work on those girls a little longer before you dragged me off. I had em eatin out of the palm of my hand."

"Yeah right," the Fish came back, "I think I remember the exact words – EAT DIRT, LOSER! You just about had them eatin all right."

"Well how about you, Mr. Smooth?" Hindu shot back. "Excuse me, sir." he mocked, "Are you a wino? Holy crap you botched that one, Buddy."

"OK, guys," I jumped in to make peace. "Frank, keep calculating. What about oil?

"Well, we've used 5 quarts in 230 miles, so we're getting 46 miles per quart. If we assume 380 miles to get home, divided by 46 (the slide rule was now smoking), equals 8.26 more quarts we'll need. We have seven left, so we'll need to buy two more at 30 cents a quart. Now, let's assume the engine will work harder up here, so, let's add two more quarts for a buffer. Now, when I add all that up it looks like $1.20 for oil and $7.92 for gas. How much is that, Shep?"

"$9.12," I shot back.

"And add $4.25 for beer if we find a case," reminded Hindu.

"HINDU! Will you forget about beer! You've already got us in enough trouble, you," Frank hissed through clenched teeth.

'OK guys. Empty-out time. Let's empty the pockets and see how much we got left," I demanded. We emptied our pockets and wallets on the ground. Hindu had trouble getting his dollar bills out from under the four year old condom he always carried, "just in case." Our total was $32.12.

'Fat City!" exclaimed Hindu, "We got enough for three cases plus emergencies!"

We piled back into the car and headed towards Basalt and a weekend of fishing. At Basalt we tuned back east, up river. The road above Basalt was gravel at that time, after the first eight miles, and Ruedi Reservoir had not yet been built. I noted the water level was low, which meant the spring runoff was complete. That meant good trout fishing.

We passed the Thomasville store, which had a Budweiser sign in the window. Hindu smacked his lips. "Wonder if they have any bums up here?" he laughed. Now we all laughed. We were in the mountains and nearing our destination. The old car was pulling her load and things were looking up. We turned left into Bud and Ellen Williams' resort. The clear, rushing waters of the Frying Pan bubbled a symphony.

"LET THE FISHING BEGIN!" I shouted, and we got out of the car to stretch.

Ellen Williams came out of the house to show us to our cabin. Ellen showed us the toilet facilities, where to pump water and where to get firewood for the iron stove. Then she issued the rules. "OK, boys," she scowled. "Here's the rules: Don't wreck the cabin. Don't bother the other guests with loud noise and have fun – that's it. Any questions?"

"No, Ma'am," I replied.

"Oh yes," she continued, "And no drinking! If there's any drinking, Don, I'm calling your Mama and you boys are outta here! AND, I'm keeping your money! Do you understand?" It was clear Ellen had experience with teenage boys.

"Oh, my gosh, no Ma'am, no way," offered Hindu in mock horror. "No drinking from us. We're all Mormon."

"Mormon, huh? Don, I didn't know you were Mormon?" Ellen looked confused.

I glanced at Hindu in disgust. He always overplayed his hand. "Well, we have Mormon-like attitudes," I replied.

"Well, that'll be news to your mom and dad. Cause they sure leave a load of whiskey bottles when they come up. Whatever..." her voice trailed off. "But I mean it – No drinking!"

"Yessum." I replied obediently.

We watched Ellen until she was a good 100 yards from the cabin, then we broke into howls of laughter. "Mormon? MORMON?" roared Frank. "Jesus Christ, Hindu, you idiot!...Jack Mormon maybe? We got a half-Jew, a Methodist and a Scandahuvian amongst us and you pick Mormon! You are such a total jerk! You always push the envelope. Your diploma next year is going to read – William Henderson, Scandinavian Jerk in training."

The rest of the trip was fairly uneventful. We caught and cooked fish. We sat on the porch in the afternoon and counted deer on the hillside. We looked at the stars and constellations, and watched meteorites fall at night. We didn't use bad language, or tell dirty jokes, and we didn't say vulgar things about women, although Hindu had been to Scandinavia and did mention that Scandinavian hooters were bigger than American hooters. He offered no details, just smirked knowingly, and would not answer our questions. We didn't bother the neighbors with loud noises, although we came close – we had a farting contest in which Hindu took first in all three categories – loudest, longest and vilest. We talked of our futures. Hindu wanted to be a vet. Frank wasn't sure, but wanted to have something to do with math and science and maybe the space

13

program. I wanted to be a jet pilot. We did get one beer each from Bud Williams, Ellen's husband, who was a bit tipsy, when he did it, and told us not to tell Ellen (fat chance!). Frank's old car held up fine and wheezed all the way home, getting better gas mileage and using less oil than she did on the way over. We never saw the old bum again, and Hindu flipped-off the stores while the Fish honked the car horn as we passed through Idaho Springs on the way home. We returned to school and were off into life realizing some of our hopes and dreams, but retaining our memories of three good friends and a summer fishing trip forever

Where Have All the Young Men Gone?

By Don Shepperd

I had just attended my 40th high school reunion. During one of the receptions an old female friend asked me, "Whatever happened to all those Academy cadets you used to bring to your house? They were really a fun bunch of guys."

I was taken back by the question. I had forgotten those days – those marvelous, wonderful, carefree days of youth when the world was our oyster. I graduated from Wheat Ridge High School and immediately entered the Air Force. When I raised my right hand on the 27th of June 1958, to enter the Air Force Academy with the class of 1962, the fourth class to graduate from the Academy, I was 17 years old. Little did I know I was beginning a journey that would be filled with excitement and adventure beyond my wildest dreams. The Academy started at Lowry AFB in Denver while the permanent site was under construction north of Colorado Springs. My Academy class went through our fourth-class (freshman - "Doolie") summer at Lowry, then moved to Colorado Springs where we were the first class to go through four years at the new location.

I was a popular guy with my classmates, since I had access to two things that all cadets wanted most – transportation and the names and phone numbers of local women. We were not allowed to own cars until our senior year. So, my parents, and our house in Denver, became the transportation hub and local way-station for many in our class. During our freshman year, before classmates began to make local liaisons, I had parties after Academy football games, which were played at the old University of Denver stadium. During those parties many of my

15

classmates met my high school friends, who were remaining in the area to attend local colleges.

"Whatever happened to Ralph Ford and that guy you called Jimmy B?" my female friend asked, as though it were just yesterday. It was obvious she remembered them well. "Boy, that Ralph was one good-looking guy, and that Jim, whatever his name was…he was the funniest guy I ever met." A lump came into my throat and my eyes misted.

My memory wafted back towards our early flying years and the Vietnam War. Strains of Peter, Paul and Mary's anti-war songs rang faintly in my ears – "Where have all the young men gone, longtime passing…?"

The official Air Force blue car pulled into the driveway and three uniformed men got out and rang the doorbell… "Sir, Ma'am, I am sorry to inform you that your son, First Lieutenant Ralph Ford, was killed this afternoon in an aircraft accident in New Mexico." The uniformed men were talking to Ralph Ford's parents…it was the military way of informing families.

Ralph was one of the finest pilots in our class. He was a natural among a group of talented young men, all of whom had risen to the "top of the heap." They had competed to enter the Academy; while at the Academy, they had competed for pilot training slots; then, competed for fighter assignments and now pursued their dreams – flying jet fighters - and they were soon to enter combat in Vietnam. They were a hard-living, fun-filled bunch, and knowing they were soon going to war, they raised a lot of hell.

Ralph was raising hell the day he died. His wing, the 27th Fighter Wing at Canon AFB, NM, was under-going an Operational Readiness Inspection. Ralph had finished his low-level route assignment and dropped the bombs from his F-100 jet. He had some gas left and decided to fly over the farm on which his local girlfriend lived. As he flew over at extremely low-level and high speed, his girlfriend, a beautiful blonde girl, came out into the yard and waved. Ralph made three passes over the farm, doing low-level rolls on each pass. On the third roll, Ralph made a fatal mistake. He kept the back pressure on the stick in just a little too long, and Ralph Ford, one of the best pilots in our class, hit the ground at 500 knots and exploded on the farm (thus, the phrase "buying the farm" - the government pays for the damage) right in front of his girlfriend and her family.

"…and you asked about Jimmy B?"

"The President is sorry to inform you that your son, Captain James M. Brinkman III, has been killed in combat in Vietnam…" It was one of 58,222 such visits performed by military notification teams during the Vietnam War. The only difference between this and the other visits that took place is that Jimmy B was my dear friend – through the Academy, through fighter training at Luke AFB in Phoenix, through a tour in fighters at Hahn AFB, Germany and then on to Vietnam - Jimmy B, the irrepressible Jimmy B, with his devilish grin and cherubic face. I never thought Jimmy B would be killed. He was one of those enduring personalities that always survived. Through thick and thin, Jimmy B and his smile always came out OK – except for that fateful day, in a meeting with that fateful bullet, in that lousy, senseless war.

I heard of Jimmy B's death in the afternoon, when I returned from a mission over North Vietnam. My crew chief met the airplane and handed me a note from the Command Post – "You received a call from Bien Hoa. Your friend, Captain Brinkman, was killed on a mission this morning." I went to squadron operations, met the Intelligence Officer, debriefed my mission and headed for the bar. I downed three martinis in quick succession, and thought about my friend and the last time I saw his smiling face (I can still see his smiling face). Then, I turned to my flying buddies some of whom knew Jimmy B – "Here's a toast to one helluva fighter pilot," I offered. "Jimmy B 'bought it' (bought the farm) this morning out of Bien Hoa." There was a murmur:

"His flying days are over
His flying days are past

17

I hope they bury him upside down
So the world can kiss his ass!!!"

"To Jimmy B – a shit-hot guy!!!"
"To Jimmy B!" they all raised their glasses and voices in unison.

It was the only thing I could think of to say and it seemed appropriate at the time, and most of all, Jimmy B would have loved it and laughed heartily.

So - "Whatever happened to all those Academy cadets you used to bring to your house?" I could have told my friend all of these stories. I could have told her a hundred other stories. I could have told her how Ralph Ford was one of seven guys who rented a big house while we were at fighter training at Luke AFB, AZ, and how four of them were assigned to Canon AFB, NM, flying F-100s, and rented another big house, and how in a few months only one, Tucker McAtee, was still alive. I could have told her Jimmy B was on line 30, Panel 47E, on the Vietnam Memorial in Washington D.C. I could have told her that on the charter airplane that took me over to Vietnam on the 13th of October, 1967, I sat in the middle seat in row 13 and that my classmate, Jeff Hornaday, whom she also met at my house in 1958, sat on my left and was killed in an F-105 out of Korat, Thailand. The entire row behind me was killed. In my row I was the only survivor. The entire row in front of me survived, but one was a POW for almost seven ears. I could have told her the first classmate I met was Don Watson. We gave him a ride to Lowry and he and I reported in together. "D Wats," as we called him, was the first classmate killed in combat.

I didn't tell my friend these stories because she wouldn't understand. I simply said, "They're dead," and offered nothing else.

"Oh," she replied, and asked nothing else. Perhaps she could see the far-away look in my eye or sense the lump in my throat.

Lilt Across My Mind
By Robin Gilbert (Marie West)

Memories of Wheat Ridge lilt across my mind like the summer breezes of 1949, the year my parents and I moved there from Northwest Denver. I was nine years old and started the fourth grade, three blocks down High Court Street, at the elementary school.

The intersection at West 35th and High Court had a big bump on the west side. I walked home every day for a peanut butter and dill pickle sandwich lunch. It was my habit to cut the time close in getting back to school. I'd head out the door running and almost every single day, stub my toe on that bump, fall down and skin my knees. For one whole year in grade school I had scabs on both knees, until my co-ordination caught up with my growth spurt.

At my home on the east side of the driveway, was an area of green grass, big trees, and an irrigation ditch, which we called "The Blue Grass Pasture." My Dad installed a 10' tall swing and monkey bar made out of 4" pipe out in the pasture. Joreen Dowling, a girl from down the street, and I slept out in the pasture almost every night one summer between fifth and sixth grades. We lay on our sleeping bags, looking at the stars (you could see the stars then, because Wheat Ridge and Denver were much smaller and darker than now) and sang campfire and Girl Scout songs. Sometimes, we would get up in the middle of the night to swing or "skin-the-cat" on the monkey bar. Memories of that freedom and sweet abandon still make me smile.

On May Day in fourth and fifth grades, I wandered through several neighbors' yards on my way home from school to gather pretty spring flowers. Those were the days, when women did not usually work outside the home, and even though they observed me inappropriately entering their yards and picking their flowers, no one ever said a word. My actions were deliberate, delicate and innocent. I think my positive intentions were evident and those observing honored them. I took the flowers home and made a bouquet for my mother. The first year Mother let it pass because she didn't want to break my heart. But, the second year, when I persisted in picking flowers from the yards of others, Mother explained about cultural rules and manners. Yes, my heart was broken, and from then on, Mother's May Day baskets came from flowers in our yard. It was not nearly as meaningful, or fun, but I was growing up.

Gary Stites and his family had two quarter horses, Lady and Robin. Gary's family had a corral adjoining our pasture. We boarded their horses in exchange for them letting me ride.

I was a charter member of "The Westernaires Riding Club." We had a synchronized mounted drill team and rode in several performances of The National Western Stock Show each January. That is probably what gave me ideas for the Pep Club Drill Team in high school. I loved to sit with pencil and graph paper and figure out those complicated formations and maneuvers.

Back on the farm, Dean Reed, Gary Stites and I rode our horses bareback, playing "Cowboys and Indians" (remember, this was 1950-51 and the term "politically correct" had not yet been coined). There was wide open territory from 35th Street south to 32nd along a single dirt lane road called Teller Street, which ran through a swamp and up the hill on the other side. We rode hard, screaming and whooping, and invariably I would fall off, knocking myself out cold, when I hit the ground. It happened so many times, I think that's why I'm known as "hard-headed." Dean Reed became a famous singing star, gained notoriety in the Soviet Bloc, moved to East Germany, married that country's most famous movie actress, and drowned in a swimming accident. Gary Stites settled in Florida and also had, or has, a Country and Western music career.

Gypsy women, dressed in long black skirts with shawls over their heads and arms loaded with bracelets, walked slowly along some of the roadbeds, gathering dandelions. When I asked my mother, "...why...?" she always said they were making dandelion wine. I don't know if she knew that, or was just guessing. I never knew where the gypsies came from, or where they went, or what they did with their lives. Now, I wish I had talked to them. Their stories might have been another crack in my shell of naivete while growing up in Wheat Ridge.

Many Saturday afternoons in Junior High, found Pat DeWan, Jerry Williams, Jim Gilbert, and I walking east on 35th Avenue to Sheridan, then north to 38th to catch a bus. We were heading for the Federal Movie Theater. Prior to the main matinee feature, there were two, or three cowboy serials. The Lone Ranger and Tonto, Roy Rogers and Dale Evans, and Hopalong Cassidy were a few of the romanticized characters, who thrilled us. The main event may have been Esther Williams cutting gracefully through the water, then being catapulted into the air on top of a magnificent 30' high spraying fountain. Oh my, with this influence, who wouldn't be looking for a fairy tale life?

After the movie, the popcorn, the bus ride, and the walk to 35th and Sheridan, we looked west to see the tall locust tree, appearing to grow right in the middle of 35th Avenue. That tree was in my driveway, a mile and a half away. There were few other trees and buildings, and with no smog, that tree was visible for miles...and a landmark.

Traffic on W. 35th was sparse. I can't even guess how many times I walked, or rode my bike up and down that street. Lois Andrews, Devona Hubka, Marianne MacDonald, Pat DeWan, Elaine and Elinor Obialero, and many other friends lived east of me. Many times, when I was walking, an adult from the community would stop and offer me a ride. Whether I knew them, or not, I often took the ride. It was safe back then, and I never gave it a second thought.

When I was 16 years old and a brand spankin' new driver, I was heading west from Sheridan on 35th. At Benton Street a little boy came barreling through the stop sign, right in front of my car. My eyes were riveted on him and full of stark terror. I was so inexperienced as a driver, I was afraid to look from side to side, or swerve to miss him, for fear another car would be in the path. My right front bumper caught his rear wheel and flipped him off his bike. I stopped – ran to him – picked him up and carried him to the nearest house. The elderly woman (probably 50 years old), didn't want the blood to drip on her rug. I was outraged, but humble, since I was the one who had hit the boy. I tearfully and hysterically asked her to call the Police. This was long before 911. A great big ole teddy bear of a policeman, who hung around the school and whom we all knew, showed up. He examined the boy, took care of him, called his mother, and then came over to comfort me. With his big, gentle arms around me, he said everything would be all right and that the little boy only had a bloody nose. Thank God!!!!!

I remember a day of rain, lightning, and thunder. Woody (?) was riding his bike home from school, going south on Teller and approaching the slough. Lightning struck him...OR...was it a smaller child who was struck and Woody used his Boy Scout training in artificial respiration to save the child's life? Memory dims...it seemed so important then, and now I can't even remember the names, or who almost died.

About 11 A.M. on a Saturday, while still in high school, I was driving west on Colfax between Sheridan and Wadsworth. I was driving my parents' 1956 Ford station wagon and a girl friend was with me. We were in the center lane with a cement median on my side. I looked in the rear view mirror and saw a car weaving wildly behind us, closing fast. The next thing I knew, he had swerved between two cars, came up on our right side, hit us lightly broad-side, bounced off and sped past. It made me angry because I had to answer to my parents for the damage. I yelled, "HOLD ON! WE ARE GOING AFTER HIM!!!" It was a car load of men, bleary-eyed drunk, sort of sagging in the seats. I put the pedal-to-the-metal and chased them down Colfax – laying on the horn, and feeling exultant, about making a "citizen's arrest." Within about three blocks, the men turned into the parking lot of a motel. Fortunately for me, there was only one entrance - the same one used for exit. I pulled my parents' car in sideways, blocking the driveway. We jumped out, ran into the motel office and called the

Police. The men were so drunk, they just sat docilely in the car. The Police came and hauled them off to jail with a remark to me, "You can't get blood out of a turnip." I guess they were referring to the damage to the station wagon, which, by the way, was minimal. But, I was Marie West - Female Cop - Arresting Officer - Colfax Drunk Squad - and proud of it!

The times were very different then. At that time the odds were those men in the hit and run car did not have guns. If that were today, the odds are they would not only have guns, but possibly an arsenal. I'm so glad to have grown up in that less-populated, less-sophisticated, less-complicated society, even though we mistakenly believed in a lot of fairy tales.

Female Bonding – Outward Bound

By Robin Gilbert (Marie West)

Outward Bound and river rafting revealed themselves to me during the winter of 1979, at an Outdoor Sports and Recreation Show in Denver at the Convention Center. My two daughters, Tracy and Shanna, were 15 and 13 years old. I was a single mom at the time. I had a strong desire to live life "full-out," go for it and not allow my "singleness" to stop me from doing the things I wanted to do.

I signed the three of us up for a week of camping and rafting down the Green River, from the Gates of LaDore to Jansen, Utah, near Dinosaur National Monument. Shanna was 13 years old, but I told them she was 14 to meet the age requirement. The safety issue, for Shanna and others, was more important to me than the letter of the law. I have lived and taught my daughters the value of independent thinking. Sometimes the reason for a law or rule gets encumbered by the letter of the law. Some will not agree with me. That's O.K. We don't have to agree. We just need to think, and protect our precious freedom to be diverse. I explained my rationale to the girls. They cheered and thought they were up to meeting the challenges of skills, good health, and strength. They had been dedicated swimmers since their introductory lessons, when each was six months old. The great outdoors was their second home. Both had lots of experience camping, from the infant seat with mosquito netting over top, right up to the present. Through Girl Scouts, all three of us had become Red Cross certified life savers, canoers, and sailors. Despite such preparation and experience, it still seemed like a monumental adventure. I felt the responsibility of what we were doing to my core.

We departed our home in Arvada for our Cabin near Tabernash for a night of transition from civilization to the semi-primitive. That night we played C.W. McCall's record, "The Gates of LaDore," over and over, our excitement and anticipation levels rising with every repetition.

The next morning we headed down the back road in "Old Blue," our ¾ ton, 4-wheel drive Ford pick-up. I hadn't driven one mile, when we spied a couple of newborn Hereford calves. Of course, we had to stop and see them up close and personal. Was I stalling? Maybe.

Two hours later, heading west on U.S. 40 approaching Kremmling and going over a bridge, Old Blue got a flat tire. I admit to having a seizure of panic, but I had to remain semi-controlled for my daughters. We were required to meet the Outward Bound group on the river bank at a pre-arranged time that afternoon. I had two young girls with me. So, who hitch hikes and who stays with the truck? I explored out loud, every scenario I could think of. The girls and I brainstormed our options. We were in this all the way - TOGETHER!

Our decision was - the two girls would stay together with the truck. I would hitchhike for help! We thought the chances of one person getting picked up were greater than three. This was 1979 and I thought the girls would be safe. If it were today, I would not leave them, nor would I hitchhike.

Two good friends lived in Kremmling. "Marilyn" would probably be working at the hospital and "Darrell" could be anywhere. A rancher stopped and gave me a ride to the first filling station. I called our friends' home, and "no answer." Their house was only a few country blocks away, so I walked. Lady Luck was smiling on me. Darrell was outside working on one of his snowmobiles (an early version) and didn't hear the phone. He might not have answered it anyway, and I knew that.

Would he help us? "…Darn tootin!" We piled in his truck with tools and headed out of town. The girls and Old Blue were OK and waiting for us. Darrell put the spare tire on, followed us into town, got the original tire fixed and back on Old Blue, and wished us well as he went back to his snowmobile. I decided right then and there, if I were going to become self sufficient, I needed to practice changing a tire on the truck, but not until we got back home. I also bought a hydraulic jack, which I could operate and that would lift the weight of the truck.

We were on the road again. At Maybelle, CO. we turned north on dirt roads for 26 miles to the Green River at the head of the canyon and our rendezvous point. We were still early, even after our delay. Some of the folks were there. Immediately, all the kids jumped in the river, swimming, yelling and body surfing. A couple of the boys dove off the high cliffs into the river below - dangerous! They had no idea where the "sleeper rocks" were located under the water. The Outward Bound instructors brought that to a quick stop.

The group was composed of parents accompanying one, or two teenage kids. Some of the parents were married, having left their spouse at home, and others were single. There were six boys on the trip; Tracy and Shanna were the only girls. The kids made friends quickly by swimming, climbing, rafting, and horsing around together. The adults took a little longer to shed some of their protective layers.

There was a widow lady from Cincinnati, who had inherited a radio station, when her husband died. She dove into unknown waters and was running the station. Her son was a tall, blond, friendly "stringbean." Neither of them had ever done anything such as camping, or rafting. Our morning meditations were held on top of the biggest, tallest boulder in the vicinity. The widow was right up there, crowded on top of a rock with the rest of us. She was good natured and a good sport. I think the widow and I were both trying to be Mom and Dad to our kids.

One of the dads was a quiet, genteel man from Connecticut, who managed a Target store. He and his son were using this trip as a male bonding opportunity.

The only other mom on the trip was a southern belle from New Orleans. She had reluctantly dragged herself off the golf course and out of the country club, to make this sacrifice for her two sons. Their dad traveled a lot with his business. It became readily apparent these boys were not used to manual labor, co-operation or teamwork. On Outward Bound trips, everyone packs gear, cleans rafts, sets up and tears down camp, cooks, does dishes, paddles, and "captains." By the end of the week, the boys' self esteem had risen several notches and they were actually enjoying taking responsibility.

On this trip were eight teenagers, six parents, three instructors and three rafts. Each raft carried gear, supplies, and people. Packing and securing everything in the rafts, to prevent losing it if the raft takes on water, or wraps around a rock (rarely do they flip), is a real art involving lots of labor. The instructors were Heather, Coulter (Mountain Man), and a second guy whose name I cannot recall. They were competent, good teachers, patient, and FUN!

One night we were all sitting around the campfire on the sandy river beach, the evening meal having been eaten, dishes done, and gear put away. The temperature was divine, with a slight breeze and the sun slipped behind the canyon cliffs. Someone spied several Mountain Sheep way up on a high rocky ledge on the opposite side of the river. We watched them until it was too dark to see. Suddenly, we heard loud mutterings. Up the shore of the river, covered with bear skins and a raccoon hat, came a Mountain Man! He introduced himself, saying he was checking his trap lines. He joined us around the campfire and proceeded to tell us the "gol darnedest" tales I ever did hear. It was magical, and it was Coulter.

The section of Green River we rafted has many tributary streams. Typically, we would raft in the morning, stop for lunch, then hike before resuming our trek down river. Hiking up one clear, cold, fast-moving creek, we found a waterfall. It was early afternoon on a hot day. The sun was blazing, and a dip in that ice cold water was just what The Great Medicine Man ordered for some of us. One at a time, we gingerly waded into the water and ducked back behind the little 4' high waterfall. I sat in the hollow of the rock and watched mesmerized as the water fell 2' in front of my face, every tiny droplet sparkling with refracted light as the sun hit it. I leaned back and smiled - this was all pretty close to heaven for me.

Then, on up the trail a mile, we climbed some big boulders to the top of a huge rock outcropping. A tiny stream of water had been flowing over the top of this smooth, gigantic rock for thousands of years. The water eroded a trough a foot wide and six inches deep before flowing over the edge to a pool 30' below. Some of the group stood in the pool at the bottom; others on top, took turns sitting in the trough with our butts damming up the water. After 60 seconds, or so, the butt with person attached, would roll out of the trough, allowing a swell of the backed-up water to gush over the cliff, drenching the campers in the pool below. "Butt-Dam Falls" blessed us with our only showers of the week.

On another day, and on the other side of the river, we retraced the steps of the Anasazi Indians hundred of years ago. Lingering petroglyphs and pictographs in sandstone caves suggested the Indians had spent some time there. One large cave could have provided shelter from winter winds blowing in from the northwest. Another cave at the confluence of the Green and Yampa rivers, could have been a refuge for weary travelers. Who knows? It was all speculation, but fueled our imaginations and was confoundedly interesting.

The kids had no trouble bonding. Their high energy flared out in all directions, creating some hilarious, mischievous, and nerve wracking pranks. On a night close to the end of the week, one of Mother Nature's favorite little critters played a prank right behind the kids. Some of them had been assigned the task of making instant Jello pudding cheesecake for dessert the next day. The rest of the younger set wanted to help. One of them got the bright idea to stay up all night around the campfire. I'm not clear whether this was some kind of endurance feat, river ritual, or none of the above. I woke up about 4 a.m. and quietly, bare feet in the sand, padded in their direction to take a "peekaloo" (family word). The kids were all asleep, sprawled every which way, and "Mother Skunk" and her odoriferous little family were happily devouring the cheesecake.

The next day was dessert-less and quiet because the bleary-eyed campfire patrol could hardly stay awake. We parents made sure they got plenty drenched in the water fights that day - Parents' revenge!

Going through Brown's Canyon was lazy business. The solid rock walls were straight, steep, and high, while the river was slow and deep. Some of us jumped overboard, preferring body surfing for several miles over riding in the rafts. Floating down the river on my back, feet downstream, listening to and watching the cliff swallows was my idea of attunement to nature and luxuriating pleasure.

Around a few more bends in the river, and our trip was over. But, just like in high school, the experiences we shared will last a lifetime. To this day, Tracy, Shanna and I still refer to "Butt Dam Falls" and giggle - female bonding.

Spring Break – 1958
By Dennis Shields

Billy Epperson moved to Wheat Ridge in his sophomore year, when we were seniors. In spite of the fact that he was behind us in school, he soon began to run with the senior and junior crowd. He regaled us with wild tales of his previous home, New Orleans.

When spring break approached, three of us were ready to make a major leap and go to the "Big Easy." Bill Weiss, Dick Leebrick and I all schemed for ways to make it happen. Weiss drove a '54 Ford of dubious reliability, Leebrick's '50 Mercury was not much better, and I had a '53, cobalt blue Ford Victoria with a new engine, but it was lowered all the way around and slow as molasses. Surprisingly, my step-dad stepped up to the plate and suggested we compute the mileage, pay him in advance, and go to Louisiana in my mother's 1956 Nash Rambler station wagon, taking his credit card to insure we had funds for gas. The Rambler was brown and white, and had real naugahyde plastic upholstery, with little cowboys and Indians embossed into the fabric. The only car less cool would have been a Henry J.

We each saved or scrimped up $100, paid up front for the anticipated gas, packed the Rambler and were off. The car had recently been fitted with four recapped tires, purchased at a bargain price. We left Colorado in a snowstorm, and soon found ourselves driving across the vast wasteland of east Texas. Weiss searched the dial for acceptable music, and we took turns driving. Within a few hundred miles, we began blowing out the recaps with surprising regularity. As we lost each tire, we would stop at the next town and purchase a used tire with the credit card. We were soon running on a mixture of bald and patched tires, and blowouts, some at 80, or 90 miles per hour, became the order of the day.

As we proceeded south and east, Weiss found more and more music to his liking. In the small hours of the morning, he became agitated and excited, and when he turned the radio on full volume, we all heard, for the first time, Chuck Berry. Things were looking good and sounding good.

Driving straight through, we eventually crossed into Louisiana, and stopped at a Dairy Queen for some food. When we pulled into the lot, we saw two drinking fountains on the side of the building, one labeled "White" and the other "Colored." Leebrick immediately walked to the "Colored" fountain, took a long drink, looked at the locals and said, "Never had no colored water before." We ate up and left without incident.

In spite of our tires, we made it to the city, and found a hotel right at the edge of the French Quarter. It may have been called the St. Charles. We had a huge single room, walk up, with a balcony looking down on the street. Every morning, at 5:00 AM, the trash crew would pick up garbage right under our window, and Weiss would go to the balcony and carry on a conversation with them, in his recently developed version of the New Orleans patois.

We started each day at the Café du Monde, drinking chicory coffee and eating the fresh fried sugar covered pastry. The drinking age in New Orleans was 18. Both Weiss and Leebrick were legitimate, and I had a fake ID. As we cruised down the narrow streets of the Quarter, we were in heaven. Not only could we go into the clubs, the nice guys standing in front all but pushed us through the musty velvet curtains that hid the good life from the street. Whiskey sours were the order of the day, and we even bought some rot gut cheap whiskey to have back at the hotel, in case we got lucky. Wild women came up to us in the clubs and <u>WANTED</u> to sit with us. They all wanted a drink, which cost a lot more than our whiskey sours. We soon figured it out. Behind those velvet curtains there were floor shows, and we saw a mixture of women, from gorgeous to lamentable, twirl tassels and grind away to scratchy music. Pretty great stuff - Hey, remember, Eisenhower was still president, Elvis was cut off at the waist on the Sullivan show and Buddy Holly was still making music. We were livin'!

Weiss heard some music that he liked, and we ended up, one evening, in a club off Bourbon Street, where a young man took a real liking to the three of us. Naïve as we were, we eventually came to realize that his interest was, well, sort of unusual. We left. I still recall the song playing in that bar - "He's got the whole world in his hands…"

One day we walked into a garden, apparently private, and when someone started to chase us out, went through a door and found ourselves in the living part of a house. We said, "Hello," to the folks, cut through the house and safely made it back to Bourbon Street.

As we left a club one evening, Leebrick was in the lead. When we got out of the smoky atmosphere and back on the balmy street, Leebrick stretched, yawned, and looked back at the two of us and said "I could sure use a piece of …!" I think he meant chocolate, but no sooner had he uttered, "piece of…," when a cabbie drove around the corner and screeched to a halt. The rear door flew open and the driver said, "…Blonde, brunette or redhead?" A large New Orleans cop was standing on the corner and he ushered us into the cab, telling us, "Y'all have a nice time, ya hear?"

We went swimming in Lake Ponchartrain. We were having a great time until some of the locals shared with us the riveting tale of how shark attacks had recently killed several swimmers. Our water experience was mostly Berkley Lake and the Lakeside Plunge, so what the hell, we fled the water, in all likelihood screaming. Only several years later did I realize that fresh water shark attacks were really pretty rare.

Time and money were both gone, and we headed back to Colorado with less than two dollars between the three of us. Again the plan was to drive straight through. Around 3:00 AM, with Leebrick at the wheel, we saw flashing red lights behind us. We had been clocked at 82 miles per hour in a 15 zone, through the heart of New Boston, Texas. Justice delayed is justice denied; so, we were lucky that a Justice of the Peace just happened to be open for business, and trial was held at 4:00 AM. Leebrick was guilty; fined $15, with court costs of $16....Busted big time, and Dick in Jail.

Since this was long before ATM access to money, the judge suggested we might wait for morning, buy tires with the credit card and try to sell them to get Leebrick out. Hmmmmmm. Weiss and I were allowed to stay in the jailhouse and could visit Leebrick, where he was in solitary confinement, while the trustee, held on a murder charge, was out and about mopping floors. The next day we called my folks who wired the funds, and our odyssey continued without further drama. We rolled back to Colorado on bald tires but with lifelong memories.

The Sixties – Early To Middle
By Dennis Shields

ESTES PARK: The cop had my gun in his hand, and was talking to Sarah. I had ripped all the buttons off my white bartending shirt and was sitting on the little couch in the living room of the rented cottage. Big conversation between those two and I wasn't invited to join. Knew the cop. Had busted me for speeding a couple of years previous and was a decent guy. Used to come into the Horse when I was on duty. Decent. He kept the gun, and I never saw it again.

Same month, I was headed up to Estes from Lyons in the Olds. Had a cold and had been drinking Herbsaint all day at the Foothills. A '54 bottle-- 110 proof. Snow coming down speeding knew the road. Sliding. The fucking boulder was just there. People gathered around dark out woman yelling he's drunk and then red light flashing. Nat Lacey, park ranger no jurisdiction, friend hid the Olds and took me home to Sarah. Nat was killed a few years later in a freak accident in a campground.

Years earlier: Springtime party fake ID my friends Jerry, Donnard and Frank. At the Horse shots and beernostingers. Dawn in the mountains no glasses barefoot where the fuck am I. Wander wander see the road aha the cabin. Feetbleeding half blind up to the cabin Donnard "Jesus Christ, if I drank like you do I'd do something about my drinking." I was 18. Jail in Fort Collins.

BOULDER: Maxwell street Claydon there Sarah working New Years talk of sending me to a monastery. Leithoff had been over earlier and taken me out for a few beers, I'm sure he is fucking Shana. No money no booze maybe Jim will lend me a hundred. Earlier fight in kitchen between Dale and Roger, Roger definitely hitting on Sarah, scared of getting busted for awol. Dale later kills himself by drinking cyanide, but that was later.

Years earlier: Boys were down from Estes Gary Ray and Butch. Driving dead Dad's Dodge. Sink Tulagi Timber Tavern Gary "Let the dumb shit drive, he's too drunk to walk!!" Laughter loosely corner VW broken glass metal rending flee. Snuck the car back to Denver. Gary died in 1998, cancer. Don't see Butch or Ray anymore.

EL PASO: Sober sister sends for besotted brother Continental turbo prop wearing only suit but enough miniature VO's to make the flight. Nice lady from Nebraska fascinated by artist in waiting now landing suddenly running down runway flashing lights and voices of sister Fred and Lew. Who the fuck are these people? Ma Plinkett's rest home, IV and tranquilizer, Pa Plinkett is blind. Two days into it, the dt's set in. Spinning spiders. Scary spinning spiders up the chest. By the end of the week I am eating.

DENVER: Thanksgiving, 1967 jail pacing no glasses crowded who are these people what town am I in Brighton I think. Must be in for drunken driving but where is the new convertible let's see Holiday Inn on 25 talking to Shelly stingers holiday drink no trouble. Trouble. Five arresting officers car wrecked impounded out on OR 9 AM lets see $3.00 and some change there must be a bar open somewhere running ah there-- "Coors, please-- thanks." Money gone now call George miss thanksgiving dinner but full fifth of scotch at home.

Via Venice bad night drunken Judge fight with Kenny and the Judge in the kitchen. Blood all over the white tiles Kenny punches the fucker out, Get them out the back door, relax then Joe is there I passed out behind the bar blood all over my jacket. Sarah gone, Gloria gone Joe puts me in his Cadillac and I pass out. One night a mafia puke threw his holster at me while I was behind the bar. His holster.

Years earlier: Painting the house snuck suit down in back of Rambler Coors all day collect pay head for Colfax. Cowboy bar-- who the fuck are these people? Girl laughing cowboy yelling are you a communiss from Boulder?? Off the stool on the floor ribs broken driving the Rambler on unknown road see kiosk ask "Which way is Boulder?" Front of trench coat and face covered in blood. Toll taker freaks out.

DENVER, NEAR ZERO: New apartment unemployed hands shaking constantly. Wake up fine then who am I where am I how did I get here. Terror O my God. Shower 2 miniatures of vodka and a Coors puking washing till some stays down. Better have some coffee. Fell down the stairs sometime between Thursday and Sunday. Can't write, can't think. 127 pounds and pukes blood every morning. Alone alast along the riverrun, by bend of bay............

The author quit drinking on December 17th, 1968. He is now a mediocre tort/trial lawyer, drives a new Corvette and has a cat named Squid.

Then...
By Gale Newell (Gale Taylor)

I knew it wasn't right from the first day. How could I, the daughter of a teacher and granddaughter of a retired school principal, be in the "Bluebird" reading group? There were the "Cowbirds." I knew I didn't belong there. And, there were the "ROBINS". I knew I belonged there. That was my place. It took the teacher several days to realize it, and then I joined the other robins in their little circle of chairs.

I rode bikes with Gary Stites...to his house, and then, to mine. I really had the BIG crush. In the fourth grade, out in the annex, Miss Boland told us not to chew too loudly with our potato chips - she had headaches. We all loved her, so we did abide. I was not so happy on Valentines Day. I was used to getting Gary's biggest valentine. When the valentines got passed out of the beautiful silver and red crepe paper box, it was very public that the new girl had caught his fancy. Her name was Patti Glenski. She got the big Valentine you punch out of the front of the valentine book! I got one just like all the rest of the class.

I rode my bike to school until I couldn't stand the embarrassing clank of my metal lunch box against the handlebars. It finally got to me. I lived on Quay St. and it wasn't far. So, walking was okay, too. I walked to school behind my brother at his insistence. He said I was so tall people would mistake me for his girlfriend. Sometimes I walked home for lunch with Marilyn Randall who lived across the street. We were pals from the time we were toddlers. We marched around, arms straight and up in the air, yelling, "Heil Hitler!" until the neighbor asked us to quit. Marilyn's playhouse was a big part of my childhood. We tried to paint the inside once, mixing the oil based color with water to make it spread farther - my second lesson as an artist. The first came when Marilyn and I used crayons on the side of my white frame house. First mural! - Not appreciated. I cleaned it all off, alone; Dutch Cleanser and me. Marilyn probably scraped her paint off alone.

I moved to that house when I was two years old and lived in it until I was a Junior in High School. My father decided to see Seattle and Boeing as his new place. I said goodbye to Blue and Gold Day and the floats and Homecoming. Johnny Parker and I had our last date dancing at Elitch Gardens. He gave me a rhinestone necklace and earrings that I wish I still had. My folks didn't like each other, so they didn't like Seattle either. We moved back to Wheat Ridge, after my Junior year, and I got to remerge with the class of 1958 Farmers. We moved to a modern cul-de-sac on Allison Court. I had learned to adjust to a new school in south Seattle, Burien, after living thirteen years in one house. I hadn't had such an adjustment since the Obialeros, Gerry Heaston, Lois Andrews, Shirley Eroddy, and Beth Fenwick, all tall like me, had come from other junior highs to merge with us at WRHS. I had not had much competition before that. Now, these girls were as smart as me, or smarter. My place was shaky again. I needed to regain composure.

I was always working to find that comfort place in school, I was struck with, "What place is this?" when I received the DAR Good Citizenship Award, voted by my peers as the female good citizen of the class of 1958! None of you remember that? I do. And, I've periodically felt obligated to live it down. It was probably March, or April, when it happened. My mother winced, saying she'd prefer to not go to the luncheon held in the honor of the winners from Lakewood, Wheat Ridge, Golden, and Arvada high schools. I acted as though I didn't want to go either and told the counselor so. But, I got my lapel pin anyway. Only days after, I succumbed to the swirling smoke of my friends, all of whom smoked. Do they now? The Obialero twins, Elinor and Elaine, and Sharon Hinst and I, all sat around my kitchen table puffing away; them teaching me how to breathe in and out and look sophisticated. My father walked in the door, in full view of my lesson in non-good citizenship. He said, "Hi," walked cool-like through the house and left us to our burning embers. And, my burning ember had left my hand to burn a hole in the appliqued and embroidered tablecloth.

I never got the hang of smoking, nor liked it much, so smoking's one habit I haven't had to give up. In the 70s I did try again. One night, after putting my two sons to bed, I went outside the house and hid down by the garage and the garbage cans; practicing again, so I could be cool when a joint was being passed around at parties. It made it easier to go to a Led Zeppelin Concert.

I taught Art and Leadership in public schools for 30 years. I often felt hemmed in by institutionally made up parameters. And, when I got the chance with a student teacher colleague to make "Alice B. Toklas brownies," we whipped up a batch. Next day, we sat rebelliously in the faculty lounge washing them down with milk. We spent the rest of the day trying to function and carry on in the classroom - it was heavy. The paranoid good citizen, came to fore. The fun disappeared in minutes. This was definitely not my place!

In the back seat of Shirley Eroddy's car, I had many before and after school moments. All her passengers, including Judy Norman and me, were with her the day we hit a pole caving in the side of her car. Driving down 38th St. towards Wadsworth on another afternoon, Elvis came on the car radio. How Shirley drove, with all that excitement and squealing, and arms waving, was a wonder to me. I faked it on that one. I never really liked Elvis as much as everyone else did. He didn't reach me until, "Love Me Tender...," but I squealed anyway. I couldn't do the arm thing. I secretly had a cache of Nat King Cole records, 33s! and listened to them, when no one else was around to make fun of me..."They try to tell us we're too young...Too young to really be in love... They say that love's a word, a word we've only heard..." - ah, Wheat Ridge! Why did my mother say those were the best years of my life?

And Now...Finding My Place on the West Highland Way

By Gale Newell (Gale Taylor)

During the spring, after my 60th birthday, I spent two days and thirteen miles on Scotland's cross country walk, experiencing myself and "Campbell," my grandson. We traveled from Crainlarich, north of Glasgow, to Tyndrum where we bunked the first night. Then, we walked to the Bridge of Orchy on the second day. We climbed over stiles, walked through spring rain and wind gusts strong enough to tear the map from our hands. We navigated mud, boulders, and sometimes, a narrow path worn many inches into the terrain by the previous walkers. I was often breathless carrying my pack on the uphill climbs, while Campbell found the energy to toss stones into creeks and waterfalls and the frequent puddle.

The morning of the first day, on the hardest and most blustery section, I felt extremely anxious. I was always eager to know where we were going, I consulted the map often and felt relief, when a passerby would update us on our progress. My anxiety must have shown because Campbell would ask, "Where are we now, Gramma?" After pointing to a landmark, a farmer's fence or a stone bridge, he would then say, "Are you sure, Gramma?" Well, no, I was not sure. The map, passing comments and the occasional wooden post with a Scottish Thistle symbol were our only guides. At least, that's what I imagined on that first morning.

After nearly sharing our rainy lunch with an aggressive dog, we began to see the sun, more and more. The terrain became more level, and it was easier to cross. We saw baby lambs, black-faced sheep on the open trail, and giant mastodon-like Highland cows. We passed the ruins of St. Fillian's Priory, designated as a spiritual place by Robert the Bruce. We trudged up and over a rise. Spread before us was the epitome of the picturesque Scottish Highlands. A herd of wooly white sheep were being escorted by a pair of determined black and white border collies. It dawned on me, as if I was seeing the first light, that we were surrounded by such secure beauty, I had no reason for my nagging concern. Who cared where we were? I tallied, for my analytical need, the number of times we found the next signpost, just when we needed it, and the frequency of instances we met walkers with essential directions. Concern changed to security. I could feel my body shift and my face relax. And, it became a game to discover the next synchronistic delight. We were walking in the right place, "My Place," which was continually announcing itself. We sang and made up stories, and held hands when the path was wide enough. Although we'd done some of this earlier in the day, now I was celebrating a new comfort, not filling a need to reduce anxiety.

That evening, as we planned our return to the trail, I wondered out loud where the next signpost would appear telling us where to begin after breakfast. Campbell said, "I know, Gramma!" as he enjoyed a plate of "haggis, taters, and neeps" in the hotel restaurant. "I already spotted it, when we bought our sweeties and crisps for tomorrow." Our Place announced itself again in a five year old boy. Now the Grandson and the Gramma are planning to head South from Crainlarich before the summer ends. With a new map and a new direction, Campbell is saying, "Loch Loman, here we come!" And Gramma, remembering that "My Place" will always show up, is saying, "Gimme' that bug juice, Campbell Man."

Sixth Period American Bandstand
By Mike White

During our senior year, a number of us congregated at Terry Hagerman's house during sixth period to watch American Bandstand. This was made possible chiefly because Mr. "Flash" Holdeman, the physics teacher, was somewhat oblivious to what went on in his classroom.

The physics/chemistry room was arranged in such a way that all the desks were up front by the blackboards and demonstration table, while the three lab benches were lined up in the back of the room, which conveniently had both a front and back door. After "Flash" (not to be disrespectful, since I met him as a fellow student at the University of Colorado some years later and found him to be a really nice guy. But, when you're 18 and more interested in impressing your peers than your teachers, he is "Flash") took attendance, he would become so involved in his lectures that he didn't notice that each time he turned to write on the board, one more person would slip to the back row, then around behind the lab tables, then out the back door. By the end of the class he would be lucky if he had 5 or 6 students left, but he never noticed.

Sixth period was when a lot of the girls had cheerleading, or drill team practice, and that was very laxly supervised, so some of them would join us as we made our way to the parking lot, got our cars and headed off to Hagerman's house.

Terry's house was a safe haven because his mother worked as a waitress during the day and the house was empty. We were smart enough to park our cars down the block and around the corners, so that we didn't draw attention to ourselves. Thus, seemingly safe and snug, 10, 12, or 15 of us, would sit daily in the living room in front of the TV watching Fabian sing, "Turn Me Loose," smoke cigarettes and drink cokes.

One afternoon as we listened to Dick Clark introduce, "the next Elvis Presley!" someone looked out the front window and yelled, "IT'S HAYCRAFT!" Pulling up in front of the house and heading for the door was the Dean of Students, the dreaded Mr. Haycraft. Apparently he was on to us and had called Terry's mother and gotten permission to come into the house in search of the nasty truants.

Kids bolted over the couches and chairs and headed for the backdoor and out the back bedroom windows, through the back yard over fences and scattered to the four winds. When Haycraft entered to house, the blaring of Bandstand, smoldering ashtrays, spilled cokes and knocked over chairs were all he encountered…no students. He began nosing around the house and upon opening the hall closet door, encountered Tom Hoff and Cynthia Chaney cowering behind the coats. Nice try!

He had his quarry and hauled them off to be disciplined. They never squealed and I can't remember what their ultimate punishment was, but the administration began requiring that "Flash" take attendance at both the beginning and the end of his Physics class and American Bandstand was deprived of its Wheat Ridge teenage audience for the rest of the school year.

Expatriate Repatriation
By Mike White

Raising kids overseas is an ambiguous experience. Whether it is good, or bad for them, is a question to which I'm still not sure I know the answer.

In 1966, after getting a Masters Degree in Chinese History from C.U. and teaching three years at Bear Creek, Betty and I took our two kids, ages four and one, and left the known world for the mysterious Orient. I got a job teaching at Taipei American School in Taiwan. We still held WWII visions of the Far East as a place where Japanese soldiers threw babies in the air and caught them on their bayonets ... too many Saturday matinees at the Coronet, or the Oriental, watching John Wayne movies. We soon learned that life goes on elsewhere on a day to day basis, just with a different flavor, and an unfamiliarity that lends a bit of excitement to the routine.

The kids were spoiled by the attention of two full time "amahs," and Betty and I weren't opposed to having someone to take care of the basics, from cooking, to cleaning, to laundry. The amahs certainly contributed to our yearly decisions to extend our contracts, and that kept us there for seven years. We loved Taiwan and often, when visiting friends and parents in Wheat Ridge, we would get to the point where we couldn't wait to get "home."

Our kids got some exposure to the Vietnam War. Every Thanksgiving and Christmas, when we were in Taiwan, we went to the Seadragon Club, which was the R&R disbursement center and picked up a couple of kids, 18 or 19 year old "grunts," and brought them to the house for turkey and all the fixin's. They seemed to be grateful, but also wanted to get out into "the community" as soon as possible to spend their $500 on the things that R&R was really all about.

We had two especially interesting guests at separate times. The first was Vic Bird on an R&R from the jungle war. We were shocked, when an unexpected, but frequent, traditional "fire crackering" of a new house next door sent him diving to the floor for cover in our quiet little living room. We all went out to Taipei Air Station and drank all night and tried to dance the Texas 2 Step. Coincidentally both of us ended up in Texas, but I still can't do the Texas 2 Step, even when sober.

The second visitor was Don Shepperd who had flown into Tainan on the southern end of the island to have his plane serviced by Air Asia (a.k.a. Air America, a.k.a. CIA). Don said the domestic flight on China Airlines from Tainan to Taipei where we lived was as scary as any mission he flew in Vietnam avoiding AAA and "boxcar" sized Surface to Air Missiles. Don also kindly invited me and Betty to visit him at his airbase and "hootch" at Bien Hoa outside of Saigon. He assured us it was secure. We actually purchased our tickets and were excited about the upcoming Vietnam adventure, when Betty got cold feet. It seems she heard about a few rocket attacks in Saigon - it was called the Tet Offensive - Betty was always a lot smarter than Don and I.

Our youngest daughter, who was born in Taiwan, spent her first three years while we were at work, in the amah's quarters with Ah Ying and her children. When we came home from school, we could hear all the kids chattering away in Taiwanese, but we couldn't distinguish our daughter by sound. Today, she doesn't know a word of Taiwanese. I've often wondered what would happen under hypnosis? There's a great doctoral study for someone.

After leaving Taiwan and being so enamored with the Far East and oriental people and cultures, we spent the next two years in Singapore. By that time we had four kids, and once again they were taken care of by the amahs, who were now Malay, as opposed to Chinese, but no less devoted to the children.

When we moved from Singapore to take jobs in Isfahan Iran, we had become accustomed to a certain life style that was beyond what we could afford in the States. We were spoiled. Iran quickly brought us back to reality. Household help was expensive, unreliable and in some cases downright unpleasant. For the first time in nine years we found ourselves trying to handle all the standard duties of household and family maintenance in a culture that didn't provide the luxuries that most Americans take for granted - no dishwasher, or clothes dryer; no central heat, or air conditioning; no supermarket, or mall. During the winter I had to fill four heaters twice a day with "naft" (kerosene) that I pumped from a large drum out by our front gate, and then carried through the "barf" (snow) into the house. Daily, Betty would try to wash Levis for four school kids in a washer that had a two-pair jean capacity. Shopping was accomplished in bits and pieces at strange stores, which had odd combinations of wares. One store carried coal, eggs and cigarettes, while another might have vegetables and soft drinks. The only thing they had in common was that each storekeeper was dedicated to cheating each and every patron, foreigners and Irani alike.

Having been raised in the 40s and 50s with Ozzie and Harriet, June and Ward Cleaver, and Father Knows Best as examples, the entire work load of washing, cleaning, cooking, making beds, etc. fell to the woman of the house, who also happened to have a full time job as counselor's secretary in a high school of 600. The kids were given chores, but they had no experience in doing what amahs had always done for them and were quick to come up with the "pressing homework" excuse, when it was their turn to do the dishes, or take out the trash, or clean their rooms.

Such conditions can only be endured so long until something, or someone, cracks. Of course, it was Betty. I think the final straw occurred one evening, when Betty was about to cook dinner, and saw that the sink was piled with undone dishes. Each kid pointed a finger at the other, passing the blame. Betty disappeared into the bedroom in a rage, and no one ate again until the responsibility for all household chores had been delegated and commitments made.

One vivid memory is of our youngest daughter at age seven, standing on a step stool, doing the dishes during an Ayatollah-imposed nightly blackout with wax from the candles that provided the only illumination dripping into the dishwater. Out of necessity, our kids learned responsibility.

Our two oldest had spent all of their formative years in overseas settings, from July 1966 until February 1979. When we were evacuated from Iran at the height of the Revolution, we passed the Ayatollah in mid air. He landed in Teheran, February 1st, and we passed him on our way to Ankara, Shannon, and finally, New York.

I ended up getting a job in Princeton and began looking for a house, while Betty took the four kids and moved into the Fatzinger residence at 7301 West 44th Avenue. Our oldest son started Junior High in the old building on 38th where Betty and I attended high school, but our oldest daughter, who was in her junior year, had to attend Edgewater High School. Having lived most of her life internationally, she had nothing in common with the kids at the school. Edgewater was in a stagnant, no-growth area and lacked even the worldliness of the burgeoning suburban schools. Cliques were formed; everyone knew what experiences counted and what made one cool. Having visited the Taj Mahal the previous summer, certainly wasn't in the cool category; even mentioning it made one really uncool.

I was sitting alone in my rented room in New Jersey the night Betty called to tell me that Kim had quit school. I got Kim on the phone, intent on giving her my wise counsel and getting her to go back. The conversation ended on this note, "Honey, you should be able to fit in, you have gone to American schools all your life." She wept in reply, "Yes, Dad, but not in America!" She reentered high school, after we found a home in Princeton, but she had learned her lesson. It wasn't until she was a couple of years into college that she would even admit to her friends and classmates that she had lived overseas and experienced peoples and cultures that most others had only read, and perhaps dreamed about.

Now that our kids are much older, the oldest is 38 and the youngest 29, they have a different perspective on their international upbringing. Some of it was good and some of it wasn't, but then that's not much different from growing up in Wheat Ridge.

The Class of '58

Writes a Book

A collection of original stories by the Class of 1958
Wheat Ridge High School — Wheat Ridge, Colorado

Edited by

Don Shepperd

Our new book is just out - *The Class of '58 Writes a Book* - I put it together for our high school class 50th reunion which will be held in Wheat Ridge, Colorado in September 2008. We were the "Farmers" (gasp!) and the rules were - one story from school days and one from later in life - it is one of the darnedest collection of stories you'll ever read - the things that happen in life, some planned, some not; some hilarious, some tragic - and what happened to the authors after high school - you'll relate and enjoy.

The book is available on Amazon, but if you buy it, do me a favor and buy it from the publisher: www.authorhouse.com - call up "Book Store" and type in the title: *The Class of '58 Writes a Book* or call toll-free 1-888-280-7715 - same price, but the commission thru AuthorHouse is three times Amazon.

Also, I wanted to embed 107 photos, but it became technically challenging without the originals and very expensive based upon 2-300 predicted sales...so I decided to put the photos on a CD. Enjoy

Don Shepperd Cell 571-212-

Handling Touchy Subjects
By Lois Kropp (Lois Andrews)

The subject of enduring pain while growing up is not a new one. We all experience it in varying degrees. Growing up is a joy for some, a trial for others. Our early lives are a mixture of joy, sadness and discovery. I think God allowed it to be that way, and gives us the choice of how to respond, so we will have the opportunity to learn how to deal with it all later in life.

Our early times in Wheat Ridge were different from today. Today the TV is full of exposes and stories of war, violence of all kinds, murder, rape, divorce, abuse, homosexuality - all taboo subjects for radio, TV and newspapers in our day.

I have discovered a number of women about my age, definitely over the hill, maybe several hills, who remember nothing of their childhood. My memories of childhood incidents, feelings and relationships are dear to me. They invoke nostalgia and all kinds of emotions, and I have gone to great effort to resurrect some of those experiences and relationships. I want to better understand, and even wallow in those memories. Why, I ask myself, would someone not remember anything? Sometimes the answer may be - to avoid the memories and - PAIN.

During my 35 years in health care, seeing patients one on one in many different settings, but always where the talking and revealing came from the patient, I have heard many stories of painful childhoods, not the least of which involved unspeakable abuse...unspeakable in our times and for decades, until some brave women, such as Marilyn Van Derbur spoke out and gave many others her reasons and paths to heal, soothe and console. Of course, hers was only one source of pain in a childhood, but it was certainly the most unspeakable. And, it did occur in our childhood days, but remained hidden.

Oh, I had my painful moments throughout childhood too. Being 6' tall in a world composed of mostly shorter people wasn't easy. But, there were always shining stars like Devona Hubka and Marie West, who looked me in the eye and carried themselves with pride, beauty and grace. They were my height and gave me someone to emulate. I eventually learned to carry my 6' frame with pride, and now with 2" of it having disappeared somewhere, I wonder - am I a different person now? Does the absence of 2" change the essence of who I am? Does the presence of unspeakable pain, past or present, diminish the essence and the beauty of life for the woman and the child?

Dealing with pain is a universal problem of growing up and often a subject of reflection, but one way we were protected from "touchy subjects" in our day was "naivete." With today's daily flow of news, movies, interviews, talk shows and soaps, I don't think there is a naïve child left in America. But, a word that describes our childhood times well is - NAIVE! - big time naive!

My naiveté is nothing short of a joke to my kids. I am not sure I ever heard the word "homosexual" until I was well into my 20s. It was then I was gently told by my mother the cause of my cousin's suffering - it was "mental illness." In those days homosexuality was considered a mental illness, and my cousin suffered unspeakably. Somehow, it didn't burst my bubble - I remained naive.

Yes, homosexuality existed in our time, and so did "sexual abuse." I was appalled, confused, and mistaken at the time, in my interpretation of my father's one, or two outbursts about some men's "mistreatment" of their daughters. It never occurred to me until years later that he was speaking of "sexual" mistreatment - abuse. He was talking in code. That's what we did then with "touchy" subjects. His clumsy attempts to be kind and protective to a couple of my girlfriends in whom he recognized the signs and suffering by-passed me. He understood. I did not. My friends never talked to me about it, nor to my father, but he saw it. Years later, when my friends and I engaged in frank and honest adult discussions and they revealed what had happened to them within their own families, his insight became apparent. Such innocence and ignorance is probably not possible today, and that is a good thing.

That my parents were aware of the signs of sexual abuse in friends, even then, amazes me. They succeeded in protecting me, and that too is amazing. It was the culture of the times. Thank heavens things have changed - a little. At least now we can speak about such things. There is help available. There is acceptance, love, protection and prosecution available. Has the magnitude of abuse changed? Apparently not, and I feel a heavy heart, when I hear of the many abuses and indignities suffered by women in varied cultures around the world. Women have come a long way, but we still have a long way to go. The consciousness of the world seems to be moving in the right direction - towards greater good for all; towards knowledge, publicity of wrong-doing; towards prosecution of criminals; towards help for those affected. I pray it is so. We paint a picture of our times as simple and idyllic compared to today - simple, yes, idyllic, no. Like today, we had many terrible problems - we just didn't talk about them.

When Columbine happened, I took my son, then almost 30, with me to see the beginning of the huge memorial of flowers and stuff that was arriving at the park. A newscaster caught us; me crying and Russ in shock. The newsman asked Russ what he was thinking, and he said we all felt pain growing up, but this wasn't the way to express it, though he never found out just how to express it himself. Russ protects me too, never telling me of such anger. Hmmmmmmmm…touchy subject.

Final Project for Science of the Mind 11 – Lloyd Barrett, Instructor Karen

By Lois Kropp (Lois Andrews)

34 years ago, after having undergone the prodding, probing, poking and questioning required in those days to establish infertility, I was determined to get the doctor's signature required to be considered for adoption. I marched into the doctor's office, hopped up onto the receptionist's desk and smiled at the nurse behind the counter. We had become friendly during my many visits, and she returned my smile knowingly. She fetched the doctor, himself the adoptive father of three, and he, sensing the obvious - that I was immovable until he completed the required paperwork - retreated to do his job. Delivering the paper work, he informed me that I was one of his few failures - not conceiving under his care, and that he knew as soon as the adoption was consummated, I would find myself pregnant. Somehow, that was irrelevant. I knew I wanted to adopt a child. What ever else happened, was up to Someone Else.

Within days, the phone call came: "You may pick up your daughter today. She is a real cutie!!!" That was Oct 12, 1967. The bonding was instantaneous. She gazed into my eyes, seeing therein the depths of my soul and the love and commitment for her life and future wellbeing that was deep in my heart. Already, plans were being made as to where I would bide if the birth parents dared to change their minds. This child, this beautiful ski-jump-nosed, smiling redhead, would be my joy and the light of my life forever, and no legal hang-ups would change the destiny of our lives together.

In the following days and weeks comments and questions by the social worker from the adoption agency led me to believe that the giving-up of this child had been a painful process; that the birth family participation had been grievous and difficult, and that they were nearby; pictures were not to be displayed, and conversations amongst my friends and contacts should be kept to a minimum. Somehow, this alerted rather than frightened me; my intuition was the birth family must be close-by, supporting me. I remained curious as to their identity, but more in awe of the legacy of my child's natural inheritance. She was more beautiful in body and spirit than nurture had a right to claim. The nature of her was the object of my wonder and curiosity for all those years.

34 years later, my daughter and I are still close She is married with a daughter of her own, and events find her suddenly living in my house with her family while plans are made for a first home of their own. Only two days after their arrival, a phone call sent her reeling into a new set of relationships and feelings about which she had never bothered to think, or fantasize. Her birth mother wanted her to know of breast cancer in her birth family and had been looking for her for a long time. Suddenly, here she was, right where she was supposed to be - nearby.

My earlier intuition proved correct. She is the natural born child of the younger sister of a friend of mine from high school days; a beautiful woman with a "hole in her heart" who loved her child at birth enough to wish for her a full family and a better life than she felt confident to provide at the time. Watching and participating in the reunion has been a re-birthing experience for me. I am most grateful for the love of this woman, who not being ready for motherhood, gave me the joy and everlasting relationship for which every mother hopes. But, I am also grateful for her courage to come forward now, to let my daughter know that she was given in love, and remembered each day of her growing up with heartfelt longing and love. Now, my daughter has a new set of grandparents whose smile and nature are already familiar to her, and a new secondary family - brother, sister, niece and nephew, and on Easter Day new twin nephews for her and cousins for her daughter. Somehow, life seems richer for all of us. The true mother-daughter bond of 34 years can never disappear. Our bond is stronger now than ever. But, this new family knowledge and relationships make it all the more complete.

We are fortunate to have this rich and wonderful experience. Not all adoption circles end so happily. Life is good; all created by Goodness and Love. Expectation of good in all things brings new life experiences into joyous fulfillment.

Mister Hall
By Victor Bird

I wonder if anyone remembers poor Mr. Hall, who taught "Agriculture" during his first and last year of teaching? Mr. Hall had been a star Southeastern Conference track athlete at Rice University in Houston, Texas and majored in Geology. After graduation from college, he worked for several oil companies and finally ended up exploring for oil in the wild jungles of New Guinea (present day Irian Java) with the attendant head-hunters, disease, and complete lack of civilization. He had a wife and four children. I speculate these were conceived on home leave, since they didn't live in New Guinea with him, but I never met his wife and children. Maybe he married a native girl, but I am digressing. He said he left the jungles of New Guinea because of loneliness, desperation, and missing the bright lights of civilization. He felt that he might make a difference in this world by teaching in the bright lights of civilization at good old Wheat Ridge High.

I remember his first day in class. Norman Vieira (a burly football player and wrestler; a gentle soul who was forced to fight all those bad guys who picked on him), Dick Cook (a student aide to the Dean of Men, or so he claimed, since he was always in the office), Terry Hagerman Marcheso (famous for throwing his typewriter out of the window during Typing class and causing Miss X to quit, after 30 plus years of teaching), and I (a quiet, unassuming, non-opinionated student in quest of knowledge) sauntered into Mr. Hall's first floor classroom, having finally "graduated" from the basement classrooms the year before. I first noticed there were no girls in the class - "Oh, tarnation!" Second, the majority of my friends were there; and third, the class genius, Larry Keith Thomas (a close friend of all due to his brains) was present, having already assumed a desk in the front of the classroom prepared to take notes and raise the class average. We all took desks wherever we wished, fully anticipating the regular drill of being reseated in alphabetical order. But, it didn't happen. We looked at each other and instantly realized that we had freedom (SET MY PEOPLE FREE!) to do as we pleased and that we would be responsible for "breaking in a brand new teacher."

Mr. Hall came into the classroom with one of those old leather briefcases that looked like an overnight valise. He attempted to start by calling the class roll. Dick Cook immediately jumped up and took the paper from Mr. Hall's hand, telling him that he knew everyone in class and it would be an honor for him to take the daily roll and relieve Mr. Hall of this menial task. Mr. Hall was overwhelmed at Dick's kindness and proceeded to tell us the administration had not anticipated such a large class enrollment and he didn't have a sufficient number of books. After the "ah, schucks, and darns" subsided, he related that until we received the books, he would give us interesting lectures and have guest speakers and films, all about agriculture. He started to tell a little of his background as an introduction to the first lesson. He never got past the questions about New Guinea. We milked that one for the remainder of the week and at every other opportunity that presented itself. We were especially inquisitive about the bare-breasted savage women and wanted pictures!

We had frequent visitors to the classroom. Coach Schwartz burst into the classroom with neck veins pulsating at least twice a week. His History class was next door, and he felt we made too much noise. This often occurred, when we had extremely interesting lectures on such subjects as collecting and spreading manure. My fear, along with others, was that Coach Schwartz would collar us at practice and take revenge by demanding some type of extracurricular inhumane football drill to help us grow and become shining examples of student athletes. Fortunately for we Ag students, it never happened.

Mr. Haywood, the dreaded Dean of Men, made regular forays into the halls to catch the miserable, uncouth, uneducated student attempting to be in the halls without a pass, or purpose. He often visited our class. We wanted to be friendly, but it was always a one-way conversation with Mr. Haywood. He was a mild-mannered man, but often felt betrayed, and one day we had a glimpse of that madness that must eventually infect all school administrators. I'll give him one thing, his spewing, spitting and loquacious invective was done without one word of profanity - Admirable! We always felt his outbursts were conceived to help him in his quest to construct the perfectly quiet idyllic hallway at Wheat Ridge during class periods. Unfortunately, he failed. During our tenure at Wheat Ridge he never found Danny Hershberger, not even once. Danny constantly hid behind the statue of Abe Lincoln, when Mr. Haywood was afoot. Mr. Haywood never thought to look behind Honest Abe for a truant Danny. We all remember the day, when Danny jumped out from behind Abe and punched the lights out of the Geometry teacher, but I am digressing again. Other teachers would open the door to our classroom, view the chaos, shake their heads and walk away. The class members always felt these teachers were being very rude. We would gladly have said, "Hello," if any semblance of courtesy had been rendered.

The day we thought we would all be expelled was when Coach Hartzog, whose classroom was immediately below us in the basement, brought a stack of test papers that had somehow "fallen out of the window." Coach Hartzog taught Geography, and if he caught you talking, cheating, or doing anything other than memorizing capitals and countries, he made you do push-ups whether you were a boy, or girl - a women's libber ahead of his time! For the uninitiated, those were the days, when schools didn't have air conditioning. The windows were left open and the exceptional classroom had a fan. The drill was: if there was an assignment, or test, we would take Larry Thomas' paper and pass it around the classroom, so everyone could copy. Someone would make enough commotion to distract Mr. Hall. When he finished putting out that "fire," another student would start something else, and so on until everyone had a chance to copy what we needed. This often went on for twenty minutes. Mr. Hall never learned to collect papers at the end of the period. Dick Cook would make a big show of collecting the papers receiving the best of cooperation from all students. Once done, he would say, "I have collected all of the papers, Mr. Hall, and will put them in your in your box." Mr. Hall would nod, smile, compliment Dick and lament the fact that no one else was as courteous and helpful. As soon as Mr. Hall turned away, distracted by another classmate, Dick dropped the papers out of the window. When the bell rang, there would ensue a mad dash out of the classroom, and Mr. Hall was left to wonder where the papers were. The result of Mr. Hartzog finding the papers was Mr. Hall's instruction to Dick to be more vigilant, to watch the papers and to report immediately any one who messed with them. I would like to report that there were no more occurrences of missing papers; however, it is rumored some were dropped out of the window on a windy and blustery day.

The introduction of guest speakers always turned into a circus event. Mr. Hall went to great efforts to arrange these on our behalf. I don't know how the County Extension Agent tolerated being the target of spit balls, but we enjoyed it. What made it even more interesting is that he returned a couple of times, after his first experience - a courageous and dedicated public servant. Mr. Hall was livid at our conduct, and vowed never to have guest speakers again. It was a sad day. We liked having guest speakers at which to shoot spit balls, but we loved making Mr. Hall livid even more. He had light sandy hair and a fair complexion. When he got mad, it all turned one color . It was a fascinating phenomena and worth seeing time and again. Dick Cook always apologized for the class and told Mr. Hall he would beat the tar out of anyone who did it again. Dick carried a reputation as the most accurate, proficient spit-baller in the class. We would all agree with Dick and say how sorry we were. Mr. Hall would forgive us and tell Dick not to harm anyone.

Our Ag class provided the majority of training for Mr. Brockman's Audio-Visual class students. Mr. Brockman would send equipment from his class to be used by ours. Inevitably, the movie projector that had been set up would malfunction. All the boys would crowd around the projector to help fix the problem with each student giving his opinion of what was wrong. We would then start a fake argument, shove each other, and cause general mayhem. Of course, the object was to avoid seeing the film of the day. This went on for a couple of weeks until Mr. Brockman sent one of his Audio-Visual miscreants to run the projector. "Oh, tarnation!" again. None of us wanted to mess with Mr. Brockman. He was also the PE teacher, and we had visions of running laps for the complete PE period for the rest of our high school days.

Mr. Hall, as I look back on how rowdy and inconsiderate we were, even though at that time it seemed like fun, we apologize. You were one heckofa nice guy trying to improve our brains. We were unappreciative jerks. We could have learned a lot from you, especially about bare-breasted New Guinea women. Later in life, after I retired from the Army, I often thought of you as I taught Biology to junior high school students. From your class I learned the tricks of the trade - It took them five years to run me off.

Lieutenant – Vam Co Dong River Basin Long An Province, South Vietnam, 1966

By Victor Bird

The ground looked like a patchwork quilt of different hues and shades of green forming various geometric figures interwoven with muddy waterways bordered by brilliant green nipa palm. Scattered throughout the quilt were clusters of five to ten thatch roofed structures surrounded by exotic trees and vegetation. Occasionally there were circular craters filled with blue-green water, the results of a bombing missions, long past.

As the helicopter made large descending spirals, the pilot motioned for the lieutenant to put on a headset and the pilot turned on the intercom. "Get your gear squared away and ready. We will be landing soon. I'll ask the unit to throw a smoke grenade to mark and identify their position."

Over the intercom, the lieutenant could hear the radio conversation between the pilot and the unit on the ground. "Hairy Dog 40, this is Yellow Horse 41, over."

"Yellow Horse 41, this is Hairy Dog 40, over."

"Dog 40, this is Horse 41. We have a passenger for you. Throw smoke, over." A puff of yellow smoke, increasing in intensity appeared on the ground about a mile ahead of the helicopter. "Dog 40, this is Horse 41. Identify yellow smoke, over."

"Horse 41, this is Dog 40. That's affirmative, over."

As the helicopter came closer to the ground making it's final approach to the yellow smoke, tracers and small arms fire erupted in the air. As the lieutenant looked down, small holes appeared in the metal skin of the helicopter. Thumping sounds were heard. There was no place to hide.

"Horse 41! Horse 41! Landing zone is hot! Cannot guarantee your safety! I say again, landing zone is hot! Abort! Abort! Over!"

"Dog 40, this is Horse 41. On final approach. We're coming in."

The pilot motioned to the lieutenant again, saying over the intercom, "We'll do a touch and go landing. As soon as I touch down, jump out. The crew chief will throw your gear out. Unfasten your seat belt now. Good luck!"

As the helicopter touched down, the lieutenant leaped out, sprinted for the nearest rice paddy dike, and dove for the ground behind the dike, chambering a round into his carbine at the same time. "Welcome to Vietnam," he thought.

The flight from the United States was uneventful. It seemed odd to fly into a combat zone via a commercial aircraft complete with flight attendants and full service. What made it different was all of the customers were in military uniform. The normal noise one would expect from a passenger compartment was subdued. The passengers were either attempting to sleep, reading, or trying somehow to calm their anxieties of the unknown fate that was to befall them. With a short two hour layover in Hawaii during the middle of the night, the aircraft proceeded on and landed in the middle of the afternoon in Vietnam.

"All personnel assigned to United States Forces Vietnam, to the right! Officers and Noncommissioned Officers, to the buses! All other enlisted men and women, to the trucks! All personnel assigned to Military Assistance Command Vietnam, to the left. Load on the buses! Baggage will be delivered to you. Hurry! Load the vehicles!"

All of the first tour personnel dog-trotted to the vehicles with the objective of getting a preferred seat. The men who were returning to Vietnam walked cautiously, their eyes flitting from one object, or scene, to another to discover what was different, out of place, or what action they might have to take. The veterans walked on the balls of their feet, bodies tense, yet relaxed at the same time. Their body language was one of being poised and ready for action. They loaded the vehicles decisively and with the objective of getting off the aircraft parking apron quickly.

After a week's orientation, including a little language study, the assembly and disassembly of World War II weapons given to the Vietnamese forces that had not been in the United States inventory for over ten years, a list of no-no's to stay healthy and alive, and being issued a World War II .30 caliber M1 Carbine with thirty rounds of ammunition, the new "advisors" were given their field assignments and told to await transportation to their new unit.

An American sergeant appeared immediately after the firing stopped, waved and yelled, "Over here Lieutenant! Leave your personal gear. Some soldiers will bring it to us. The VC (Viet Cong) just wanted to welcome you to the area." A couple of Vietnamese soldiers ran for the gear and placed it in a small hooch.

"Welcome to the battalion, Lieutenant Bird. The Old Man is with his counterpart, the Battalion Commander. I'm Sergeant Ghoulson. We'll go directly to the hooch where we'll be staying tonight, and I'll try to fill you in on what you need to know."

The hooch was a ten square foot building with a packed dirt floor and made out of palm fronds. There were no window openings. Inside, mosquito nets were hung over sleeping gear lying on the floor with a homemade wooden table and five three-legged stools. Outside of the hooch was a large water barrel. Rain water was collected during the monsoon season and used during the dry season. The water was used for drinking and cooking. After lifting the lid, pushing away the mosquito larvae, dunking your canteen in to fill it , and adding water purification tablets, you were good to go the rest of the day.

The latrine was located outside the hooch with two poles extending over a pond. One would balance one foot on each pole. Privacy was guaranteed by palm fronds surrounding three sides, as the user squatted to do business. During the dry season, the farmers would net the fish that had been fertilized with human waste dropped into the pond and sell them as a cash crop at the market.

I often thought while I was in Vietnam that maybe I could one day teach high school and tell stories to the class like my old Agriculture teacher, Mr. Hall. Then, I would chuckle and think of the many good times we had in his class - someone putting some kind of ink on his head so that every time he rubbed his head the ink would smear and the spot would get bigger and bigger. He never did understand why the class was laughing at him, and my thoughts of teaching would drift off...and I would come back to the reality of Vietnam.

"Lieutenant, you and I will work together," said Sgt. Ghoulson. "When we are on combat operations, normal movement, or on any other thing where someone might get into trouble, we will go with the lead company and its lead platoon. Most of the time we will be right behind the point squad where we will be able to influence the action. We have only one 105mm artillery howitzer to support us. There are no U.S. ground forces anywhere in the area. When you call, 'Fire for effect!' expect no more than three rounds from the Vietnamese artillery unit. The guns are ones the U.S. turned in for salvage and they aren't too accurate. So, we depend on helicopter gunships and air strikes."

"The way we have been operating is, I carry the radio in the morning and you carry it in the afternoon, or vice versa, whichever is your preference. The Old Man, Sergeant Wilson, and the radio operator will be with the Battalion Command Group. We will be his eyes and ears and keep him informed of what's going on. It's time to eat. I'll get you introduced around at dinner."

I was taken to meet the Commander. Lunch and dinner were usually with the Vietnamese Battalion Commander and his staff, plus the American team. "Welcome Trung-uy (Lieutenant), to the battalion," said Dai-uy (Captain) Bey. "You have come at a very fortunate time. Tet (Chinese New Year) will start in a few days. We look at a new arrival at this time to bring us good fortune and much success. That's why the VC gave you a nice reception, when the helicopter arrived. I will introduce you to my staff at dinner. Let's take rice."

Food cost $30 per month. A typical meal was composed of sliced tomatoes, onions and lettuce (a big no-no according to my orientation in Saigon), pineapple soup with a large fish head, or chicken, or duck, cut up into thumb sized pieces (bone and all), and large containers of cooked rice. Sometimes we would have pork, but it was mostly the skin and fat with a minuscule piece of meat attached. No beef was available. One chicken would feed 12 people. Always, with every meal, came "nouc mam." Nouc mam was the juices of salted, rotted fish mixed with a few exotic spices. Nouc mam was used for flavoring everything - the universal Vietnamese Worcestershire sauce. Rice was always the main part of the meal. Other items were only there to augment the rice. One would fill his mouth with rice, using chop sticks, and stab a thumb-sized piece of chicken, duck, or fish, for a little flavor. About three bowls of rice did the job - in many ways.

After dinner, the sun began to set. The sky was spectacular with hues of gold, orange, and red just for a moment. I never tired of the beauty of the Vietnamese sunset, and this was often the time I thought of home and my family. And, suddenly, as if a dark curtain covered the sky, it was pitch black. This occurred night, after night. First, a brilliant sunset, followed immediately by total darkness. As soon as the darkness descended, the noise of the insects and other creatures began a loud cacophony. I thought the noise would never let me sleep and would mask any movement of the enemy. It was only later I discovered it was the silence at night that was dangerous. The silence meant that someone, or something, was out there.

"Lieutenant, wake up! We move out in 15 minutes. Get your gear squared away and saddle up. We will move with the lead company. I've got the radio." It was still dark, but the noise of men getting ready and joining their units was evident. The Vietnamese NCOs were giving orders fast, bringing order out of disorder, and in the process of becoming completely ready, when the order was given by their officers to start the tactical movement.

All of a sudden a tremendous blast occurred! One squad of men, crossing a bridge to secure the other side, was suddenly blown to bits by a homemade VC mine. The movement had not even begun, and we lost seven men to the enemy; ten others were wounded. I had my first taste of combat and my first opportunity to call in a helicopter medical evacuation.

We saw no other action that first day, and after a fifteen mile walk through the countryside, arrived at Can Guioc, the district headquarters, where we were to spend the next 30 days training, relaxing and allowing some of the soldiers to go home on leave and enjoy the Tet holiday season. We even slept in an old French villa that had no electricity, or water, but had tile floors, windows with glass and a real outhouse with a porcelain commode.

Our time had passed and it was time for one of our sister battalions to rotate into Can Guioc for some rest and relaxation. We started into what would become our daily routine. Before dawn we would move to our daytime position where we would patrol the area looking for the enemy. As soon as it got dark, we moved to our nighttime position where we would set up ambushes, hoping we could spring a trap on an unsuspecting enemy. We never slept in the same place twice and constantly roamed around in our assigned area looking for a fight, or if we got some hot intelligence of a massive enemy troop movement, hid.

It seemed when we moved in daytime, we couldn't go a mile without a sniper shooting at us. The first time, I hit the deck wondering why some SOB was shooting at me. After all, I really hadn't done anything to him, so why shoot at me? I decided quickly I wasn't doing any good laying behind a rice paddy dike and I couldn't do my job looking at the ground, so I began to ignore the sniper fire; they never hit anyone anyway. I began to think of myself as invulnerable, as though I would never get hurt.

Being American soldiers from the greatest Army in the world, we felt the responsibility to teach our Vietnamese counterparts the proper way to conduct combat operations. One night I convinced the lead company commander to make a stealthy move to a location distant from the rest of the battalion. We would move silently and set up a company sized ambush along a known infiltration route, kill a huge number of the enemy, and become legends in our own time. The main requirement was total silence. Packs and equipment was taped, so there was no possibility of noise. All had to understand the route, so there would be no talking. Everything was done exactly the way we learned in Ranger School at Fort Benning.

We were wading waist deep, single file across a rice field. There was enough ambient light to see the two men in front and the two men in back. A "swishing" noise was heard, then again the same sound. Barely heard, came a whisper, "Keep the noise down," in Vietnamese and English. Suddenly, an automatic weapon opened up shattering the stillness of the night. The column went into a defensive mode. Were we discovered? Were we being ambushed? What is going on? The talking, yelling, and noise sounded like the halls at Wheat Ridge High School, when we changed classes.

"It's me, Lieutenant. I fired my carbine," said one of the American NCO advisors.

"What in the hell happened? Don't you know you have blown the whole operation and everything we were trying to teach the Vietnamese?"

"Sir, I was going along and this large snake swam at me. I tried to move it away several times with the stock of my carbine but it kept coming back. I couldn't get rid of it. It was too big to grab, or crush its head with my rifle stock, so I had no other choice but to shoot it. I was afraid it was going to bite me."

My reputation as a steely-eyed combat trainer came into question that night. The Vietnamese soldiers fished the dead snake out of the water, and we ate it for dinner.

We received some hot intelligence one night that we were completely surrounded by three VC battalions. Our only choice was to hide. We set up in a rice mill where my new NCO, a fearless young man from the inner city of Chicago, assured me I could count on him to save us from being captured, or killed. I told him thanks but I could take care of myself. No light was to be used or shown. The night wore on. I fell asleep.

A horrendous, loud scream woke me up! It was my NCO. He was shining a flash light around the inside of the rice mill. I knew immediately we would be found and have a real fire fight on our hands, then finally killed.

"Turn off that light! What happened, Sarge? Don't you know you have given us away and we're probably about to be killed?"

He was shaking and said, "Sir, I am afraid of no one, or anything, except rats. And, one crawled across my chest when I laid down. When I was a kid in Chicago, the rats would bite sleeping children and disfigure them. My sister lost part of her nose and two of her fingers. I'm really sorry, but I just lost my cool."

The night passed, I thought about how my beautiful wife and baby daughter were going to survive, after my death, and I gave heartfelt thanks to my Maker when the dawn arrived. Checking in by radio, we found we had received the hot intelligence message in error. There were no hordes of VC. I asked around to see if anything unusual was heard during the night. No one heard anything, but they did say that they had caught some nice, fat rice paddy rats that were really good eating. I declined their invitation to that sumptuous meal. My sergeant's secret was safe forever. We never spoke of it again.

The only time I felt really successful was the night I got my Vietnamese counterpart to move to a new and better position. He had selected a clearing at the top of a small hill. The only hill in a four mile radius; the perfect spot to fire our mortars to calibrate their range; the perfect spot to use as a guide, when attacking at night; the only distinguishable landmark on the map, other than canals; the perfect spot to attack; in short, the worst possible position one could pick. All of my arguments fell on deaf ears.

He said, "Trung-uy, you sleep there and I will sleep here next to you. We have plenty of security and will get a good nights sleep."

Only one thing to do - spread out your poncho; make certain your weapon is loaded and functions properly; that everything you need is handy; lay down; cover yourself with your mosquito net; say your prayers, and be ready at the first crack of a bullet passing over your head to meet your Maker.

Again, a loud scream. "Trung-uy! We move!"

"What's wrong, why did you scream?"

"A little green snake crawled over my chest! Very poisonous, very dangerous!"

I knew the snake. We called it "the two-stepper." After being bitten, take two steps, sit down, die. It was the green bamboo viper about a foot to 18" long, one of the most poisonous snakes in the world. My reputation saved by a snake.

Somebody said it best, "Combat is days of boredom interrupted by moments of sheer terror." And, most of the time that was the case. Every day we awoke knowing that we may, or may not, look into the eye of the tiger. In other words, we knew we may, or may not, be engaged in mortal combat that day.

We traveled around a fifteen square mile area of operations, never sleeping in the same place twice and very seldom spending more than a few days in one place hunting the enemy. We were fairly successful in small unit fights and I honed my combat skills by using helicopter gunships, working with Air Force and Navy pilots, and occasionally having an artillery round fired. Out of all the fights I got into, I only had scratches from shrapnel, the hair parted on my arm, and bullet holes in my clothing. My feelings of invulnerability increased because I never got hurt - endangered, yes! Hurt no!

The only things I carried other than my combat gear was a shaving kit, paper to write letters, a poncho liner for sleeping, and a mosquito net. We got a change of clothes and a helmet full of water for bathing once a week. That's the only thing Mr. Shepperd, or Mr. Calvert, didn't teach me in Boy Scouts - how to get clean from head to toe, washing and rinsing, with only a helmet full of water - In Scouts I had learned to live without electricity, running water, or the other amenities of our American life, but cleaning with insufficient water was something I never learned.

My duffel bag with the rest of my clothing and personal stuff was stored at Regimental Headquarters. I saw my duffel bag twice in six months, the day I arrived and the day I left.

But, there were little things that made our life enjoyable, like going into a small village and buying a piece of ice that we could use to cool the warm Vietnamese beer that was preserved with formaldehyde. Or, a soldier climbing a coconut palm tree to get you a coconut. Or, watching your bodyguard get two men to argue and fight and if it wasn't fierce enough to jump in and beat both of them. Or, saying hello to "Rainbow," a soldier that had his front teeth capped in different colors. Or, someone sending you real American food and getting Ho Chi Minh's revenge for a week. Or, taking the stale, dry popcorn that would be used to protect the things sent from home and seeing the pleasure it gave the children as they ate the stale, dry stuff.

After a great deal of thought, I realized I only wanted three things in life. One, a nail to hang my hat on. Two, to be able to sit down rather than squat to do my business. Three, to be able to sleep in the same place every night. Home and family were beyond my ability to influence, or comprehend; they were too distant and too much of a dream. My life was at the level of basic survival.

To me the war was simple. The government messed with the people in the day, and the Communists messed with the people at night. If the people made up their mind which way to go, the war would be over in a day. Unfortunately, the Vietnamese people as a whole were very gentle and compassionate and just couldn't make that decision. All the Vietnamese farmer wanted was to be left alone to make enough money to get drunk and burn some kerosene oil in front of his ancestors shrine at Tet and raise his children.

Every so often the Vietnamese Regimental Commander would come up with a combat operation that by using all three battalions would rid the countryside of the VC once and for all. These normally were gigantic walks in the sun with nothing accomplished other than making the civilian populace miffed.

On one occasion, it looked like a good plan and we might accomplish something. The plan was to load two battalions on Vietnamese Navy river troop transports and make an amphibious river assault into a known VC stronghold that we were previously told to avoid because we would incur too many casualties. The other battalion would form a blocking position, and the two battalions would force the enemy into the block and hence defeat the bad guys so badly they could never recover.

I was with the lead platoon that disembarked from the first boat to hit the shore. Three hundred men were offloading behind the unit I was accompanying. I carried the radio and got separated from my sergeant. It was during the dry season, after the rice harvest and rice straw was scattered all over the fields. We were about three hundred yards from the river, when all of a sudden, the fields erupted on both sides of the friendly force with scathing gunfire. We had walked into a battalion- sized ambush!

The VC had dug foxholes and covered them with rice straw. We were in the killing zone. I ran forward. I looked behind to see who was with me. There was no one. The rest of the soldiers were running back to the river, some were trying to reach the boats that had offloaded them. I was all alone and an enemy machine gunner was firing at me. This I could handle, but it was a .50 caliber, or bigger, and the rounds cracked above my head and I couldn't tell where the bullets are coming from. I didn't know which way to turn, so I ran. I ran from corner to corner of the rice field with bullets chasing me all the way. It looked like an open field defensive football running drill where Coach Schwartz would move his hand back and forth and we would run backwards in the direction of his hand. I spotted a small mud house built on a rise that had been mostly destroyed. I ran to it for cover. As I lay there, the machine gunner crumbled the mud plaster layer above me, then crumbled the next layer, then the next layer. Two more inches and it was bye, bye Birdie. All of a sudden the gunfire stopped. My radio crackled, "Rainbow 5, this is 6. What is your status, over?"

"6, this is 5, I'm here alone about three or four hundred yards ahead of everyone else and there is a guy that doesn't like me and has me pinned down. It's kind of lonely out here."

"5, this is 6. Can you direct air or gunships?"

"Roger, 6. Get any immediate flight you can. If we can get a FAC (Forward Air Controller) to help us, ask him to come up on this frequency." Well, the day improved, after that. An Air Force FAC was in the area just waiting for something to happen to make his day. I quickly told him what was going on, where I needed help, and asked if he had anything available. Within minutes, the Air Force jocks had a field day dropping napalm, bombs, and rockets. The FAC and I took any airplane available and had a ball. When I called for immediate air support, every jet in the air came to where I was and dropped, or shot, everything they had. It was a great show and saved a lot of lives. It was also the first time I spent a couple of million dollars worth of Air Force ordnance assets to keep myself and my buddies alive. Eventually, the rest of the battalion joined me, I was alive, but had bullet holes in my fanny pack. My shaving cream burst making a mess, but I didn't have a scratch; another day with nothing to write home about.

We had 43 killed from the ambush and 57 killed from drowning. I don't remember the number that were wounded. We never found a dead VC, which wasn't unusual, since the VC always carried their dead away from the battlefield, so we wouldn't know how much we had hurt them. I know we got a few because napalm and burning flesh have a distinct odor, and the odor was there that day. Mr. Machinegunner, thanks for running out of ammunition, or deciding you wanted to live to fight another day.

Not long after that operation, we on another patrol and had just stopped for the day. My boss handed me his radio handset and said, "Major Harding wants to talk to you."

"Battle 6, this is Hotel 5, over."

"Bird, you are out of uniform and I want you to get squared away, over."

How did he know that? I was sitting with my shirt off, no boots or socks, and had pretty well gone native. He was 15 miles away. Besides, he must really be mad because he's not using proper communications techniques, his pet peeve.

"This is Hotel 5, roger, over". I made certain that I answered correctly. I didn't want him to get any angrier.

"Get with your boss and have him give you a set of Captain's bars and get in uniform! And, by the way, Captain Bird, congratulations. Battle 6, out."

This was a total impossibility. I had only been a First Lieutenant for 18 months, had only been in the Army four years. Everyone knew that you had to have at least 42 months in grade as a First Lieutenant and at least six-seven years in the Army to be even considered for Captain. But, I accepted the promotion. It meant I would earn about $500 a month. Not bad for a 26 year-old kid.

Being promoted also meant that I would have to move. The policy was six months total immersion with the Vietnamese and then six months where you could eat American food, speak English and become acculturated back into the American way of life.

About July of 1966, I moved to Duc Hoa, the home of the 25th Vietnamese Division. My three basic desires were met. In addition, I had a cot to sleep on, showers and clean uniform every day, roast beef and potatoes…and I started another six months of adventure. But, that's another story.

The Kid Who Didn't Fit – Pat's Story

By Pat Wilkinson (Pat Stephens)

About five years ago I was in Denver, and had the need to see where my life began. I went by the first home and the others that followed, seeing that they were not there anymore....torn down to make way for progress. Did they ever actually exist? Where had I really come from?

Has anyone noticed, when we reach our 50s and 60s, we have an overwhelming urge to "go back?" Does this mean we have reached the dreaded status of SENIOR CITIZEN? No Way! I laugh, when I describe someone in their 60s, or 70s, as being an "older person." I'm there, but that's NOT me. I will stay young - no "old" labels. Oh, yeah! Just keep the face cream, makeup and skinny clothes coming, say to hell with it and trudge along...slowly.

Senior Week 1958: We worked for twelve years to leave school, only to return daily and flaunt our superior status as seniors over the lowly underclassmen.

June 5, 1958: The day began rainy, gloomy and cold. This was Graduation Day, but was this an omen of our future? We had to go the Calvary Temple in Denver for the long awaited ceremony. The rain stopped. For me it was a day of great joy and anticipation until late afternoon. My sister, with whom I lived, ruined my dress. My brother-in-law called and said he couldn't make it. My parents, who were divorced, were not speaking. So, I cried and was a mess. Hopefully people thought these were tears of joy. It was not joy.

After the ceremony, everyone was going to Elitch's Gardens; the old Elitch's on Tennyson Street in west Denver. I could not get permission to go, and so began the reality of "adult" life. These tears would not be the last.

But, back to my beginning. I was born and raised in Denver. My parents divorced, when I was two, so I lived with foster parents until August 1956 in a seedy neighborhood.

When I was 15, I moved in with my sister and her family on Dover Street in a suburb called Wheat Ridge. What a change for me! - a beautiful home, city and real neighbors! I was in heaven. My next door neighbor was the one and only Elaine Sponsler. She was funny. She was her own person even then. She was my friend. I began my junior year at WRHS, September 1956. Scared isn't half of what I was feeling. I knew no one. Yes, I knew Elaine, but she wasn't in any of my classes, so I was on my own. Since my last name was Stephens, I was listed alphabetically by Bill Stuerke, Gary Stites, Dave Sutcliffe, etc. They became my friends. Dave, long gone, but fondly remembered, was my first date at Wheat Ridge for Homecoming 1956. I felt I had been accepted, but not so. Outsiders weren't accepted very readily. This carries on through life, but it was so hard, when I was only 15 years old.

November 1956: The great day came to go to Golden and get the "big D" - a DRIVER'S LICENSE! I passed it in a 1950 Buick sedan. I couldn't do it now - drive the big car and parallel park - no way.

My memories of the 11th and 12th grades are scattered and dim. I didn't really participate in anything! My single goal was to get out of school, get married and live happily ever after. That was the way our generation was "trained", by TV and even in church. So, I went hunting. Marriage meant security. Where was Women's Lib in 1958?

If this sounds sad and unhappy, not so. I had tears, but I also had fun. I have certain memories that will always be there and which have sustained me through tough times. I know this doesn't make sense, but I miss those days, and yet, I don't.

1956 wintertime: In the always alphabetically organized classes, my life changed - somehow, seats began to change and I got a steady boyfriend - Dick Brazzell. He had a 1950 maroon-colored convertible and I tied my scarf around his rear-view mirror - how romantic. Hey, I belonged! In the spring of 1957 we were driving up 44th Avenue, and a new voice came on the radio...his name was Johnny Mathis. I was hooked and still am. Life was good. Dick and I wore "steady shirts."

Then, Elaine Sponsler introduced me to the first true love of my life - a FOOTBALL PLAYER from Golden. I did the unthinkable and told Dick good-bye. Little did I know he would leave WRHS, the school he had attended for 12 years and go to Arvada. That was a shattering time. In 1999 we talked and wrote. He's happily married and he's still wonderful. I hope he has forgiven me. And, how did my first love turn out? Today, 43 years later, we are still the closest of friends. In January of '58 we became engaged for all of 3 days until my sister found the ring, took it away, and I was forbidden to see him. Heartbroken, I didn't give a damn about senior year, graduation, or anything else. My life was over. I tolerated the passing of time until I could graduate.

Thanks to Cliff Miercort, I had a date for the Prom. There were fun times at the church basement at 38th and Wadsworth on the weekends. Where are you Jack Oliver? You loved to dance! There was one episode of my wearing the Golden High School letter jacket to school. Needless to say, WRHS was offended. Bill Stuerke "threatened" that poor jacket. I never wore it to school again. I smoked my first cigarette outside the school with Janna Scherick. We were supposed to be at the basketball game, but we were "big girls", who could finish off a pack of Marlboros. I went home, "puked" all night and was accused of drinking! One Halloween a bunch of us sneaked into Crown Hill cemetery. We thought we were such devils!

I was kicked out (asked to leave sounds nicer) of our Senior English class, because Dave Sutcliffe and Dick English took over the class. It was funny, very funny, but the teacher became irate. I just laughed more, and more, and we were all very nicely sent to the Dean's office - it was worth it.

Bill Stuerke, (I miss you, Bill. I know you are in heaven with the good guys) was a dear friend. We only dated once right after graduation. Fake IDs in hand, off we went to Sam's on Lookout Mountain. We must have drunk more than we thought, because on the way home, we decided to awaken a Justice of the Peace in Golden and get married. The man was furious and sent us on our way. I next saw Bill in 1960 in Oceanside, CA. He was one of "the Few, the Proud, the Marines" - no more chubby baby fat - trim, fit, tan, manly - he was beautiful in uniform. I was a new mom washing diapers in a laundromat - small world and we talked for hours. We laughed. We were both glad the Justice of the Peace threw us out - Life.

Life Looks Up and Life Goes On – A New Kid No More

By Pat Wilkinson (Pat Stephens)

In 1958, when as a high school senior, I broke off my engagement at the insistence of my sister, I thought my life was over. I was wrong. In 1960 my life started over and things started looking up - I married the world's best man. Yes, he is one of the perfect ones; well, most of the time. We have just celebrated our 40th anniversary, so I did something right. We didn't and don't have wealth, but we have each other and have had a wonderful life - most of the time.

Early in September 1984 our phone rang...the unbearable had happened. Our oldest son, age 24, was gone, killed in a horrible accident. Our lives fell apart. Our love was tested. No one is prepared for this - the worst thing you can ever do is bury your child. We have another grown son, a daughter nearing 40 (ooh, how can this be?) and, BEAUTIFUL GRANDCHILDREN. Life goes on.

And so, to the class of 1958, my old buddies - we were the last class of the original school building. We had a song, "Graduation Day," by Johnny Mathis, I think. I hear it once in awhile and I remember our class. To the people who were my friends - with great fondness:

To Elaine Sponsler - you know you are a hoot, plus you were Miss Englewood Speedway Queen and one of the funniest people I know, but the worst double-date "fixer upper" I've ever met. You were great at finding me sneaky ways to see the guy from Golden. You taught me I could tell big white lies and get by with it. Shame on you!

To Dave Sutcliffe (God rest your soul) - thanks for asking me out on my first date. It was the first time I felt I belonged.

To Cliff Miercort - thanks for asking me to the Prom. I smiled inside.

To Janna Scherick - thanks for making me puke from smoking Marlboros - I knew cigarettes were bad for me.

To Dick English - thanks for taking over the English class. I'm still laughing about it. To the football player from Golden - I hope you are still running for touchdowns. You were a good guy.

To Dick Brazzell - you were special and still are. I'm glad I knew you. You gave me the courage to stay in a "new" school and I have never forgotten it.

To Bill Stuerke - may God hold you in the palm of his hand - Semper Fi.

To Don Shepperd - thank you for putting this Best Seller of a book together. It gave me a chance to write things I've thought about for years.

The last reunion I attended was our 10ᵗʰ reunion in 1968 - we were just kids. The boys were in Vietnam. The year 2000 seemed remote. We had so much life left to live and so much to get done. Now, as shadows appear on the western horizon, I am feeling the pull to go home; back to Colorado, after 20 years in Las Vegas. It's time for another life. Where did those 42 years go? Did we make a difference? I think we did. We were good kids. Keep it going class of 1958 - Wheat Ridge here I come! - a new kid no more!

I Coulda' Been Another Bob Cousy

By Doug Rhinehart

I am not sure at what point in my adolescence I mapped out my entire secondary education goals and objectives, but I had a solid plan that was pure in its simplicity. It was so clear it shone like a distant beacon on a winter night. In fact, it could be summed up in one word - BASKETBALL! For a few years, basketball flowed through my veins and out my pores. Basketball was the first sustained passion in my young life and I shamelessly and completely gave in to it.

As a teen-aged hormone factory, I also had a passion (OK, a lust) for girls and with my basketball plan I had that part all figured out too. By being a basketball star, I reasoned, the thing with girls would take care of itself. It was elementary. At WRHS in the mid-fifties the jocks had all the good looking, sexy girls; the kind of girls we used to drool over in study hall; the ones with the really tight sweaters with "kazooms" pushing out the stretched fabric like a couple of tent poles.

Basketball would solve many other looming teenage problems as well. My grades would be taken care of, because I would have to stay eligible in order to play. It would be a royal pain in the ass and would take away time from shooting baskets, but I was willing to make that sacrifice. Basketball would also solve the omnipresent problem of being popular. Once again, it was so simple and obvious - at WRHS the most popular guys were the jocks.

In my perfect teen world, I would have been a three-sport hero, but it didn't take me too long to recognize my shortcomings. Baseball was definitely out. I never had any pretensions, or even dreams, of being a baseball player. I was too damned scared of that hard, unforgiving ball screaming towards my pretty face. I loved football and I played it in 7th and 8th grades and my during my Freshman year, but I was a "shrimp." That was one of the nicer names the bigger guys called me. I found it wasn't a whole hell of a lot of fun getting squashed by guys bigger than me, and that was 99% of the team. Thankfully, others of diminutive stature, such as Vic Bird, Bill Henderson and Don Shepperd were also on the team and shared some of the pain.

I began playing basketball about the fourth, or fifth grade, and quickly fell in love with it. I found that I had pretty good shots and I spent hours working on them. When we moved to Wheat Ridge and our new house on Teller Street during the summer before seventh grade, I talked Dad into mounting a hoop and backboard on the roof above the attached garage. I immediately began shooting baskets, and like magic, it began to attract neighborhood kids my age. They would come riding slowly by on their bikes, and we would slyly check each other out. Finally, a tentative wave, or a mumbled, "Hi, howya' doin?" was ventured, and soon we were shooting baskets together. Thus, I began a very dear friendship with Carol Piper and Nancy Quante. Later that summer, they introduced me to some of their friends and their friends would shoot baskets with me. By the time school started, I had made quite a few friends. It seemed my plan was working!

My dad would get mad at me for playing so much basketball, because the ball hitting the backboard, or bouncing off the hoop, would reverberate through the house like a bass drum. But, I was not deterred. I had to work on my shots. And, did I ever work! I practiced endlessly on my jumper, set shot, and free throws! I practiced hour, after hour, day and night. When it started getting dark, I turned on the headlights of the car that I parked at the end of the driveway and put a table lamp, minus the shade, in the front window. I would practice hour, after sweaty hour, in the middle of the day throughout the summer. That pretty much killed one of my favorite alibis for not mowing the lawn, "Dad, it's too hot." When winter came, I shoveled the driveway free of snow, much to my dad's great astonishment, and continued shooting. I would shoot until my fingers cracked and bled.

I also worked long and hard on my "Bob Cousy behind-the-back-pass." Cousy passed the ball from the ball hand to the other hand behind the back without travelling. That may not seem like such a cool and spectacular move considering today's game where players from pros to snot-nosed kids are able to do indescribable things with a basketball. But, we're talking about the 50's, when a behind-the-back-pass was unheard of. Bob Cousy of the Celtics was the first player I saw do it. He was a guard and my plan was to also be a guard, so I just had to learn how to do it. It had no practical application, because if you were so stupid as to pull such a "hot dog" move on the floor in a real game, or even in practice, the coach would go apoplectic. If he didn't kick you off the team, he sure as hell would sit your smart ass down on the bench.

In junior high, the basketball program wasn't much. We didn't have games with other schools, so each homeroom would have its own team, and we would play each other. Just about every able-bodied boy in a homeroom was pressed into service. So, you could end up with some guys, who were pretty good with the basic skills, and others who dribbled the ball off their shoes and couldn't make a basket if the hoop was as big as a swimming pool. But, it was all we had, and we made the most of it. Besides, we got to wear UNIFORMS and play in front of our peers. It was a start. Each Friday afternoon, the whole school would go next door to the high school and everyone was forced to watch ten skinny, uncoordinated kids in ill-fitting and mismatched uniforms run up and down the floor desperately trying to score a basket.

I eagerly awaited high school where my plan was sure to come to fruition in spectacular fashion.

Freshman basketball could have been so good. It was a definite step up from junior high. We played regulation games with other schools. We had good looking uniforms, even though some of us unwittingly made an early fashion statement - we had very baggy pants. But, for me that was about the extent of what was good about Freshman basketball.

We had a coach who didn't know diddly squat about basketball. Coach Cooper was a hell of a nice guy. He never got mad and didn't rant and rave if you made a mistake, but, he was a track coach, not a basketball coach. In college he held some sort of world record in the pole vault, which he told us about repeatedly.

I think we practiced one, and only one, basic play, where the guard would pass the ball to the center, now called "the post". Both guards would then break around the center and he would either hand the ball to us and we would go in for a lay up, or he would take the shot, or he would pass to one of the forwards. Well, the other team didn't have to be a bunch of Larry Birds to figure out our complete offensive scheme, and we were soon pretty much finished for the game.

I felt I was doing pretty well. I had a good shot and with Coach Cooper's style of basketball, that's about all that was required. I wasn't a starter, but I was usually about the first off the bench, so I should have had plenty of playing time to improve my game and get a chance to move up to a starting position. However, Coach Cooper had no confidence in the subs, so he never sent any of us in unless the game was a total lost cause. So, the starters would pretty much play the entire game, then be totally wasted by the fourth quarter, and we would go down in flames yet again.

During my Sophomore year, I still felt fairly confident that I could make the Junior Varsity; however I noticed that some of my skills had fallen behind the guys who had started regularly on the Freshman team. Coach Proctor was the quintessential coach. He was tough, demanding, unforgiving, and took no nonsense. You lived in dread of his meltdown stare. Or even worse, you might pull a blunder that was so stupid it wasn't even worth his time to chew you out. He would just give you a quick, but devastating glance, before dealing with others who were not such complete morons.

I came to realize that my ball handling skills weren't as good as they could have been. I should have spent more time practicing my dribble and learning to dribble with both hands. But, I was confident that my shot would get me on the team. There would be two cuts, and whoever survived those would be the J. V. team. I had little doubt that I would survive the first cut. Those were the guys who considered basketball as a second, or third sport. They never really spent much time shooting baskets and rarely played in neighborhood games, because they weren't much good at it.

The first cut came one night, after practice. The coach announced that a sheet was posted in the locker room with the names of those who were still on the team. Even though I felt fairly confident, I still remember that huge burning grip in my stomach and the increased breathing as I crowded up to the list. My eyes quickly scanned the list, but I didn't find my name. "No problem. I just need to go down the list one more time, methodically." I did, and with the same result. "How could that be! There must be some mistake? There *has* to be a mistake! I'll look again!"

As I went through the list one more time, I was aware of the intense emotions of the guys in the locker room. Some were dejected and were telling a friend in mournful tones that they weren't on the list. Others were excitedly announcing to anyone and everyone that they had made it and were getting slaps on the back from others, who had also made the cut. As I slowly turned away from the list, I knew I was going to have to face my friends, and when they asked if I had made the team, I was going to have to find some way to tell them that I didn't. I was shaking, having a hard time swallowing, and my face felt like it was scorched. I wanted more than anything to be able to go unnoticed to my locker, get my clothes and get the hell out of that room!

To make it as difficult as possible, the first person I encountered as I headed for my locker, slapped me on the shoulder and with a big grin declared, "Hey, we made it, didn't we?" Somehow, I conveyed to him that I didn't. I don't know if he was just being a good friend and wanted me to feel better, but he told me that there must be some mistake. And then, he said, "Christ, you should have made the team before me!"

The word spread quickly and other friends came over to offer solace. I was burning with humiliation as I quickly dressed and left the locker room. Outside, it was dark and the air was crisp. I had a long walk home and I had time to go deeply into and through a variety of emotions. I became angry and furious at the coach. It was his stupidity; his oversight! "He obviously had it in for me! After all, my friends were adamant that I should have been on the team!" Then, I again became confident and knew that there was a mistake. "First thing tomorrow I will go to Coach and get it all cleared up." Then, I became incredulous. "How could this *possibly* have happened? I had it all planned out. All my plans were made." Now, what was I going to do? I took a deep breath full of the cool fall Colorado air. "My life is ruined, that's all there is to it."

And then, the tears started. "Christ, I don't want to cry! Don't I have enough shame already without crying like some girl who didn't make the cheer leading squad?" But, the tears came and rolled off my cheeks as I plodded toward home. It was a very, very long walk.

"Whatcha' Takin' a Pitcher of?"
By Doug Rhinehart

I was born and raised in the West and I love it with a passion. The landscape is a deep part of me, and I feel I am a part of it. Thus, it makes me sad to see change come - I know, don't tell me, "Change is inevitable," but that does not mean that I like, or welcome, all of the changes I see taking place. Thus, for my photography, I find I am drawn to the lonely, isolated places in the West where the vast landscape predominates, but a man-made remnant, or two, is left to symbolize our struggle for a foothold in such an unforgiving and relentless environment. Such places hold a silent and sad beauty, and they must be searched for, as they are not a part of the force-fed scenery one finds along the sterile corridors of an interstate.

Though my contacts with people in such out-of-the-way environs are few, some of the ones I have had, have been interesting, funny, enlightening, and even potentially dangerous. Many encounters begin with an observer's curiosity.

A few years ago I was pursuing a photographic series dealing with objects snagged on barbed-wire fences. Even though not much of significance came from the series, one encounter that I had with a local resident has remained as a memorable experience. On some desolate road in southeastern Colorado, I spotted a single old high-top sneaker hanging from the top strand of a roadside fence. I immediately stopped the car and got out my camera equipment. I set up my camera and tripod close to the shoe, and as I worked with the composition, I became engrossed in what I was seeing in the viewfinder. I was intrigued with the old shoe barely hanging by one shoestring to the barb. I wondered how and why it came to be there. I wondered how long it had been there and where the mate was.

After taking several frames, I picked up my equipment, turned to walk back to my car and noticed an old, dusty pickup slowly approaching and pulling to a stop on the other side of the road. I thought the two farmers inside, about as old and as worn as the truck, might own the land and were just checking on what I was doing.

The old guy who was driving slowly rolled his window down and very deliberately rested his arm on the door. He leaned out and methodically pushed the brim of a battered hat up on his forehead, revealing a bright band of untanned skin. I figured my best tactic was to be friendly and appear unthreatening. I gave them a smile and greeted the driver with, "Hi, how ya doin'?"

He stared at me for a few increasingly uneasy seconds, ignoring my greeting. "Whatcha' takin' a pitcher of?" he asked as slowly and deliberately as he had rolled down his window and adjusted his hat.

Ahh, yes…that oft-repeated question once again. I pointed and volunteered, "…That old tennis shoe hanging on the fence down there."

A few more seconds went by as he glanced at his buddy, and then continued studying me. His timing was as keen as any actor's. He likely did not know what a pregnant pause was, but he certainly had the technique down. "Ya wannit?" he drawled, as he turned again to his cab mate and they both chuckled.

My discomfort level rose considerably, but I figured I might as well laugh along with them. "No", I replied, "I'll just leave it there for the next crazy photographer." I felt some relief, when they laughed a bit at my reply. Hopefully, we were moving to a more friendly ground and any moment now they'd be asking me to go have a beer with them. But, the questioning continued.

"Where ya from?" I replied I was from Aspen, up in the mountains. I soon found myself starting to explain to those two old birds my aesthetic sense. I said that I liked photographing on the plains because of the play of space and light and that I found the distant horizon line was..."Well, I'll tell ya what. Wherever you're from, I'd suggest when ya git ta home that ya go see a doctor." Pause, eyes still locked on me and a smirk began as he lay on the clincher, "'Cause you're sick!"

Laughter erupted from inside the cab and my inquisitor rolled up the window, put the truck in gear and slowly pulled onto the road, leaving me standing there with God-only-knows what kind of a expression on my face. I watched the hats on their heads in the back window of the pickup bob up and down, back and forth, as I'm sure, they repeated the punch line several more times and slapped their knees harder with each telling.

As I put my equipment into the back of my car, I envisioned them heading down the road to the local "Mom's Cafe", just dying to tell their story to their friends and anyone else who would listen.

* Editor's Note:
The author is a world class western photographer who has displayed in many shows and galleries across America.

Small World

By Nancy Keyes (Nancy Winslow)

When I was growing up on 44th Avenue in Wheat Ridge, it was a small world.

The apple orchard stretched from our house to the neighbor's barn. Those neighbors, the Briggs, I didn't know very well because their kids were friends of my big sisters, who were eight and ten years older than I was. But, I do remember their dad pretty well, because the day I was trying to help my Mom do the wash and didn't let go of the sheet soon enough, it was Mr. Briggs who came with a crow bar and pried the wringer apart. We all marveled at how I had wrung my arm out clear up past the elbow and hadn't broken it.

The corn ran in rows from our house on 44th Avenue clear down to Clear Creek. There were big poplar trees down by the creek and more of the same big trees up in back of the Wheat Ridge Dairy past the grain silo and the barn and the cow pastures. My Dad watered our garden, the lawn, and the orchard from the irrigation ditch out front. It was great fun to get the neighbor kids, Jill Daniels, or her brother, or Sharon Baumert to sail stick boats on a perilous journey through the culverts and catch them on the other side.

Sometimes, I'd go to my Grandma's house which was diagonally across 44th, next to Steve Fairchild's house. She raised chickens and sold eggs and I loved to take my shoes off and run and jump from bin to bin of chicken feed. I guess it was the closest thing I knew to walking barefoot on a sandy beach. My Grandma didn't like it much, because it would mix up all the different kinds of feed, I guess. Anyway, whenever she caught me doing it, she would shoo me out. But, I did get to put little chicken rings on tiny baby chicken feet in the spring. That was a lot more fun than running away from chickens with their heads cut off, which I also did, since my sisters had me convinced that they were running after ME!

It was a small free world that I loved dearly: a few little houses, several big barns, lots of trees, the Dairy and my Grandma's.

Even by fourth grade, all that started to change. And, the changes came more quickly than a young Tom-boy, who was feared at the local elementary school, wanted. Track housing replaced corn fields. Lots of new "sissy kids" showed up at school, who did things like, "get married" during recess time. No more long lunch hours so I could go home and wrap celery. By sixth grade, my own Grandma and Grandpa subdivided, and the day the bulldozers came to clear out the orchard, the young Tom-boy hugged and kissed every one of her apple trees goodbye and cried, and cried. You see, she knew them all, had climbed them all, had spent hours in their arms reading books, telling stories, making animals out of clouds and hiding out. Only the soft spoken, whispery Miss Boland, who always wore an artificial rose in her dark hair, and whose own life it was rumored was tragically altered by the death of her fiancée in the war, seemed to care.

By the time high school days came, the class was more than ten times the size of Mrs. Wilson's first grade class. Some of that was because kids from two other schools had all become Wheat Ridge Farmers. Still, much of the increase was the result of those new houses, which had sprouted kids where the corn used to grow. But, even with more and more kids, Wheat Ridge remained a sheltered, naive and homogeneous world.

There were morning announcements on the PA system given by the new principal, Dr. "You Row Your Boat and I'll Romine": "Would the person who removed a typewriter from Mrs. Burman's class please return it? The following people are to report to 8th Period study hall: Owen Owen, Ron Simone, and Bob Southern. Class elections will be held on Friday following the Assembly."

Assemblies were something else. All four high school grades would file nosily into the then big, heavily blue-curtained auditorium. Frequently, the first part of an assembly, after the pledge of allegiance, of course, and announcements, would be enduring as Mr. Shelton's off-key band played really old songs. Still, the auditorium was a great place for passing notes, or rolling marbles down the slightly inclined floors. And, sometimes we would get to hear some really good singers from our own ranks perform. Gary Stites with his country and western songs was our class favorite, while Joan Cline who sang "You'll Never Walk Alone" was from the class ahead of us, and Dean Reed, class of '56, sang songs like "Company's A Comin'" with a real twang.

Dean Reed also worked at the Wheat Ridge Dairy, and whenever I'd wander across 44th to get a chocolate malt, I'd hang out and talk with him. He was a thin guy with a crew cut who was on the track team and once raced a donkey up Pike's Peak - a race I think he won. I remember thinking that caper was kind of bizarre, but outside of that, Dean seemed like a real "country boy". Somehow, maybe because he wasn't one of the football heroes, I always thought I was the only one in my class who knew Dean at all.

When Dean Reed reportedly "defected" to the Soviet Union, it not only made headlines in the local papers, but absolutely shocked everyone who heard about it. It was unclear how it happened. Rumor had it that Dean, after graduating, wasn't making it as a singer and drifted down to South America where he was married and was indoctrinated into communism which every one in Wheat Ridge spelled with a capital "C." "Defecting" in those days was REALLY a big deal and the mark of a traitor, which I suspect, sometimes rested heavily on him. However, Dean Reed did achieve fame and fortune there, and we shook our heads as we heard that he had become the Elvis Presley of the Soviet Union. He had, after all, been a part of our small, mostly innocent world. That world was filled with Blue and Gold Days, building floats in garages, or barns, football games followed by dances at "The Barn," which was really some kind of rec center. It was there that I first saw Phil Vieira do "the Bop" and someone else do "the Twist." After hearing that to learn the Twist, you should pretend you were drying your backside on a stationery towel, I went home and practiced for hours in the kitchen with the radio going full blast. My mother, as I recall, was less than happy about these sessions. Back at The Barn my girlfriends would get broken hearts and go sobbing into the restroom, or out to a car, when their boyfriends danced with someone else. It was there where my own high school boyfriend, Stan Nikkel, first asked me to dance, though it wasn't the Twist. For some reason, when I think of The Barn, I remember Linda Fitting always looking for Jim Snapp.

Of course, we had high school dances as well. The gym took hours to deck out with twisted crepe paper hanging from the hoops and across to the bleachers. One year, when "Cherry Pink and Apple Blossom White" was popular, the gym was all decorated in pink and white. Bands would play, and we would slow dance the night away, almost always ending with a rendition of "Blue Moon." And, each couple had "its" song. "Earth Angel" belonged to one couple, "Melody of Love" to another, and "Cherry Pink and Apple Blossom White" to Nancy Quante and Craig Lancaster. Even today, when I hear those songs, I immediately think of the people to whom they "belonged".

Signing yearbooks, writing endless notes, going to the Frosted Scotchman or Berry's drive-ins, putting people in trunks to sneak into drive-in movies, and occasionally ditching school were all part of the scene in those days. Since I was too tall for most trunks, I was spared. But, I definitely remember shutting the lid on Bonnie Harris. Besides that, there were parents who didn't want their kids dating and many's the time that four, or five of us, hid Dick English down on the floor of the backseat so "the girls" could pick up Pat Glenski. Some of the guys actually owned cars, but most of the girls I knew had to borrow their parents'. Bill Henderson's cars, like many others, were constantly breaking down. I remember driving up Wadsworth with my hand on the floor on some small button feeding the car gas while he steered, after his gas pedal had fallen off. Another time, he called about three in the morning, and my not too happy Dad and I went almost to Golden to pick him up, after a couple of wheels had fallen off his Nash Rambler.

Graduation was a sad time for me. I was very uncertain of the future and knew that a group of close friends would go separate ways. However, the day itself proved unexpectedly funny, when the diplomas were passed out, and mine was BLANK! I started passing it up and down the rows, and those seated next to me were all laughing it up. Seems I had forgotten to pay a "library fine" of some 36 cents!!!

Fast forward (not a term we would have known in 1958!) to May 1995. I am in a country called Kyrgyzstan . It is one of the new countries which have come into being as a result of the collapse of the Soviet Union. When I am asked to go there to teach English for a U.S. AID project, I have to buy a new map to figure out where I am going. Turns out that this country is in Central Asia bordering China and many other "stan" lands. Biskek is the capital city where I will be living. Trying to get a handle on what this place is going to be like, I call a friend from Wheat Ridge days who is at the Pentagon and who I figure can get me some information. A few days later, thanks to Don Shepperd, a lieutenant calls and tells me all about Kyrgyzstan. When I ask him if there is any place in the U.S. that might be like Biskek, he says, "Have you ever been to Denver, Colorado?"

Biskek is exotic and fascinating, and like Denver, is situated on a plain snuggled up next to the Tien Shen mountains. Soviet-built, western European style opera houses on one block contrast sharply with the street vendors' rounded woolen yurts on the next block. Men wear white triangular felt hats with black tassels and black designs. They can and do sit for hours in the Asian squatting position, sometimes playing chess, or having a cigarette in their western suits. It is a small city with many government buildings where in 1995 the statues of Lenin still stand. An outdoor market for food contains women in babushkas hawking homegrown strawberries, onions, carrots and potatoes. A vendor with a leafy branch from a nearby tree swats flies congregating on the hanging sides of lamb and horse. One booth sells frozen "Bush's legs" - those are drumsticks imported from the U.S. under one of our aid programs. I feel a very long way from home.

The people are mostly Asian, though some Russians have remained despite independence. My classes are made up of engineers from the Kyrgyzstan Energy Company. We meet eight hours a day and have lunch together in the cafeteria. Out of the twenty five, I have only a handful of women and only two Russian men, both of whom are named, Sergei. They have asked for English classes in order to prepare them for the team of American engineers who will be coming in our wake to help them privatize. Because their English skills are generally weak, or non-existent, my co-teacher and I decide to institute an afternoon of cultural exchange. This will force them to try to use their new language to communicate with us. We will explain to them as best we can cultural things we know about the U.S. and they will explain to us things we are curious about in their culture.

Since it is their turn first, we decide to limit their explanations to telling us about certain people we have heard of in the short time we have been here. This is, after all, generally much easier than trying to explain governments, or religions. So, we ask the first few "volunteers" to tell us about a poet whose name we had heard ever since our arrival. They go to great lengths in their preparations and we are fascinated to learn that the man is an ancient poet along the lines of Homer. His epic poem, which is thousands and thousands of lines long, tells the history of the people of Kyrgyzstan. Even now, certain people are selected whose life's work is to recite his entire epic poem from memory. They show us a videotape of a "reciter". Mesmerized, we watch the person using hand and head motions to signal changes of pace in the story, all the while sitting in a cross-legged position. Though we understand not one word of Kyrgyz, we somehow know the reciter is telling of battles lost and won, of drought and famine, or days of plenty.

Next, it will be our turn, and we need to prepare information about some famous Americans. Who do they want to know about? Someone suggests George Washington. "Well, OK we could tell you what we remember learning about George, but it is probably not a lot more than you already know yourselves. How about someone more current? Who else have you heard of that you would like to know about?" Another student suggests John Kennedy. "OK. That is a good suggestion." We teachers remembered Kennedy well and would be glad to talk about him. "Anyone else?" One of the Sergeis began waving his hand wildly in the air. "Yes, Sergei, who would you like to know more about?" Sergei replies, "Dean Reed"!

Chills run up and down my arms as I put his name on the board and explain that I went to high school with Dean.

Later, my students would take me to the Arts Museum in Biskek and show me a huge photo hanging there of Dean Reed in his heyday on tour in Biskek. As I gazed into the familiar face in the photo, I tried to find, but couldn't, the answers to the many questions I would liked to have asked the man from Wheat Ridge so far away from home.

The Bridge
By Nancy Keyes (Nancy Winslow)

The war began in earnest in April of 1992. Can it be that only two short years before, in April of 1990, I sat in such contentment by the bridge in Mostar? Mostar is an hour or so drive on a winding, tunneled mountain highway from Sarajevo where the Fulbright Scholar program had placed me at the University of Sarajevo for my first overseas teaching assignment. The first time I went to Mostar I was the guest of a colleague, also a Fulbrighter. Nick, my colleague, was new to Mostar but not to Yugoslavia having spent the previous year in Niksic. Like the native Yugoslavs, in the few weeks since my arrival, I had developed a fierce loyalty to my city, Sarajevo. One of the first arguments I had with Nick was over the relative goodness of Sarajevo "pivo" (beer) as opposed to the relative mediocrity of Niksic "pivo".

From the top of a minaret with a tight spiral staircase, we looked out over the small city of Mostar. Old red tile roofs, gray and semi-white, almost-adobe houses and apartments cut through by the stream of green, a most indescribable black and blue-green, the river Neretva. At intervals white threads of bridges spanned this slash of darkish green. Later, as we walked the old, old bridge, I would hear the story of how it had been built. It had taken nine years from 1557 to 1566. The builder, I was told, was ordered by the ruler himself, to make a new connection between one side and the other. It was to be big enough for carts to go each way, and it was to be sturdy. On completion of the bridge, the ruler and all the people of Mostar came out to celebrate. A crowd of onlookers watched from the spit of earth below which the river itself had deposited close to its side. The first people began to cross. Moments later, the bridge collapsed, hurling all into the blue-green water forever. The builder was marched to prison post-haste while the ruler fumed over the loss of time and money. Finally, the ruler ordered the builder to try again. But, this time it must work. This time if it didn't work, the architect would be publicly executed. Convinced that the new structure would also collapse, on the day that the last white stone of the incredible Mostar bridge was slipped into place, it is said that the builder was running for his life and already several miles away. But, hold it did. Hold it did for more than four centuries.

The old bridge, "stari most", worn by the millions of steps of the millions of people, millions of horses, and myriads of carts that had crossed it, was smooth as silk. The stones, polished by constant rubbing, shone in the noonday sun. Elevated in the middle to a very slight point - not a rounded Roman bridge - it echoed the windows of the old Moslem houses. The incline to the middle of the river was steep enough to make walking without sliding backwards on the glass-like surface difficult. Knowingly, this architect of past times, provided cross sections of smaller, raised stones forming a horizontal line to catch backward sliding animals, carts, and people. Modern engineers looked at the bridge and wondered how without cement, without steel........ How had he made it hold? And how was it that after four and a half centuries, that in this century no engineer, no ruler, no person had figured out how to keep people from sliding backwards?

Atop the stone side rails at the far end of the bridge in their bathing suits stood young men shivering and goosepimpled. As tourists crossed they would try to cut a deal. For a pack of cigarettes, they would jump from the bridge into the sunlit forest green water many feet below hoping to miss the rocky outcroppings near the shore. I couldn't watch. When I opened my eyes, I saw the same thin body climbing out of the water onto the rocky sides and coming up the steep hill with a smile to claim his prize.

Wandering the curving, narrow streets on the other side of the river, we passed cooper shops with Turkish tea sets, a stone sculpturer's studio, and souvenir stores. Intricately patterned rugs, predominantly white, red and black, in the kalim, flat woven style brightened the street. The shops, housed in buildings some as old as the bridge itself, had rounded arches for doorways just tall enough to stand in and sported shutters made of decorated metal, closed and bolted to keep goods secure. Metal braces, forming triangles against the buildings, held small projecting roofs above the heads of those entering from the cobblestoned streets. Above the roofs small arched windows were crisscrossed with heavy metal bars from the same ancient times as the bridge itself.

Later that night wandering through the city-village in search of a restaurant, we found ourselves again drawn to the river and the old bridge. Descending a stone stairway, we came upon a small, very old house with a patio big enough for two welcoming tables outside. Inside, the white adobe walls smelled musty despite a small fire glowing in the hearth. With yellow light and clinking glasses, the coziness invited us to linger. After dinner and at least one bottle of Zilavka, a clear and crisp white wine of the region, we mellowed Americans gave up our exteriors and melted into the setting.

At tables across the way, men brought out their guitars and began strumming. They raised their voices in full force at times to plaintive melodies. The lyrics of these songs passed down through generations, added to or changed, told the regions' stories - sometimes of struggle, but more often of love, unrequited. Some songs seemed almost familiar by now though I had crossed the ocean only a few weeks before. Ivo, a friend in Sarajevo, had translated several for me, whispering their words softly in my ear as they were being sung. A favorite of mine was, "Yellow Quince," Zuta Dunje. The words told of a man whose love for a woman ends tragically and who forever after is reminded of his lost love by the perfume of yellow quince. And, this old song, dating back also to the 1500s, caressed the dimly lit walls that night.

The songs, sung with emotion, were not only from, or about this very specific region, but about all the other regions of the country as well. Some were gypsy songs, some Serbian, some Croatian, Montenegran, Macedonian. The strains of the melody told the native listener of its

97

origin, but the songs were sung by all. Women could and did join in, but clearly men held the center stage.

I observed to Nick that this was surely not an American scene. In Colorado, where I grew up, men were said to have sung round the campfires under the stars. But, I have never seen it except as a demonstration for tourists. Nick said he had heard that American men were assholes compared to their romantic European counterparts. In my efforts to stay objective, I maintained that American men were simply different, that there was no need to put a value judgement on the difference. But, we did agree that singing by men in the U.S. is usually assigned to entertainers, or reserved for those who mumble through, or chime in with the national anthem before a ballgame.

Complaining slightly, Nick said men in the States are emotionally deprived. By this he meant that men miss something in life because of their inability to relate emotionally even if they have strong feelings and are as sensitive as women. Men must hide their emotions. No crying allowed, romance is for "chicks", and a night out singing with the boys would bring smiles indeed. So, American men end up keeping stiff upper lips, keeping feelings to themselves, and keeping everything inside - all the while knowing what they lack. Frequently they are so successful that the squelch is permanent and emotional ties impossible.

Our conversation was coming to a close. These differences we were observing just part of the education of stepping out of one's usual pair of shoes. James Baldwin once said he had to leave the U.S. He had to be out of it to "see" it. I was to learn what he meant - for by living abroad, my appreciation of my own country increased by exponential amounts. It was then that the truly magical freedom of the U.S. became real. It was then that the specialness of choices was not drowned out by the daily routine of violence.

Suddenly, an American song interrupted the flow of mysterious notes - the strains of a song by the old group, the Kingston Trio. "Hang down your head, Tom Dooley, Hang down your head and cry." Their version of Tom Dooley was a salutation and an invitation. When we looked up, the men with the guitars were smiling and beckoning for us to come and sit at their table. And, so we did. They played. We sang. They played. Then, they sang by imitating our sounds though they had no meaning to go with the words. We sang. They sang the words we provided. They played. We sang. We struggled to remember words. They played. They wanted words to twenty songs, or more. We tried to supply. They REALLY wanted words to Bob Dylan songs. We tried to explain that NO ONE really knew the words to Bob Dylan songs. They sang a rendition of Old Suzanna. Suzanna, in their version, came not from Alabama, but Louisiana. On and on into the night...

Finally, with hoarse throats, we immerged, laughing, into the dampness. Above us, the warm, yellow lights had been turned out. Arm in arm, we stood for a long moment and looked up at the dark shape of the magnificent bridge against the evening sky...

On May 23, 1993, the white stones, which had held for four centuries, became victims of war. Explosions shattered the air, and the broken bridge slipped into the forest green waters of the Neretva forever.

A Letter from Dave

By Dave Sutcliffe as written to Doug Rhinehart

The following is a letter written to Doug Rhinehart from Dave Sutcliffe, following the 20th class reunion in 1978.

August 22, 1978

Dear Doug,

It was two weeks ago today that I set out to prove that you can go home again and survive. Transformed perhaps, but none the worse for the wear....There were good reasons to go back there and touch home. Everybody that showed up was a good reason as far as I'm concerned. I'm sorry, really sorry about the ones who didn't for logistical reasons and tragically sorry about those we probably drove off. I can't deny the pleasure in standing among old friends. It's nice magic and it certainly transcends a lot of personal events and details that at that moment, anyway, became very unimportant. An almost forgotten Colorado accent came forth and said, "Hello, David, where have you been?" And I loved it! We're still shy, that's what.

Watching all those eyes meet again and, of course, knowing all the things that couldn't, or wouldn't, be said, but wondering anyway just what would happen if they were, knowing all the while old enemy time is working against us all. (However, I have been recently reminded that the death of the caterpillar is the birth of the butterfly.) And, so we sat and stood, and I suppose laid (I certainly hope so!) and tried to squeeze it all in...knowing from the beginning that we couldn't, still the moment itself was to be enjoyed and it was. I delighted in seeing the generous, good-natured people that I grew up with. Many of them seem like family to me, and in many ways I remain closer to them than I do my own somewhat scattered relations. I'm especially grateful to those who bothered to organize the event itself. They did an extraordinary job of providing us all with a lovely weekend...a magical memory to take home and savor with all the rest of our mental clutter. Now, we can either hope we make it to the next one, or make a vow to vanish, and never appear again. In any case I'll be there one way, or another, and I hope they are all there again. I'd like to see them drag even a few more in out of the bushes...that would be nice. Oh, would I love to see an encampment of all those people...a three-day mountain rendezvous-fiesta. What with modern advances in wine, women, and song, we couldn't miss. I suppose the class of 1958 could ---- up anything, but the attempt would be well worth witnessing.

Did you see all those beautiful little kids? I really regretted not having my family with me. It was very obvious that the dimensions of all our lives had been enlarged by all those miniature likenesses of ourselves, and it seemed appropriate that they should at least all meet each other, at least once in their lives. My kids certainly missed something valuable, and I'm sorry.

Finally, I'm very grateful that Tom Hoff didn't have me arrested. That was nice, thanks, Tom.

Well, this letter has taken me over two weeks to get out and it still reads like a crossword puzzle. I must face my first day of school tomorrow (with kids present) and I am genuinely dreading it. I've already gotten into a potentially serious (insubordination) conflict with the principal, and it looks like I may have to make some heavy duty decisions in the near future. I'll let you know more about that later. For me this is the last day of summer, and it truly saddens me. I feel like I'm about to be returned to my cell. A depressing thought, indeed. I know I'm pretty spoiled, but freedom is a very infectious phenomenon, and believe me I'm totally infected...virulent actually!

Dave

* Dave was a popular member of the class of '58 and a good friend. Dave's promise was prophetic: In his letter, speaking of the next reunion, he said, "...I'll be there one way, or another..." Dave was at our 30th reunion in 1988, but only in spirit. He died of cancer in March 1988. His memorial service was attended by about 30 of his friends and family at the opening day of the baseball season at Milwaukee County Stadium. He made all the arrangements before he died. It was one of the most amazing events I have ever attended. He was a good guy - Doug Rhinehart

A Tribute to David, July 26, 1988

By Doug Rhinehart

It was in the middle of the night and we were somewhere in the middle of the state, returning to my place, after our twentieth high school reunion. David was going to go back home with me and spend a few days before he had to return to Wisconsin. We'd been on the road for a couple of hours and had been talking non-stop about the reunion and seeing our old classmates again. We both expressed several times what a hell of an experience it had been. The night was made bright and cozy inside the car as we shared our observations and feelings. We were both struck by the obvious fact that we had all changed to some degree over the twenty years. However, it had been a great source of amazement and amusement that in many ways people had remained the same.

We were in complete agreement that the "Ladies of '58" had definitely weathered the twenty years a lot better than the men.

We became quiet and allowed the hum of the curving, mountain road to accompany our reflections. David asked if I wanted to hear a tape that he had brought. He said it was his favorite and one that he had listened to a great deal on his drive from Wisconsin. It was, "The Outlaws," and featured among others, Willie Nelson. Willie was David's favorite singer. As we drove on through the blackness, listening to the music and feeling the warm elation of having spent a rewarding weekend with old friends, I was particularly taken by one song that Willie sang. It was, "Yesterday's Wine," and seemed very appropriate. It gave words to what and how we were both feeling. I said that to David and remarked that I liked his tape a lot.

A few days later, when he was getting packed and ready to drive back home, I noticed the tape lying on top of the player and I handed it to him. "Nah", he said, shaking his head and walking on past. "You keep it". I replied that I could always buy my own copy and he would want to listen to it on his drive back home. He stopped and looked at me and said with finality, "No, I want you to have it."

David's joy and love of giving to others has always astounded me. There are many things that I can learn from his life and many attributes that I would like to adopt in my own life. His capacity for giving and sharing is one I don't believe I can ever match. I can only hope to emulate it. His generosity could and did extend from small things, such as the Willie Nelson tape, to more sweeping gestures.

In one of Dave's last years of teaching high school, he volunteered to coach the girls' softball team, after no one else wanted to take on the task. The team was a pretty sorry bunch. They had produced few, if any, wins the year before and things didn't look any more promising the year David agreed to coach. Nevertheless, David felt they were deserving of the time and energy he devoted to them. He also promised that at the end of the season, he would take them all out to dinner. The girls probably expected something like a Big Mac with a Coke, and that would be fine, because no one had ever done anything like that for them before.

The day before the dinner, Dave simply told the girls to come to school the next day, "dressed up". Just minutes before school let out, three chauffeured limousines drove up to the main entrance and, in front of all their classmates, the girls were driven away in style. They drove around Milwaukee for over an hour, during which they made phone calls from the limousines to boyfriends, mothers, and anyone in the world they could think of calling. They then were driven to one of the more exclusive restaurants in the city for a very elegant dinner, all paid for by David. Those girls may not have won many games that season, but they were treated like winners and they felt like winners that evening.

It is an awesome and impossible task for me to pay adequate tribute to David. I feel I could write a book and it would not do justice to the person David was…and is. I would not begin to give form and substance to the full and vigorous life that he carved out for himself. To be sure, his nearly fifty years of living were similar to all our lives. He had his allotted quota of pain, loss, disappointments, and unfilled dreams. By "society's standards," a phrase he abhorred, he was not the model for exemplary citizenship. He could be as profane and as irreverent as anyone I have ever known. If you go back and look at the group photo taken at the twentieth reunion - who is the only one in the group giving the finger? David was not a saint, nor did he have any desire to be one. Thank God, because he would have been intolerable as a saint!

David was David. He figured out how he wanted to live his life and he even determined the best way to face his own death. And he did both.

I would like to propose a toast:

> *"And to taste yesterday's wine,*
> *Yesterday's wine, yesterday's wine.*
> *Aging with time, like yesterday's wine.*
> *We're aging with time, like yesterday's wine."*

To David Sutcliffe…

5355
By Elle Raeder (Elinor Obialero)

"5355". Only the address numbers are left from the family home on West 38th Avenue. Everything else is gone, replaced by another of America's dreary strip malls.

When mother died, the four of us needed to divide her personal belongings. We each picked a number, then selected from our parents' treasures. Passing up beautiful crystal vases and valuable sterling silver trays, my fingers surrounded a set of four black wrought iron numbers: 5. 3. 5. 5.

"5355", our family commonly referred to our 38th Avenue home as just that, its address. Our home was located in one of the most visible areas of Wheat Ridge, close to the Denver city limits, near Sheridan Boulevard. It is now a frenetic, high traffic area, but it wasn't always like that.

Dad bought "5355" for Mom in 1940. They needed more space, after we twins were born. It was perfect for his apple, peach and cherry orchards, for his fruit and vegetable gardens and for the chickens and ducks that became childhood playmates. My nursing career began when Mom noted that a baby chick was ill, and I ran and got the old red enema bag and attempted to use it. The idyllic lifestyle and landscape, along with my father's wine making from bountiful burgundy grapes, was heaven. We came away from childhood with an idyllic quality of innocence.

As time passed, population growth paved the way for commercial development and urban sprawl. Everything we needed was now within a block, or two: the grocery store, the cleaners, the Standard service station, Case's famous flower and produce stand,

and the lumber yard, just to name a few. The vacant land next door made way for a Fourth of July firecracker stand. Our blue spruce trees became the target of small fires each year from bottle rockets. Later in the Summer, the "holy rollers" salvation tent filled that same vacant space. The wailing congregation along with the folksy hymns was cheap entertainment. The cool night breaking the summer heat allowed for the fervor of healing and souls being saved. You could live your whole life on 38th Avenue and not miss a thing, or so we thought. Early life never veered too far off the beaten path. Indeed, we found moments of true excitement and bursts of sheer joy. We took it all in as we prepared for real life.

After leaving Mountain View Elementary, we headed for better things at Wheat Ridge Junior High and Senior High School. Notice, I use the term "we" a lot, because as a twin, that is the way "we" thought. Sometimes "we" walked and later got rides from a classmate heading up, or down, 38th. In junior high, a frequent stop was the A&W Rootbeer hangout. The salty, delicious fries smothered in catsup, washed down with crowd pleasing humor and Cokes, made for guilt-laden worries about the pimples sure to come.

In 1954, they tore down the three lovely homes to the east of "5355" and built a Safeway, much to the chagrin of our parents. We and our friends used the store's parking lot and my Dad's old '37 Dodge to learn how to drive. Learning to shift resulted in intense jerking and convulsions of laughter. We soon figured it out and we were on our way driving down 38th Avenue by ourselves, seeking excitement that existed beyond our idealized lives at "5355". Everybody, would gather at our house with just enough money to go to the corner and buy 45 cents worth of 19 cent a gallon gas to get us to Carl's Pizzeria. Pizzas were a new thing to our area and they were the rage. There, for around $2.75, eight of us would share a sausage and cheese combo. Each friend put in whatever he could that day. Everyone was so fair with the small amount of money that they had, we were never short. We then drove back home with no gas to spare, waving at friends along 38th, and the friends always seemed to end up at our house for the next couple of hours. Our parents loved all the kids and offered more food and drink.

"5355" was always a hub of activity. Starting before school, some of our girlfriends would come to change into unapproved daring outfits and apply lipstick, not allowed in their own parent's homes. Our mother was not fooled about what was going on. But, so wise in knowing what was really important, she spawned a protective aura around all of us.

During the high school years, more than one homecoming float was built in our large garage. We produced many a winner hidden in veils of secrecy from the rest of our talented class competition. We were sometimes so thickly sweet in our friendships that it is no wonder they continue today.

Life was not perfect though along 38th Avenue. At the "Creamery" across the street from the high school all of the "toughies" hung out, and we were told more marijuana was sold there than the dairy products that they advertised. Drugs have been around a lot longer than most would admit, but we were never tempted. It was a quiet time, but even in the Fifties there were those, who seemed to be living dead-end lives that were going nowhere.

I also remember in 1957, while sitting at a Farmer's football game, I joked that the Safeway was on fire as fire engines left their station and headed east on 38th Avenue. It was! Racing home from the game, my heart pounded as I saw our property encircled by firefighters with hoses on our roof, saving our little French inspired home from the raging fire next door. The fire was horribly frightening with windows exploding and cans popping late into the night. It ended with nothing more than a heap of glowing embers and charred debris.

That same year, police sirens screamed down 38th and stopped across and down the street from our house. I was sitting in the car with my "steady" boyfriend. My mother had not yet switched the porch lights on and off signaling for me to come in immediately. It was entertaining to watch 38th Avenue's action and discuss our future while restraining ourselves from "necking" too much. My boyfriend and I ran to see what the commotion was. What our naive eyes saw was startling. Left dead with a visible hole in the patrol car windshield and one in his head was a Wheat Ridge policeman. I wished I could have saved him. This experience cemented my decision to become a nurse. I was headed for University of Colorado's School of Nursing. My college decision made.

Elitch Gardens was ten minutes down the street from "5355." Our dad and Mary Elitch were close friends. Consequently, that was where we worked and played each summer throughout junior high and high school. Conveniently, the Trocadero Ballroom at Elitch's was a great place to be taken by our boyfriends.

Also on 38th Avenue was the #13 bus line that led us into the "big city" of Denver. Music, dance, cooking and swim lessons were regular activities for us. Also, the orthodontist, shopping and lunch "downtown". Because we were not allowed to drive into the city, the #13 was our ticket to freedom.

38th Avenue has become worn and weathered. The landscape quilt needs to be rewoven, reclaimed, and revitalized both on an aesthetic and a social basis. The future brings some good chances for tear down and redevelopment. As hard as it was to see our beloved high school demolished and replaced, it was the correct thing to do. Now, the rest of 38th Avenue must be improved upon. The grand old avenue leading to the heart of the city must always be kept grand. Change brings good and bad, mostly good. This premise provides optimism for the future.

The intriguing part of writing about our past is to make all of us scratch the surface of our lives and ask the question - is this all life is? Have we achieved all our childhood dreams? Would we really like to have lived in a different time? And, most important, can we pass on an improved world to the next generation?

The Nurse Faces Real Life
By Elle Raeder (Elinor Obialero)

My heart was beating fast that first day. As the large metal ring's key unlocked Door #1, then Door #2 slammed with its own tremendous force, I find myself standing on the smooth as glass polished floors. It was my first day as a psychiatric nurse in the men's locked ward at the Colorado Psychiatric Hospital. It was a long way from "5355," our old home in Wheat Ridge. Nothing here was as sweet as my young life had been. Ironically, nothing here was as clean as the shiny floor made it seem.

I quickly passed the cells, ominously fronted by real prison bars. I thought I knew what to expect. I did not know that the criminally incarcerated state insanity pleas would be housed in the same area as the safer non-criminal patients. I thought they brought the criminals just for the day from the prisons, rather than they being kept here for three week evaluation periods. My job was deciding if their horrible deeds were driven by insanity, or cunning, similar to the popular movie "One Flew Over The Cuckoo's Nest".

My position description clearly stated that I was to interact with the patients. They had a plethora of problems raging from the common unsuccessful suicide attempts to paranoid schizophrenic murder. We had to medicate them and give them electroshock and insulin shock treatments. In general, we had to keep peace among highly agitated individuals.

It didn't take long to put faces to the textbook descriptions that we covered in the many psych classes that tried to prepare me for this. However, I wasn't in the least bit mature enough, when it came to some of this black, dirty stuff. I quickly learned about some of our society's darkest secrets that led people on the worst paths of emotional and physical destruction. I grew up fast, and in many ways, became far wiser than I wanted to be.

Easy to understand and observe were the obsessive-compulsives and the manic depressives. In that day, your family could commit you. Harder to understand were the sociopaths and the psychopaths along with the catatonic schizophrenics and the paranoid schizophrenics. There are ones to this day whose names, faces and problems were so impressionable to me that years later they are not forgotten. Stark reality replaced the storybook life that I led in Wheat Ridge.

There was J.S., the youngest person ever to see the inside of CPH. Frail, thin and animalistic, he was an eleven year old schizophrenic, who was smart enough and healthy enough by the end of a year's hospitalization that he begged me to take him to my own home. Sadly, his future was bleak because both parents were in the state hospital with the same diagnosis.

There was L.M., now behind those bars, who was later put to death in the gas chamber after killing his wife and three of his ten children when his wife found him naked in a field committing incest.

There was the handsome J.C., a 36 year old sociopath, who had taken tens of thousands of dollars from everyone with whom he made contact. He was a con man, had been in prison for the same, and couldn't stop his chronic behavior. He looked and spoke so normal that I could picture being his victim too. I quickly learned not to be so trusting.

Then, there was the 18 year-old boy, whom after reading his chart, I knew why he was in tremendous turmoil and had tried to commit suicide three times . His step-father forced him to commit acts only the devil would concoct. Predictably, his fourth suicide attempt was successful.

I learned from the in-depth histories of these patients what created the other side of our society. It opened up a horrific part of life to me. I had read novels and seen movies, but my experiences far surpassed them with true-life horrors. Such abnormalities should never be allowed to exist.

The Monday I quit as a psychiatric nurse started out routine. As I was passing out medication making sure the patients took it, one of the patients, who viewed me as his girlfriend, attacked me. He thought my weekend absence meant I was unfaithful. I was knocked across the large, ornate pool table in the day room. I picked myself up off of the floor and wrote a complete account of this terrifying incident in his chart. I decided that I needed a more normal work environment. I had spent a year in a field that is still little known to the average person. However, this world of insanity would remain with me for a lifetime. Ultimately, I find myself just as compassionate for the mentally ill as I do the physically ill. All American citizens need to be more aware and more understanding towards them. Many mental hospitals opened their doors and sent their former patients into the world unprepared for mainstream society.

Real life can be tough.

Trains, Raging Hormones and Trouble

By Bob Walden

Trains, trains...I think my fascination with trains and traveling really took off, when I was 16. We had an Exchange Trip for 30 of us from Wheat Ridge to Plant City, Florida. We sat up in coach seats night and day all the way there and back. What a trip! Bob Brown and I fell in love with Plant City girls and almost went back to see them the next summer. At that age it was amazing how deeply in love you could be in just a few days...raging hormones.

Fast friendships were built on that trip. Eric Siverts and I are still close. I think that's where we started calling Robin Marie West, "Buns," and Randy Schafer, "Beaner." As I remember it was all Don Shepperd's fault. Interesting things happened on that train. In New Orleans we got Don Shepperd really drunk on beer and had trouble trying to keep him from flying out the 8th story window of the hotel...trouble. It was no surprise, when he ended up as a Jr. Birdman at the Air Force Academy.

Trains, trains...I can't remember many of the guys from the senior class on our   exchange trip, except maybe, Stan Nikkel. We junior guys were the rowdies. But, I definitely remember some of the senior girls. They furthered my education. Sharon Sanders and I became so fascinated with a human embryo specimen at the Museum of Science and Industry in Chicago that we made the bus late. Boy, did we get crusty looks, and not just from the teacher chaperones. Sharon and I got to ride in the "Vistadome" together all the way back from Chicago. I still really like Vistadomes...trains and raging hormones...

The exchange group that came to Wheat Ridge from Plant City was a pretty rough and tough crew. We took them ice skating at the Denver Coliseum Ice Arena. It was their first time on skates. I got into a situation that started as a full-blown rumble with a Hispanic gang, but the Plant City guys finished it. Somewhere in the scuffle I remember hearing something about brass knuckles and switchblades. It all broke up when the cops came...hormones and trouble...

The Plant City exchange crowd had a shoplifting ring going at home. We found out about that later, after they carried away half of Central City. It was the middle of winter and the Central City merchants opened the town up, especially for the 60 of us. They were really unhappy, when half their town disappeared. The Plant City crew left the Central City train, but only because it wouldn't fit in the bus. I thought the school disciplinary meetings over that one would never end. At the time it was a really big, serious deal. Finally, we took up a collection to try to calm down Central City and preserve our reputations. Of course, the Plant City group had already departed for Florida with all the loot. I was a little slow on the uptake. I remember thinking, "What are they all doing sitting in the back of the bus trying not to giggle, and why are all their coats mounded up over something?" I just didn't get it until the teachers called the disciplinary meeting over the merchant's shoplifting complaint. Plant City - young hoodlums ...trouble...

While in Plant City we performed an Old West skit about a mining town for their High School assembly. Our song went:

Cocaine Bill and Morphine Sue went strolling down the avenue
He sniffed once and she sniffed twice
But she sniffed the most, 'cause she sniffed so nice
Oh, honey, have a whiff
Oh, honey have a whiff
Oh honey have a whiff on me, on me...

Hey, were we ahead of our time, or what? One of our teacher chaperones, Miss Sayre, actually suggested the song. Can you believe a teacher doing that today?...trouble...

My wife, Leslie, and I met, when I was a senior. My cousin, Gary, went to North High School with Leslie, and we met at a party at his house. Leslie's old boyfriend, Denny, was harassing her. So, I took Gary down to Denny's house and "chose" him. In those days that meant, "Come out and fight!" He wouldn't come outside, and later Gary told me it was a good thing, because Denny's three big brothers were right behind him. Gary was trying to figure a way to slam the screen door and hold them inside... hormones...raging hormones...and trouble...

But, what goes around comes around. Little Mouse (Don) Payne beat me up across from the school behind the grocery store on Teller Street. It wouldn't have been so bad if he hadn't still had a cast on his broken arm. Actually, it was off by then, but it was still on when he "chose me" in the first floor boys lavatory. Mr. McGaffey broke up the affair, but Mouse got back to me later. That hurt. Tough kid...lots of hormones...

A sociology test somehow got copied at the school office and passed out beforehand. Everybody got 100% on the test and the teacher, Mr. Ellis, freaked out. He said the guys in our class were all going to end up in prison. Boy, did we fool him! Some of us are still out. Some of us even became generals and doctors. There's probably a "fine line lesson" there somewhere?

Well, my memory "train" has turned into an emotional roller coaster. But, then, that's what high school was all about for me...hormones... raging hormones...and trouble...

Trains, Less Hormones, Still Trouble and a Change in My Life
By Bob Walden

Later in life I became a dentist. Even later, I found The Lord. It has made a tremendous difference in my life. I still ride trains, but left my hormones behind...unfortunately, I still find trouble...

While riding across Romania on a night train I wondered, "Why do I like trains so much?" This was crazy, but maybe it went all the way back to our Plant City High School exchange trip. The Romanian track was so rough I spent more time in the air than I did lying on my bunk. I can usually sleep almost anywhere, but banging against the walls kept waking me up. I went down the corridor to the glorified hole in the floor that passed for a toilet. I was thrown against the wall so hard it ripped my shirt. Urine was everywhere, of course, and not just mine. Maintenance and cleanliness was a joke. On the other hand, in the Frankfurt airport, a lady was mopping between my feet as I used the urinal. Now, that is cleanliness and maintenance carried to the extreme! I'm not sure which is worse, but they were both different experiences.

So, what am I doing on a train going across Romania? My wife, Leslie, and I were medical missionaries in Timisoara, Romania. We were there for a year doing some dentistry, but mostly bringing in surplus medical and dental supplies from the U.S. to the Romanian doctors. In this desperately poor former Warsaw Pact nation, the doctors were fairly well trained, but they just couldn't get medicine, supplies and working equipment to help their people. Leslie and I traveled here in Jesus' Name to bring them some hope. We shared with the doctors and patients how we felt they could ask Jesus into their hearts to forgive their sins and give them new life. We often saw hope spring to life in these beaten-down people. One precious three year old, Andreea, looked like our granddaughter, Monica. Andreea was severely burned over the bottom half of her body, when her dress caught on fire on an open heater. When my good friend, Dr. Doreen Dobrota saw her, he was shaking with rage over the way she had been neglected and left to die by the rural doctors near her village. It was too late for Andreea, so all I could do was stand by Andreea's bed and tell her, "Jesus loves you," and show her a picture of our Monica. I was on my knees next to her bed, in tears, asking God to heal her. My heart was broken over this precious child's suffering and pain. God chose to heal her by taking her to be with Him. I'm comforted to know I will see her again. Next time I'm looking forward to a smile, when I kiss her forehead.

Another victim was a wino, who fell asleep in a drunken stupor next to an electric heater. He burned his legs so badly the doctors amputated them at the hip. He knew he was dying and was really afraid. Dr. Dobrota translated as I helped this Jewish man ask Yeshua into his heart as his personal Messiah. He died in peace, shortly thereafter.

The Romanian street children living in the sewers, sniffing glue, were another heartbreaker. The former dictator, Ceausescu (Chow-chess-cue), forced the people to have babies. He would then take some blood from each child, have it typed and cross-matched to his blood, then exchange it for his own. By doing that, he thought he had discovered the way to stay perpetually young. It didn't stop the bullets that later killed him, and I don't even think they were silver. While at a ski area near Brashov, I could look down on Dracula's castle in Transylvania. Was it just a coincidence that Nikolai Ceausescu got the bright idea to exchange his blood with baby's blood? I don't think so! They would go from baby to baby with the same unsterilized needles. That is what caused the AIDS epidemic in the children of Romania.

Corina was one of the AIDS children. I got to hug her and tell her Jesus loved her....more heartbreak...more trouble. Romania was hard duty, but oh, do we love the people there! They love and pray for us too. Four of the doctors there and their families are our friends forever. We are working on getting foundation money to assist them in helping their own people.

So, I'm on the train with my good friend and interpreter, Eugen (A-o-gen) Perianu, on the way to visit my friend, Dumitru Duduman, in Botoshan in Moldovan Romania, which is on the other end of the country. Dumitru smuggled hundreds of thousands of Bibles into Romania and the Ukraine. The Romanian Secret Police, the Securitate, tortured and beat him within an inch of his life several times for smuggling Bibles, but he wouldn't stop. The last time they used bare 220v electric wires to torture him. While it was happening he said, "God, just let me die." But God said to him, "You won't die but your captor will." All of a sudden, his torturers went running up the stairs. The man in charge had dropped dead of a heart attack. The Securitate left him alone after that.

Dumitru spoke often in the U.S. and used the offerings from his speeches and proceeds from a book about his life to build a beautiful and wonderful orphanage to rescue the street children and bring them up knowing Jesus as their Lord. He built a church behind it shaped like Noah's Ark. "...to take the children in and save them." He took me up on the Ukrainian border across which he used to smuggle Bibles. As we looked past the guard post he said, "Bob, as bad as things are here, they are worse over there." I said, "Wow!" because I couldn't imagine how they could possibly be any worse.

Nancy Winslow has stories from Kyrgyzstan. It's a rough life in that part of the world too, as witnessed by the American climbers who just escaped from being held hostage there. My partner just tried to get into Northern Iraq. Saddam Hussein has put a $50,000 bounty on any American caught in Iraq. Trusting God is why it works for Leslie and me to go to places like that.

My fascination with trains is still with me. I still find trouble wherever I go. I left my raging hormones behind long ago...or maybe I'm just using them in a different way for the Lord...

"The Next One Will Be Better"

By Stephanie Moore (Stephanie Poe)

From the time I was in kindergarten until eighth grade, my family and I moved every year. Never very far, but as luck would have it, every time our residence changed my school district changed, too. I was always "the new girl". Shy to begin with, it was painful to have to make new friends every year. Just when I managed to feel somewhat at home, off we'd go.

Finally, in eighth grade, my family moved to Wheat Ridge. And though we continued to move every year, it was just blocks instead of miles. Miraculously we remained in the district. Fitting in was still difficult, but little by little I began to make friends. In my sophomore year my parents finally abandoned our vagabond "renters" lifestyle, took the plunge and became homeowners. We bought a house on 37th Avenue, close to Kipling... and across the street from Jay Criche.

Mr. Criche taught Drama and Speech at Wheat Ridge High. He introduced that shy girl to a fascinating world -- and he changed my life forever.

A long-time movie fan, I was in love with fantasy and make-believe. I'd made up stories for as long as I can remember. At age twelve, I devoured movie magazines, and pasted pictures of my favorite stars all over the walls of my room. I would become a movie star, I'd decided. Much to my chagrin, my family lacked the insight to have been native Californians -- Hollywood seemed a million miles away. I grew up a little and packed my dreams away until, at sixteen, I signed up for Mr. Criche's Drama class. Discovering the world of drama and the theater was intoxicating. Like an alcoholic's first drink, or an addict's first drug,

I was immediately hooked. It was as if I'd had a whiff of something delicious, and now, finally, I got to taste it.

I couldn't get enough. I read every play I could get my hands on. I'd always loved reading fiction, and here was something even more powerful, it seemed. Distilled to its essence, here was the very stuff of life – no long, rambling descriptions, but instead, life as the characters on stage were living it, here and now.

I was fascinated by Mr. Criche's lectures, and enchanted by his passion for his subject. He loved the theater, and wanted to share it with us. His knowledge of the theater gave him an air of (what seemed to me then) incredible sophistication and depth. Instead of droning on about equations or photosynthesis, he enlightened us about tragedy and comedy. He had a lively wit, a warm laugh, and his tweed jackets smelled of cigarette smoke. I suppose I had a crush on him.

I tried out for the school plays and was cast in some roles. "Seventeen", "The Man Who Came to Dinner", "Plain and Fancy", and "The Glass Menagerie". My shyness disappeared on stage – I could be someone else. Marie West was the star, and I yearned to be as talented as she was. I realized even then that, despite how much I enjoyed being on stage, I was not destined to become an actress. But, I loved the theater. Drama and comedy were like air and water to me – I had to find a way to have them in my life.

If play practice ran late, as it often did, Mr. Criche would offer to drive me home. How privileged I felt, being in his company, sharing our thoughts about the play. He'd pull into his driveway, and I'd get out of his car and walk across the street, my head spinning with daydreams and fantasies.

Toward the end of the year in Drama class, Mr. Criche gave us an assignment. We were to write a one-act play. I don't remember what I wrote about, only that it was dull and uninspired, and certainly lacking in technique. The assignment was much harder than I'd realized, and I was frustrated that my effort was so pathetic. When Mr. Criche handed our plays back to us, he warned us that the grades were very bad. He was disappointed in us, and he didn't mind if we knew it. There was a large "C-" on mine, and a notation that read something like this: "This is trite and uninteresting. The characters are stereotypes. But it <u>is</u> a play, and it can be criticized, which is more than I can say for most of the others I read." I was crushed. It wasn't just that I was ashamed of the C-, it was that I'd failed to live up to Mr. Criche's expectations. He must have noticed how hard I was taking this, because he stopped me after class. "Try again sometime," he said. "I think this is something you could do – and the next one will be better".

Although I wrote dozens of short stories and a couple of very bad novels, it was many years before I tried again to write a play. It was a play for the screen instead of the stage, and I wrote it in a university extension class. It, too, was sorely lacking. But I heard Mr. Criche's words... "the next one will be better".

I saw Mr. Criche a few times after I graduated, went to college, and married. But we soon lost touch. How often I've wanted to thank him for giving me a safe place to hide my shyness, for introducing me to a world that has fascinated me for forty years, and for helping me live my dream.

Do I Dare?
By Stephanie Moore (Stephanie Poe)

1988
Do I dare?

I see an article about a screenwriting class at UCLA Extension – "Writing the Thriller". I've taken the only screenwriting class offered through UCSD Extension here in San Diego, and I loved it... I've never felt more invigorated. I'm hungry for more information, and the best place to find it is at UCLA. The catch is, it's a hundred miles away, and I have a husband, four children, and a full time job as a paralegal. But I obey my instincts – this is something I must do. I pay the tuition, adjust my work schedule to leave at 3:00 on Thursdays, and venture – though I don't know it yet – into new emotional as well as geographical territory. With rush hour traffic, I barely arrive in Los Angeles in time for the 7:00 class. The class is dismissed at 10:00, and by the time I pull into my driveway back in San Diego, it's almost 1:00 in the morning. But I'm wide awake... planning the thriller I'll write: Let's see... there's this woman who's married to a politician, and her crazy ex-boyfriend thinks that...

1991
Do I dare?

My roller-coaster marriage has taken a final plunge, and this time, the wheels have left the track. My husband and I are divorcing. Amicable, but painful. Our four wonderful daughters are safely out of the nest, and I have a decision to make. The prospect of climbing the legal ladder seems less and less enticing. I want to write movies – I want to make people laugh and cry. I decide to move to Los Angeles. I'll get a job, and continue to take classes at night – I get euphoric thinking of a half-hour round trip to campus instead of a six-hour round trip. I find an apartment, pay the first and last months' rent, the damage deposit, and fill the car with gas. I have thirteen dollars left.

1995
Do I dare?

I've become an Angelino – I get my bearings when I finally accept the fact that Wilshire Blvd. and Santa Monica Blvd. actually *intersect* (!). San Diego (the part I was fortunate enough to live in) was calm and green and bucolic. And there were places to park. Los Angeles is fast and clogged with traffic and urban, in a fun, flashy, sprawled-out way. And where in the &#%$@ are you supposed to park?!

I'm at UCLA, in charge of the newly-created certificate programs in Screenwriting and Producing at the School of Theater, Film and Television. I work with dynamic, inspiring people whose screenwriting books I've read. I interact with aspiring writers whose dreams I understand. I'll never get wealthy there, but it's a great job. I've continued to write – I have seven screenplays "in my trunk" now, but I still have a lot to learn. I've taken our certificate program in screenwriting and have grown enormously. I'd love to take the Masters program… but what if I didn't get in? What if I couldn't handle the workload of a full time job and the MFA program at the same time? And the biggest question: even if I did get it, am I really good enough? I can't resist trying – I fill out the application and take a deep breath.

1996
Do I dare?

Being part of the MFA Screenwriting Program at UCLA has been nothing short of amazing. The intellectual challenge, the camaraderie, the sense of purpose, has been far more wonderful than I could have imagined. I often feel as if I'm dreaming this -- I've magically been given a chance to live my life twice! I loved raising my family, and now I'm exploring an exciting new world. By some miracle, my age has become irrelevant. My classmates range from twenty-something to almost sixty. Lucky for me, the head of the program believes that people who've actually experienced a range of emotions can convey them better. Many of the people I hang out with are the age of my youngest daughter, but we have our interests and dreams in common.

A friend in the MFA Program introduces me to her friend, Mark. He's a writer/director who's had several low budget feature films made. He's looking for a new project. My friend tells him that I've written a script he might like – it's about a little girl who brings her Barbie doll to life.

Mark reads it, and we "do lunch". He tells me how excited he is about the script, and at the same time, how the subplot needs to be reconceived. I'm relieved that his ideas for the rewrite are the same ones I've been mulling over. He sees the same movie in his head that I see. He wants to option the script, and co-write it with me. The credits would read, "Written by Mark Rosman and Stephanie Moore," "Story by Stephanie Moore", "Directed by Mark Rosman". I tell him I'll think about it. I make a leap of faith and a few days later, sign the option agreement.

2000

Much has transpired. Mark and I spend almost two years developing the script, writing and rewriting and finally, marketing it. We get a marvelous Christmas present in December 1998 when Disney options the script. Another year in development, but this time it's the real thing. We sit in the office of "our exec" at Disney, and have serious discussions about such things as whether a fashion doll would know how flowers smell. More rewrites. A year later, another Christmas surprise – Disney greenlights the movie. In spring 1999, I travel to Vancouver, Canada and watch my movie being filmed. I keep feeling as if someone is going to nudge me awake – surely I'm dreaming!

March 5th. There are no chauffeured limos dropping Gweneth, Brad, or Meg at my door. No Versace gowns, no red carpet -- my guests arrive in jeans and tee shirts and climb the forty steps that lead to the front door of the house I share with David. The guests are my friends – Hollywood screenwriters and aspiring screenwriters, fellow students, some people I've known since I first came to L.A., some UCLA screenwriting faculty, and even a high school classmate – Don Shepperd – whom I hadn't seen in forty years. Fortified with food and drink (the caviar noticeably missing), we crowd into my living room, sit on folding chairs rented for the occasion, and watch as "The Wonderful World of Disney" flashes onto the T.V. screen. And then "Life-Size", and my name. There's a spontaneous burst of applause and cheering from my friends. I'm literally moved to tears by the outpouring of love and support. How incredibly lucky I am.

I'm glad I dared to follow my dreams. I look at Don Shepperd and think back to 1958 when we were seniors at Wheat Ridge High. How grateful I am to my drama teacher, Mr. Criche, who read the first play I ever wrote, criticized it honestly, urged me to try again... and assured me that the next one will be better.

In Memory of Dr. Gary Taylor
By Don Shepperd

I hated him the first time I met him. He ruined my hunting. It was 1949 and we were nine years old. I lived in the northernmost row of houses in Wheat Ridge on West 45th Place. There was nothing but wheat fields all the way to 48th Street and the trolley tracks to Golden. I regularly shot pheasants out of my bedroom window. My mother cooked them for dinner…and then came West 46th Avenue and Gary Taylor.

"You JERK!" Those words began a lifelong friendship. "You've ruined my hunting. Mom says I can't shoot out the back window anymore because of your houses."

"Well, you'll get over it, Gary replied, "But, I've got a gun too. Let's just go further north." And, we did. In addition to pheasant we shot rabbits and muskrats, and my mother cooked them all. "Muskrat stew. Ummmmmmm, BAD, but there's lots of it." we laughed. Our mothers had two rules - don't shoot towards the houses and whatever you shoot you must eat. We were careful where we shot and what we shot at. We were tempted to shoot a skunk once, but figured we could never gag down skunk stew and were convinced my mother would cook it.

Then, came 46th Place and 47th Avenue, and more streets, and they all filled up with houses. With the new houses came friends - Shirley Duden, Roberta Belec, Sandra Burbank, Ed Manor, Judith Cundall, Pat Sullivan, Frank Fishman, Dick English, Roger Bennett, Martha Huffman, Janie Van Der Schouw. Our hunting days were over, and friendships replaced bullets.

Gary and I became fast friends. We continued to hike through the fields and valleys. We watched muskrats swim in the ponds and placed pennies on the track for the Golden Trolley to crush flat and paper-thin, until all the ponds and tracks were gone, covered by houses in the new "suburbs."

In sixth grade I badly needed Gary. My girlfriend, Patti Glenski, married my friend, Gary Stites, on the playground. I was publicly humiliated - rejected - my life was over. I turned to Gary. He "felt my pain." Gary didn't have a girlfriend. We decided to be brutally honest with each other. We talked it over and laid it on the line. The sad fact was - we were skinny little nerds. It was no wonder women didn't want anything to do with us. It was then we turned to "the books."

I had a paper route, giving me a source of income - $25/month. Gary helped me fold papers every afternoon and rode his bike along side mine, chatting as we threw papers onto the sidewalks. If I missed and threw a paper into the bushes, Gary faithfully retrieved it. I had a "working man's bike," rugged, thick tires, wide handlebars to allow me to carry the heavy cloth bags for the papers. Gary had a "cool" bike; an American Flyer with red, white and blue plastic streamers hanging from the handgrips. He often hooked clothespins and playing cards onto the bike frame near the tires. The cards snapped against the wheel spokes making the bike sound like it had a motor. We were the noisiest Denver Post newspaper bicycle delivery team in Wheat Ridge.

Using the money from my paper route, I bought a set of encyclopedias from Betty Fatzinger's father. I paid for them at $5/month. Every afternoon, when school was out, the papers were delivered, and all the other boys were out chasing those "silly girls," Gary and I memorized facts from the World Book Encyclopedia. We set out to become the smartest kids in the school. We failed miserably. Larry Keith Thomas had an IQ higher than the rest of the class put together. I decided I would become a pilot, and Gary wanted to be a doctor. We would teach those "stupid women" to reject us. We were sure one day they would flock back to us, begging forgiveness. We waited for many years without result, so we had time to memorize a good portion of the World Book Encyclopedia. Unfortunately, we never found any girls that were impressed with that ability.

Gary's mom and dad owned a dry cleaning business and could seldom take time off, so Gary often went fishing with my family on the Frying Pan River on weekends in the summer. Gary was a great fisherman. Oh, how we caught fish in those old days before, "Whirling Disease," and when German Browns and Native Cutthroats proliferated in the western slope waters.

We were great fans of the Denver Bears. Curtis Roberts played second base and Gary knew all his statistics. Gary, Frank Fishman and I wanted badly to be athletes. Unfortunately, we were skinny little wimps. Instead of cheering crowds, we heard our parents yelling at us as we played football in our front yards and wrecked the lawn and shrubs. Maybe it was better that way. We studied hard and got through high school and college. We didn't see each other much anymore. Gary went on to be a successful dentist and I went on to be an Air Force pilot.

When we were kids, Gary always wanted to fly, but had bad eyesight. Military aviation was not an option for him; however, he became a civilian pilot and bought his own airplane, a red and white Piper Tri-Pacer. He envied my military flying. He wanted to hear about every mission in Vietnam and couldn't wait to hear the stories, when I checked out in my last airplane, the F-15.

I envied Gary's ownership of a private airplane and couldn't wait to ride with him. I never got to do that. I had planned that he and I would fly over the Continental Divide, look at the Frying Pan River from the air - all the holes and creeks we fished as kids. Then, we would land and fish the river once again, catch great fish and sit on the cabin porch in the early evening and drink beer. We would watch the deer on the hillside and talk about how great it was to grow up in Colorado and how fortunate we were to come from good families and grow up where there were muskrats and Wednesday Night Fights and the Denver Bears. I still have those World Book Encyclopedias and think of Gary every time I see them in the bookcase. I smile and a lump comes into my throat. He died too soon. I miss him. He was one of the best things life can produce - a good friend.

The Dentist
For Gary Taylor by Don Shepperd

Gary Taylor's parent's were, Merle and Pat Taylor. Pat's real name was, "Edra," Gary said, "But, don't EVER call my mother Edra, or she'll hate you forever." I called her "Mrs. Taylor." The Taylors owned a family business, O'Brien Brothers Cleaners, at the corner of 38th and Sheridan. For years Gary and his parents worked hard amidst the steam and chemicals to bring us our clean clothes. Those were the days before air conditioning. Gary's mother ran the counter, Merle drove the delivery truck, and Gary worked in back surrounded by oppressive heat and bad odors. I often wondered how many years "the business" took off their collective lives. It was no wonder they were all skinny - it was Wheat Ridge's version of a "polluted sweat shop." Where was OSHA, when we needed it?

By the time Gary left Wheat Ridge High School in 1958, he was one smart dude. On his college application for pre-med at the University of Colorado one of the questions asked was - What was your greatest accomplishment in school? Gary stated simply, "I have memorized the World Book Encyclopedia." I don't know if it was his sense of humor, or audacity, that got him admitted, but C.U. soon learned he wasn't kidding. Gary breezed through the very difficult pre-med curriculum with "straight-A's," no small feat.

When it came time to compete for entry to medical school, Gary decided he wanted to be a dentist. He faced an awesome schedule of competitive exams. Among the varied battery of tests was one designed to examine the "manual dexterity" of the applicant. Supposedly, a dentist had to have "good hands." Each participant was given a block of hard, chalky material and several "carving instruments" with which to shape the object of their own choice within 15 minutes. The material had to be handled carefully to prevent shattering. The aspirant was then asked to describe what they had carved and why the object was selected. Grades were assigned based upon "originality and quality of work."

For his explanation, Gary stated, "I have carved a penis. The reasons I chose it were two: First, I was worried about breaking my selected object. I have never heard of anyone breaking their own penis. Second, I think this is a 'dicked - up' way of choosing dentists." It was typical Gary Taylor - humorous, innovative, irreverent, audacious - a risk-taker - he got into dental school.

Gary received a "college deferment" from the draft. In return he chose to enter the Air Force and was assigned to a godforsaken location called, "Ajo Air Force Station," in the remote Sonoran Desert of southern Arizona. He said his closest neighbors were six coyotes and a jackrabbit. Like everything else he attacked his assignment with a sense of humor, he got married. When I asked him how he ever got a wife to move to Ajo, Arizona, he said, "I told her I was stationed in Phoenix."

Gary was always fascinated by airplanes and aviation. After getting out of the Air Force, Gary had three children, Kelly, Keith and Danica, all of whom still live in the Denver area. Kelly gave Gary his first grandchild and Gary bought the youngster a tiny flying jacket to which he attached his Air Force captain's bars. He always said he wanted to take his grandson across the border into Mexico to drink a margarita "like a real pilot."

Gary was a magnificent dentist. His office at 6th and Garrison was filled with airplanes and aeronautical magazines and souvenirs. I gave him a picture of me piloting an Air Force F-15 in a vertical climb over my base on Cape Cod, Massachusetts. He proudly displayed it on his office wall. One day, while on a visit to Colorado, I asked him to work on a particularly onerous tooth. He told me it was God's way of paying me back for all the candy we used to eat as kids. While Gary worked on my tooth, he told me of his fascination with and love for the country of Thailand. He traveled there many times. He made many friends and even donated a water tower to an impoverished village - typical Gary - generous with friends. After Gary finished working on my tooth, we had lunch. He called and cancelled his afternoon appointments, and we talked about old times and old friends. We should have talked longer. Little did I know I would only see him one more time. When I saw him five years later, he was dying.

In one of those awful twists of life, 1993 was the worst of years for Pat Taylor. In the back bedroom lay her husband, Merle, dying of a brain tumor. In the front bedroom lay Gary, also dying. Gary went first, then three months later, Merle died. Pat Taylor continued to live in the small family home at 6230 W. 46th Avenue. After the deaths of Gary and Merle, every time I visited Denver on business, I went by to see her. She never changed, always pleasant, always upbeat. Despite the loss of her husband and son, she never sought pity. She always asked how I was and about my family. She and my mother, who had moved to Texas and was in her late eighties, talked regularly. In 1996 Pat sat down on the old couch in her living room and died peacefully. She had talked to my mother two days previously. Pat Taylor was a good woman.

When I think of Gary, I am not sad. I am surrounded by warm memories of hunting and fishing and flying, delivering the Denver Post by bicycle, Wednesday Night Fights on black and white TVs at our fathers' feet, memorizing facts from encyclopedias on the living room floor and waiting for the women, who had rejected us, to come by and apologize and beg - they never did. Gary Taylor was a good guy and a wonderful friend.

Summer Camps
By Cindy Carroll (Cynthia Chaney)

"There's a mountain meadow sparkling in the dew of early morn',
and it's June in the Rockies once more..."

While growing up in the 40's and 50's in our community called, Wheat Ridge, next to the Rocky Mountains, this refrain could only mean one thing - TIME FOR SUMMER CAMP! - the time I looked forward to all year; well, almost all year; well, at least for a portion of the year, after Christmas and Easter were finished; well, actually, probably only after school got out, and the short attention span brains of children realized that it was now time for - SUMMER CAMP!!!

For me summer camps began very early in life, because I had an older brother with whom I had the normal sibling rivalry. I felt it was only fair that I get to go to camp just like him, even though I was two years younger and below the minimum age. I'm sure I made life miserable for my parents. I'm sure they felt compelled to find a camp that took VERY young kids. The result of all the pestering, whining and other things little girls do to get their way, was two weeks in a place called "Peter Pan School". For most of the year Peter Pan was a private school, but during the summer they took in all sorts of kids and called it a "camp." Actually, it wasn't really much of a camp because it was right in the heart of downtown Denver. The only outdoor area was a small play yard at the rear of the house, and there were definitely NO HORSES! And, every kid knew that summer camp meant horseback riding. But, Peter Pan did have the requisite camp craft projects. My fondest memory of that camp was the day my parents visited and took me out to lunch at the Brown

Palace Hotel. Some exciting camp it must have been for my best memory to be getting out of it!

The next year's camp came closer to the real thing. It was up in the mountains, which was far better than a city lot in Denver, but again - NO HORSES! It was the big time, though, for a little girl because it was "CO-ED," and we got to sit around a campfire at night and sing camp songs. I'm sure there were the usual life-enhancing craft activities, but all I can remember are the songs and the campfires.

Next, came "Blue Bird" day camps. Every day for one whole week we got to show up at the camp and do all sorts of "activities" - no overnights, and still NO HORSES! - as this was back in an urban area of Denver. Camp songs were big again (but no real camp fires, since this was day camp - darn!), and we had more of those exciting and life-enhancing craft activities like square braiding plastic strips into all sorts of lengths. We called them "lanyards" and thought they looked pretty cool; not too functional, but definitely colorful. I'll bet if placed end-to-end the lanyards I made during all my summer camps would stretch from here back to Wheat Ridge.

The best of all summer camps was "Camp Wahalla" for Campfire Girls! This was the real thing - up in the mountains, sleeping in cabins, campfire songs around campfires, poison ivy, and best of all - HORSES! And, of course, there were more of those plastic strips we square braided.

Camp Wahalla was so special, we had to earn our own way each year. We did this by selling "Crystal Cuts" candy. While the Girl Scouts had their one-variety-fits-all cookies, the Camp Fire Girls had our many-colored Crystal Cuts! There is probably not a child alive who will tell you that candy tastes bad, but that stuff did! It was rock hard, and no matter which artificial flavor you tried, it all tasted like petroleum mixed with sugar. We must have had the best relatives and friends in the world, because each year they continued to buy that awful candy; just enough so I could earn my way to camp. Even though it sat in my Aunt's garage year after year, no animal ever tried to get into her unopened Crystal Cut candy.

As we got older and camp got more expensive, we added Christmas card sales to our fund raising efforts. Each Fall I would gather up the books of sample cards and head to my aunts, Mom's friends, and "the neighborhood". We were right up there with the Fuller Brush Man in our persistence - taking orders for our boxes of cards. True, ours were more expensive than store-bought, BUT hey, you could get ours "embossed," AND besides, we were cute little girls in our Camp Fire Girl uniforms. Who could resist buying at least one box from us? Well, a few doors got shut with a polite, "No, thank you," but, in those days no one would think of slamming the door on a door-to-door sales call - it just wouldn't be polite. There was one very nice lady who lived around the corner on 44th and never, ever turned me down. I just loved calling on her because I knew she would buy more than one box, get them embossed, which would give me extra credit, and admire how beautiful our samples were. It didn't take much to boost the morale of children in those days of innocence.

When we were very young, Camp Fire Girls camp lasted only one week. I was usually there with Nancy Winslow, Nancy Quante and Ann Morgan. Our parents would drive us up to camp on the weekend, unload everything that we had packed from the recommended camping gear list, gave us a little money for the canteen, kisses and hugs all around, and drive back down the hill for a week without little girls giggles in the house. Could it be that they looked forward to camp as much as we did? Gear went up to our cabins, the money was given over to the camp canteen to be used against the candy bars we would buy during the week, and we tried to look brave - like we didn't already miss Mom and Dad.

As we got older, we could stay at camp for TWO WEEKS! Maybe that's why we had to sell those Christmas cards – to pay for that second week? My favorite camp activity was, as you probably guessed, horseback riding. Archery was my next favorite, except for those awful feather burns I got from the arrow slapping against my wrist as it released from the bow. The other great thing I could do as an older camper was go on COOKOUTS - This meant cooking our food over an open campfire. Cooking with Aluminum Foil was becoming a big thing. It was "so neat" to wrap a piece of meat, a potato, carrots and onions in foil; place them in the fire and actually cook them without the foil burning up - magic. What did we care that some of the food was usually half done while the other part was burned? - it was such a novel idea. I remember we had salad with these gourmet meals, because once when Nancy and I had "salad duty" and dropped the lettuce in the mud while fixing it. We rationalized that since lettuce grew in dirt anyway, we'd just wash it off and no one would know the difference. Sometimes, we had breakfast cookouts with another wonder food of those times - POWDERED EGGS and POWDERED MILK! I won't try to describe those delicacies, but I'll never understand how a world war was won on that kind of food.

Where did the magic of summer camp go? When and how did we get too old to be Camp Fire Girls? How did horseback riding lose its enticement? Out of all my many summer camping experiences, what has remained with me all these years are the songs sung around the campfires on those wonderful Colorado summer nights. Today children are always amazed that someone as old as me can sing right along with them - songs they've learned in day school or on their own camping experiences - and they are even more surprised when I can add a few new ones to their repertoire.

This year for the first time in many, many a year, I once again returned to that wonderful experience of camping and looking up at a million mountain stars high above...

"There's a mountain meadow sparkling in the dew of early morn', and it's June in the Rockies once more..."

A Walk to Remember
By Cindy Carroll (Cynthia Chaney)

It was November of 1999 when I saw the ad in the newspaper. Just a short time before the much ballyhooed Millennium would arrive. The year 2000 would also be of significant personal meaning to me - it was to be the year I retired from 41 years of working, celebrated our 20th wedding anniversary and turned 60 years old. This definitely called for something more memorable than the usual cake and ice cream. That's when the newspaper ad caught my attention: "Come join the celebration," it said, "and be part of a great cause!" Avon's Breast Cancer Foundation was advertising a fund raising event in San Francisco to be held in July of 2000. "Just walk sixty miles in three days and commit to raise $1,800 in contributions," the ad said. I sent in my entry fee, and thus began one of the most memorable events in my life.

Raising the $1,800 was a little intimidating. The most I had ever done before was to raise camp money from candy and card sales (see my earlier story) for Camp Fire Girls. With lots of advice from the Avon Foundation, I sent letters to friends, relatives, and co-workers asking for contributions, and hoping for the best. Amazingly, this was the easiest part of the experience. In very little time I had raised $4,500.

With that part done, I began serious training in the spring. From April until July, I walked over 380 miles (the distance between San Francisco and Los Angeles) and bicycled another 250 miles as cross training. I learned a few important things throughout all that exercise: Clothing, especially socks and shoes, make a big difference as the miles mount up. Burning up to 1000 calories in a long walk doesn't equal loosing weight - it takes a lot of energy bars and sports drinks to walk 20 miles. Walking is a wonderful way to really see neighborhoods. And, most importantly, breast cancer is not selective in who it hits. I met some pretty incredible survivors in the organized training walks.

The 3-Day event officially started on the last Thursday in July with registration, tent assignments and a safety video. By this time, we had lots of energy and were anxious to the point of being hyper for the actual walk to begin. The next morning, we showed up at 5:30 AM to drop off our baggage which contained sleeping bags, sleeping mats, fresh clothing, and extra shoes, all wrapped in the recommended plastic bags. Tents were to be provided. Then, all 3,000 walkers (2,900 women and 100 men) and 500 volunteer crew members gathered in a schoolyard for the opening ceremonies. The energy was incredible and contagious, and nervousness made the port-a-potty lines a block long!

The first day's route took us from San Jose to San Carlos, a total of 23.5 miles over mildly hilly terrain in 90-degree temperatures. As we headed out from the opening ceremonies at 8 AM, it was quite a sight to see 3,000 walkers clogging the sidewalks. There were people of all sizes, shapes, ages and physical abilities walking. Motorists stuck in commuter traffic honked support and spectators cheered us. With support facilities every two miles, it was easy to drink gallons of water and Gatorade, and munch on energy snacks. While this was not a race, one of my friends, a woman who has been in remission for the last few years from breast cancer and did not walk at all before we started training, was one of the leaders into camp that first night. She used to cry on the hills when we did our training walks, and now, she was finishing in the top 50 walkers. What an inspiration for the rest of us.

All I have to say about camping the first night is that lousy food and tent sleeping is as good as a gourmet meal and the Hilton, when you have just walked twenty-three miles.

The second day's route from San Carlos to Skyline was to be shorter, only 16.5 miles, with lots of ups and downs thrown in for the challenge. One of the hills we climbed was so long and steep, a mule-team wouldn't have gone up it. Walkers were dropping like flies on the way up. At the top of the hill we joined a trail which runs along a beautiful reservoir.

It was so pretty and calm, we wanted to lie down and take a nap under the big oak trees. By the time we reached camp for our second night, the famous San Francisco fog had set in. It was so windy and foggy, we could not see more than three tents away, and guides had to be posted along the paths for us to find the showers and port-a-potties. It truly lived up to Mark Twain's famous quote about his, "…coldest winter was a summer in San Francisco." We woke the next morning to puddles of water in our tents but laughter all around us. Thank goodness for those plastic bags we packed everything in the first day. Wet shoes and socks would have made completion of the event impossible.

The third day of walking began in fog so thick we had to carry light sticks for passing motorists to see us. As the fog lifted throughout the morning, this segment turned into our most beautiful route; a total of 20 miles from Skyline to the Marina Green in San Francisco. We walked along the Pacific Coast, through Golden Gate Park with spectacular views of the Golden Gate Bridge, and down to the San Francisco Bay.

And then, we had done it! 3,000 people had walked a total of 60 miles in three days and raised $6.2 million for the fight against breast cancer. The closing ceremonies were held on the beautiful Marina Green in San Francisco. Husbands, wives, loved ones and friends were there to cheer us and share in our tears of joy. For our processional parade into the closing ceremonies, special honor was given to those amongst us who had survived breast cancer. Seeing so many survivors on the platform in their pink T-shirts was a wonderful end to an incredible journey.

At the opening ceremonies, we were told that the trip would be challenging and tough enough so that we could experience our own possibilities and gain an understanding of the pain and endurance it takes to fight the battle against breast cancer. It was all that and more. So much courage and spirit touched my heart and soul. We saw people in a lot of pain keep walking and smiling, and got choked up when we passed others showing tributes to their lost loved ones. We met hundreds of crew and volunteers who worked incredibly hard and always had smiles on their faces. We watched the medical team treat thousands of blisters (some on my own feet) and attend to all manner of injuries (sometimes it looked like a war zone). Thousands of supporters along the route kept us going when we were hot and exhausted, or cold and tired. Everyday, there were tears of joy and peals of laughter. The cause, the spirit and the determination carried us through a finish that made each person feel like a hero.

When I was growing up, Andy Warhol said that everyone should get their 15 minutes of fame. I'm glad I had my 15 minutes of being a hero as we walked into the finish area in the middle of the cheering crowd.

Memories – Long Ago and Far Away

By Duane Burtis

We came back to Colorado in 1946, after the war, from Clarendon, VA. in a 1928 Dodge touring car and settled at 4300 Graves Street. The street name was later changed to Garland, because there was already a Graves Street in Arvada. I say, "We came back…," because I was born at home on Meade Street in Denver. Dad worked for the U.S. Geological Survey, and we moved around the U.S. a lot during WW II.

"Number please!" Yes, real live phone operators on every call. "494M.".…"Thank you!" In the late 40s that was Dan Brebner's phone number. Our number was "1297W." Later, a girlfriend's number in Lakewood was, "Belmont 3-2686." It's funny how some things just stick in your memory. Numbers were my thing. My elementary school library number was, "594." Admission to the Arvada Theatre was 9 ¢ till about 1950, when it went up to 14 ¢. "Highway robbery! Outrageous prices!" I thought at the time. But, the Roy Rogers and Gene Autry movies and Daffy Duck cartoons were worth it to a ten-year-old.

Friends? Back then they were determined by scarcity and proximity. Dan Brebner lived two houses north of me and we became fast friends. Anyone else close to my age was at least an iris field away, and they were big fields. Dan had a single shot "Daisy" BB-gun, one of those you bent in the middle to cock it. Then, you dropped a BB down the barrel. The BB was supposed to stick there until you fired the gun, but sometimes it didn't. So, you put your finger over the end and tipped the barrel up and down until the BB finally stuck in place. One day, it was my turn to shoot, and my finger was covering the muzzle. Dan saw a bird and grabbed for the gun. Yes, it went off. We went to his house, and his mom pinched my fingertip like she was squeezing a pimple to get the BB out. God, that hurt!!! - almost as bad as a dentist's needle.

Our stomping grounds were generally along Clear Creek, anywhere within a mile of home. One spring, we were along a part of the creek where we had a tree bridge. The creek was frozen over, but the weather was relatively warm and things were beginning to thaw. Dan was on the bridge with his gun, and I was on the ice. He shot me in the calf, on purpose, but it didn't go through my Levi's. As I was rolling up the cuff to see the damage to my leg, Dan came down to check it out too, and the section of ice on which we were standing gave way. He was near the edge and jumped to shore, while I went in up to my waist before I was able to grab a limb. About that time Kenny Lines showed up, and while I sat on the bridge, Kenny and Dan twisted my pants between them to wring them out. I have replayed that vision many times and laughed.

The tree bridge stayed in place for a long time, and under it the water flowed pretty deep. I learned to swim there one day, when my big brother said, "Jump, or I'll push you off the bridge!" I chose to jump because I knew he would do it, and then I would not have a choice about which end would enter the water first. Between such things as big brothers, rope swings in the tall cottonwoods, tubing in the spring flood waters of Clear Creek, shooting each other with BB guns, launching Cherry Bombs and M-80s with a slingshot and throwing rocks at each other with slings, we were lucky to live long enough to grow older.

We made tree swings, more often than not, from sections of black and red hose not unlike the water hoses you could find in Berkley Park. In the winter we held ice skating parties on the creek with hot dogs and marshmallows cooked on open fires, and sled riding down the trail below Randy White's barn. The trail was a steep path used by the horses to get down to a lower pasture.

One summer day, our creek turned murky, and all the fish in the creek went floating downstream, belly-up. That was in the early 50s. It was said that Coors was discharging bad water. We were told not to go swimming in Clear Creek any more. For a few years Dan and I did our swimming in the Lakeside Amusement Park pool - clean, chlorinated water - Yuck!

So much for the pre-Wheat Ridge High School days - those were the Fruitdale Elementary School days. The Fruitdale School had grades one through eight. Then, we had to pick a high school. The choices were: Wheat Ridge, Arvada, or Golden. Since my big brother and sister went to WRHS, I started there in 1954. I don't have a lot of great high school memories. The guys I ran with were Don "Little Mouse" Payne, John Rose and Gary Davis, all from Fruitdale. None of them graduated. Sometimes I wonder how I made it. For a while Gary had a 50-Ford ragtop and we occasionally played hooky. Once, we took off and went to the Safeway, bought one pomegranate each and munched on them getting the juice all over our shirts. I had never eaten a pomegranate before. God, they were messy to eat without a bowl, or something! That day we ended up out in Aurora.

Gary Davis had "the hots" for a girl that lived on Teller Street between 32nd and 38th. I don't remember who she was, but as far as I remember, she never went out with him. We burned a lot of gas going up and down Teller, after school and on weekends. The four of us usually ended up going stag to the school dances. During all of high school, I only remember going on two dates. If I had been smart, I would have gone on a third, but I was young and dumb then, like a lot of guys.

It was probably through Don Payne's influence that I went out for wrestling for three years. I only got to wrestle on the "B-squad" once. During the match I escaped from a usually fatal hold. From that experience Coach Brockman got the idea I was so loose-jointed I couldn't be pinned. Shortly after, during a practice match with Golden, I think he lost some money betting on me. The Golden wrestler that pinned me was no B-squader, I guarantee.

I also went out for Track and did some pole vaulting. During our previous years along Clear Creek, Dan Brebner and I used poles to vault across the creek and irrigation canals and whatever else to avoid getting our shoes muddy. I found out there was a BIG difference between vaulting for distance and vaulting for height. I wasn't the best in the league, but did OK.

Some of my fun memories are the football and basketball games and the Community Center where there was dancing afterwards. My sister, Jeanne, tried to teach me to dance a few times, but it didn't take. I had the proverbial two left feet, but I went anyway.

I wasn't much of an academician. More worldly pleasures captured my fancy. But, I did have a favorite teacher, Mr. McClean, who taught "plane geometry." He wore bow ties which would normally have classified him as a "dork," in my mind, but few teachers and subjects captured my imagination and interest - he did. He was a cool dude. I wonder if they still teach plane geometry?

There was a time in Geography class in the basement, when Gary Stites brought in his guitar and did his Elvis version of, "Blue Suede Shoes." I don't know what it had to do with geography, but he was good, and so was Dean Reed, singing about "The Old Knot Hole" during assembly.

I don't remember who was involved, but when water pistols were the thing with which to irritate others, I rigged a rubber battery filler with a short hose and a water gun nozzle to fight back. I kept it in the desk and lifted the top just enough to hold the tip out the side. I think I was busy hosing down Norm Vieria, when the teacher noticed the commotion, and my water gun became school property.

And, last but not least, the student exchange program: During junior year, I went on the exchange trip with North Adams, Massachusetts. They didn't prove to be as active as the previous Florida exchange group, when it came to shoplifting - "five finger discounts." Good thing, or it could have ended our opportunity to get out of town on school time. We rode a train all the way from Denver to North Adams. Somewhere east of Chicago, the "countryside" disappeared. There was no open space between cities, at least not along the railway. It was a two-week trip with one week spent with our exchange partner. My partner was, Ronald Baruzzi, who lived in Readsboro, Vermont. The town was located in a valley between tree-covered hills. I slept in an attic bedroom in a bed with down covers about a foot high. Wow, talk about warm and comfy! I played hooky one day and just went for a walk in the woods. Even though it was winter and cold, it was beautiful. The second week was a sightseeing trip down the East Coast. One day, we visited the Statue of Liberty and the Empire State Building. That night, it was party time for most of the group in a New York City hotel. We left from Grand Central on a train for Washington D. C., saw the sights there and hopped a ferryboat down the Chesapeake Bay. I recall it being an overnight boat ride. They served us some bad food for dinner, and almost everyone woke up with food poisoning. We were transported via school bus to a hospital. I think Dixie Savio and I were the only ones to come through unscathed - we were tough. From there we were put on a train back to Denver.

And that's the way life was for me in the big metropolis of Wheat Ridge, Colorado. Memories - long ago and far away...

The Utah Years
By Duane Burtis

Advancement with my corporate office in Denver led to branch manager training. Opportunity was before me, when suddenly I was offered a series of locations that, well, let's just say, left lots to be desired. Turn down one - Sterling, Colorado was acceptable. Turn down two - Price, Utah and my sincerity and dedication to the company would be questioned. We were off to Price America, Utah! Our goal as a family was the country life and thus began the great adventure.

The branch store was a cement block attachment to a "third-hand" shop next door and on the wrong side of the railroad tracks. It wasn't pretty. The most encouraging view that I saw daily was a sign above that read, "In Price to Stay." Finally, after four years, the company invested, and I oversaw the building of a brand new store. But, it was a long three years at the ramshackle location.

As a family we settled into one of three housing choices during the "boomtown era" of Utah's energy bonanza. Our homestead was one acre of weeds that came up to the armpits with a small ranch house on the desert side of the Wasatch Mountain range. It wasn't pretty. Undeterred, we were optimistic and thoughts of the pioneers danced in our heads. Armed only with a roto-tiller, shovels, rakes and sweat we slowly planted an orchard. Next came landscaping, and by year two a garden flourished. There we were, the homesteaders from Denver, working seven days a week for the company and also working our land - poor in money, but rich in livestock - we had two dogs, three rabbits, that rapidly became twenty three, a duck and a teenage son. Life was good.

I bought a prefabricated garage kit in Salt Lake City, and then it happened - the Thistle, Utah Mud Slide! The event actually made the front cover of the National Geographic magazine in 1983. Heavy, persistent moisture promoted giant mudslides. One major slide moved a mountainside filling in the valley and diverting the river. The highway and railroad disappeared. Losing the railroad was a disaster. The railroad was the cornerstone of Price's economy. It transported the area's rich, low sulfur coal to the Pacific Rim for overseas shipment. The loss of the highway cut off the main connecting route to Salt Lake City. The two and one-half hour trip became a five hour trip around mountains instead of through them. We watched the population shrink from 50,000 to 10,000 in just over a year. Houses were abandoned. The coal mining industry came to a near standstill as lucrative, long term 25-year contracts were canceled. Price, Utah's future was sealed. The community slid into a depression. Our small town adventure became a small town's nightmare.

We elected to stay in Utah and ride out the storm. We bought Honda ATC's and explored the desert. We went rock-hounding, visited Lake Powell, saw petroglyphs, pictographs and fossils and visited every corner of Utah.

We watched the Army Corps of Engineers struggle to rebuild the highway and railroad through and over Billy's Mountain and above Lake Thistle, as the area became known. As the dammed-up river created ever expanding lake frontage the Corps dug drainage tunnels from east and west and were mystified when the floor of the west tunnel barely met the roof of the east tunnel. The drainage angle was not proper, so they ran an enormous flexible pipe over the rim of the mud dam from the lake to the dry riverbed. But, the piping wasn't long enough to reach the ground and the water began eroding the base of the dam threatening to weaken it...and so it went - don't let the Corps of Engineers build your house! The highway was reconnected after a year, but daily rockslides made the trip a risky adventure. Finally, transportation connections were restored, but the international coal contracts had vanished. Other coal suppliers had been found, and Price America, Utah continued in its solitary gloom. Sadly, the desert town never recovered.

After four years of sweat and tears, we requested a transfer back to the Mile High City. We sold our house for just enough to cover the mortgage and took our collection of well-traveled household goods, two used vehicles and the teenage son back to Denver for a new start. Utah or bust!!! - We busted.

If you can't resist going to Utah, we recommend Bull Frog Marina on the eastern shores of Lake Powell and Waweep on the west. Lee's Crossing along the Colorado River below the Glen Canyon Dam is an interesting stop. When we were there, the large rocks along the river diverted the water making a three foot high wall of water midstream where fishermen stood. The Mogollon Rim outside of Mexican Hat, Utah is a drop off the edge of the earth. There Indian pictographs on slick rock walls outside of Thompson, Utah in a lonesome unpopulated canyon most worthy of a side jaunt.

Shaffer's Trail, a forty-mile jeep trail out of Moab heading to Dead Horse Point is a challenge. The trail up the face of Dead Horse Point along a narrow former cattle trail provides pause for thought - how did they ever do it?

On the desert floor we found prehistoric mud balls filled with fossils and sharks teeth. The Mormon communities dynamited many of the natural hot sulfur springs to discourage skinny-dipping - damn! But, we found one below a deep water fall in the Wasatch Mountain Range.

Cedar City hosts a replica of an outdoor Shakespearean Theatre with an annual repertoire of the bard each summer.

Starvation Reservoir matches its name. Carnivorous Mormon crickets below Green River, UT were fascinating as they zigged and zagged along the desert floor aggressively combing the sands until disappearing at high noon. St. George, UT and Mount Zion's National Park are worthy of a view.

Thus, we ended our attempt at small town living and rejoined the hustle of metropolitan Denver until our son had grown and the next adventure beckoned - Seattle, WA. Washington or bust!!! We'll see. It's a good life.

Lessons Learned
By Dixie Savio Jones (Dixie Savio)

It was 1948. The world order was finally stabilizing...at least in our homes. The early morning radio soaps included, "Stella Dallas", "Let's Pretend", "The Shadow Knows", and even "Buster Brown" was back living in his shoe. The soldiers had returned home from the war, or so it seemed; you saw lots of "men in uniform" walking around on the streets. There was even a chance you might be able to buy some "bubble gum." We had heard about it, but there was no gum during the war. We had never seen a wad and certainly never chewed, or blown the big pink bubbles that eventually popped all over our faces. And, we could now stop poking the "color button" in the "Nucla" to make it look like butter. The liquid color that Mom smeared on her legs was replaced on special occasions by real "silk stockings" that had a big seam wandering up the back of her leg. And, the sticky stuff she used to keep the "up-sweep" on her hair-do was available, along with the red henna-colored rinse to make everyone look even more beautiful - amazing how many redheads there were in America. The coal man came with his huge truck dumping these marvelous, huge black shiny diamonds in our coal bin. Daddy shoveled them every morning and night into our big stoker to keep our home comfy. The egg man, Mr. Weller, arrived again, once a week to sell the "fresh eggs." There were no eggs during the war - they all went to the soldiers. Mr. Weller also offered the colorful printed flower sacks that we made into wonderful house dresses and aprons for Mom and play dresses for my sister, Linda, and me...only Dad was not a recipient. Times were wonderful again. The war was over - we won. It was great to be safe...

All seemed wonderful again, until one particular day that still haunts me…it was early morning. The routine was always the same - Dad readying for work; Mom preparing breakfast and Linda and I racing around with excitement gathering our books for school. Breakfast was over and Mom was in the dining room "accessorizing" Dad's suit coat…folding the sharply creased, starched white handkerchief into his breast pocket, dropping gum and Life Savers in the right pocket. And then, she gathered up the change that was left on the buffet from the night before and slipped her hand into the left pocket…but her hand wouldn't drop the change. She slid to the floor, gasping for air, screaming guttural animal-like sounds, as her face twisted and drew into a grotesque mass of folding flesh. "Who is this person?" I thought, "This can't be MY MOM! What is happening?" as I accompanied her shouts with my own.

Dad hollered from the bathroom, "Velma, stop playing. You are scaring the kids!" She couldn't stop, and as Dad approached the dining room, he was aghast at the sight of his beautiful wife.

It took many months of live-in care and fulltime nurses to put our family back together. Neighbors and friends assisted with food, "setting" the girls' hair, helping with the wash and the other daily chores. Dad spent every day and every evening sitting at Mom's bedside. The diagnosis was frightening - paralyzed on the right side; blinded left eye; no speech; couldn't read, or write; little memory…only remembering Dad and "one" daughter - my sister. Today they call this a stroke, or an aneurysm, or maybe both. In those days the chance of living was minimal, and full recovery…well, not even an option.

But, Mom was a fighter.

The love in our home was never in question. We all loved one another and clung to our Mom for fear we could lose her. My sister and I dedicated a portion of each day to teaching our Mom what we had learned in school to help her regain her memory and begin to read, write, and talk again. Dad put all his energy into working, supporting us as well as a "live-in" to care for us. It was a changed world…stay out of the kitchen…you will upset the live-in…tiptoe around the house…don't wake up Mom…the kettle boiling on the stove sanitizing the needles for Mom's injections…don't fight with your sister, it upsets Mom. And then, the day on the play ground, when I heard, "Nay, nay, nay…your Mom doesn't even know she had you. That's how important you are." The tears ran down my cheeks as I ran home to Mom. "Why don't you know me? Aren't I as important as everyone else?" The question was tough…the answer…there was none.

It was a small, isolated, unthinking kids incident, but it was a big deal to me. It made a difference in my life. The kids at school felt awful…trying in every way to make it up to me. But, I just felt different…not about them, but about me!…not sure who I am; a little kid with big disappointments; "grown up" feelings and how to act, so I didn't upset anybody at home…I just wanted to be loved, not hurt anybody, and retreat into myself to find ME.

I was starting the sixth grade, and Dad announced it was time to move out of North Denver, to Wheat Ridge, a rural community west of Denver…lots of places to play; corn fields; we could even learn to ride a bike…lots of places without cars. It sounded great! But, that meant making new friends and starting all over again.

It was the greatest for me! I met a wonderful new best friend, Pat Glenski. She was THE popular girl in school. Everybody liked her…and she really liked ME. Through Pat, without her ever knowing it, and I didn't either, I began to believe I too, could be liked. I began caring about other people the way I wanted them to care about me. Two special friends that reinforced my confidence and gave me the courage to be who I am were Don Shepperd and Mike White…they told me I was pretty…the four of us, Pat, Don, Mike and me had great fun together. I began to develop new friends, regain my self-confidence and eventually was at ease with new interests and a desire to be involved in "kids stuff" once again. We had so much fun together. I thank all my friends for what they gave back to me. May I never forget how important it is to care about others more than myself. Once you do, that, you find "real" fun and happiness.

Later Life Bag Woman
By Dixie Savio Jones (Dixie Savio)

The Senior Prophecy said I was going to be "...Yul Brynner's hairdresser". My timing wasn't right for the hair business. If I had only waited, Michael Jordan might have made the difference - bald became the rage. I was never great at timing, but I decided to try leaping over tall buildings in a single bound and entered the business world.

After high school, I attended the University of Arizona. I selected it for all the right reasons - sunshine, palm trees and a GREAT basketball team. I returned to Colorado and spent 10 years with the Colorado Cattlemen's Association. I learned a lot about "bull" and met all the right people to introduce me to politics, my first true love.

Politics took me to the Governor's office where I spent a few years helping to reorganize state government and then on to coordinating "THE ATOM" in the eleven western states. No one had ever taken me for a scientist, especially after I said, "Oh, you mean 'atom', not like 'Adam and Eve'?"

Like Al Gore, who gave us the internet, I had conquered the atom; so, why not luggage?...I went to work for Samsonite. The climb in those days for a female was tough, but rewarding. I became the first senior female executive at Samsonite and retired from there 25 years later. Bob Jones had the "hottest" advertising agency in town and he won the Samsonite account - and my heart. Lucky me - he chose me over the account, and I have been married to my great, loving, artist-husband, Bob, for 19 years. Now, we are both retired, living in Castle Pines, CO. We take two, or three month, adventure vacations every year. We have been to Indonesia, Irian Jaya, Africa, China, and other exciting places.

Life has been an adventure - Wheat Ridge, Arizona sunshine, cattle, politics, nuclear energy, luggage - now, I am doing some modeling and contract television work on Home Shopping Network in Florida selling, what else??? - Samsonite bags...I guess it takes one bag to sell another?

Playing Hooky
By Jerry Jensen

Our family moved to Denver in 1954, when my father was transferred from Billings Montana, to the much warmer climate of Denver, Colorado. Because he would work in the Denver Federal Center West of Denver in Jefferson County, we would live in Lakewood or Wheat Ridge. When we bought the new home in Wheat Ridge for $18,000, I became a Wheat Ridge Farmer. A lot of us spent time seeking to change the name, what kind of mascot is a farmer? The name remains to this day, but this is not the story of my time in the halls of Wheat Ridge High, but rather out of it.

I was scarcely enrolled in the ninth grade when I was invited by my new friends to commit a daring act. We would not go to class, but instead walk the mile east to Sheridan Boulevard and visit Larimer Street. My parents had told me never go to Larimer Street because it was dangerous, so this added the excitement of risk of where we were going, to the risk of getting caught. I had not reached puberty and looked like the 5' 3" child I was. We boarded the bus at Sheridan and headed downtown. We exited the bus as it turned up 16th street and walked the block to Larimer. It was even better than I had imagined. Larimer Street in 1954 was skid row at its best, and Denver was the largest city I had ever seen. There were seedy hotels with narrow staircases littered with old drunks just sitting on the steps. Spaced between them were bars with foot rails just like in the cowboy movies. And then there were the pawnshops.

We managed to sneak into a few bars and look around before the bartender would spot us and yell, "You kids get out of here!" Tough guys leaned on the bar talking to hard looking women, just like in the movies. They were nothing like our suburban fathers who went to work while our mothers cleaned the house and prepared our dinner, where the biggest event of the week was going to church on Sunday morning. But the pawnshops were the best. The owners didn't kick us out and we could roam the glass-topped cases which held every type of gun imaginable. Actual German Lugars, like in the war, pearl handled revolvers, Colt .45s, and .357 Magnums. We were thrilled. There were watches, all sorts of exotic cigarette lighters, rings, bracelets, and more. We happily spent the morning there before eating our lunches which we somehow had kept with us. We arrived back at the end of the school day and lied to our parents about whatever actually happened at school. I wish I could remember how we didn't get caught but I don't, which brings me to the second time I played hooky when I was 6' 2", a senior, and knew better.

When Bill Weiss ,Terry Marcheso and I drove to school in Bill's blue '50 Chevy they informed me that tomorrow was to be Senior Ditch Day. While not listed in the school schedule, a ditch day for seniors sounded like an entitlement we had earned, still with risk, since neither of our deans, Mr. Haycraft or Mrs. Purvis would approve, and obviously must be kept secret from other adults, like parents. The Senior Ditch Day was in the fall, during football season. It was organized by "The boys", the most popular group of athletes and rebels led by Dick English, Dick Weber and Norm Vieira. I was only a fringe member and was thrilled to be included. My fringe status, I thought, was due to the fact that I liked going to class and took nerd courses like Trigonometry, which wasn't cool. But my wife later explained it better when she pointed out I was both arrogant, oblivious, and self-centered when I was younger, which it had taken her years to try and correct, with little effect; (this must be why marriage is so popular as a self- help tool).

The next day arrived, bright and sunny, as Bill arrived to pick me up for school. We were soon in a convoy of four cars. There were only four cars as this was "the boys" senior ditch day not the whole high school. We headed west into the mountains. The thrill of freedom was in the air and I thought we were too cool. We stopped by Central City and practiced rolling stones down the Glory Hole. Watching large boulders bounce down a slope couldn't have been better. Then we raced down the narrow switchbacks leading into Jamestown. The idea was to stay, train-like, right on the bumper of the car in front while taking the turns as fast as the first car. These two rear wheeled drive cars screeched and swerved on each turn, and we were thrown back and forth but somehow no one rolled off of the two lane narrow road and down the embankment. When we arrived by the dam, we found a chute fed by a mountain stream. Someone said, "I'm in," and stripping to his undershorts jumped in the frigid waters and slid down the chute. Who was next? Everyone, since no one wanted to wimp out. Damn, that water was cold, but the ride down the chute was fun. We were all shivering as we dressed, but our manhood was intact. We then returned to lugging stones over to the concrete dam and rolling them down its face. If you do not understand why this was so great, instead of answering questions in Mr. Ellison's Civics class, then you have never been a normally immature 17 year-old boy. The rest of that day blurs away in my memory but not the next.

I awoke the next morning with clarity of mind totally lacking the day before. I had visions of Mr. Haycraft and Mrs. Purvis looking at absentee lists with all the usual suspects among senior boys on it, I imagined them checking each one with a red pen. There was only one solution I could see, I was sick. Actually the thought of getting expelled did make me feel ill. My mother appeared at the door, "Jerry get up, you're going to be late." I moaned and rolled over, "I'm not feeling well." That was somewhat true even if it was a lie. Unfortunately, she soon appeared with a thermometer, "You don't seem to have a fever," she said. My symptoms immediately changed to stomach cramps. "My body aches," I said. She looked skeptical, but left. I tried to go to sleep but soon the phone rang. "It's the office at school calling to see where you are. Is something going on? I told them you are sick." That night I was blessed. My mother had a church meeting. My dad didn't understand why he was writing the excuse for the absence to the school when my mom always did it, and he seemed surprised that I was so willing to write it for him. Best of all he didn't notice when I put "two days," not "day," for being absent, before he signed it. Be thankful for dads who notice so much less than moms.

I didn't get expelled, but I know some of the others got in trouble. None of which prevented us from graduating or probably kept us out of a college we weren't going to get into anyway. I do remember my class friend, Dennis Glenn, didn't come. He was at football practice that day, and he was the only one that received a football scholarship to college that year. As we get older, we remember, with more clarity, the unusual days of our lives, good or bad. I still remember my two days of playing hooky. When I was in college, I told my mom about it. She gave me one of those wise motherly looks and said she already knew.

A Vietnam Story
By Jerry Jensen

This is a story that took place in Vietnam. But it is not the Vietnam that you will find today with the New Century, Hyatt, and Sofitel hotels overlooking Saigon streets clogged with cars and motor bikes. This is also not the Vietnam that some of our classmates' experienced, in the bamboo stands, swamps, and mountains of this narrow country where the mountains run north to south for a thousand miles but the distance from the Laotian border to the sea, often is only forty. That Vietnam opened for most Americans in 1965 and closed in 1973. The sounds and fury of warfare died away as the last helicopters flew off the embassy roof and the rifle fire remaining was the volleys of firing squads. The Rex and Caravelle hotels, flanking the ornate French Revival Opera House still dominated the core of the city. The hotels having disgorged Americans, filled with Russian and Japanese, and the new leaders presided over a tightly controlled stagnant economy while the rest of Southeast Asia boomed. We arrived in 1992, and not much had changed.

We were enticed to this country by a businessman who had escaped as one of the thousands of Vietnamese boat people in the 1970s, who eventually made it to Denver. It was curiosity, not ambition that brought me here, which was good because I have never made a penny to this day from our investments in Vietnam. "Do," as he was known, was from Da Nang, the seaport in the central part of the country. He introduced us to many business opportunities including, marble quarries, hotels, cement plants, rubber products, and water bottling. In 1992, Vietnam was still subject to an American embargo but I always felt that we as citizens, not the State Department should determine where we could travel and invest. This day we had traveled north from Hue, the old imperial capital of the country built on the banks of the Perfume River. Quang Tri Province is where the famous Route 9, a crazy winding road ascends the mountains into Laos and was a major part of the Ho Chi Minh Trail. We traveled through Quang Tri City the battle-scarred town which lay in the middle of the DMZ during the Vietnam War, where we were to meet the company that wanted a hotel built in Dong Ha, on the river. Dong Ha was the capital of Quang Tri province and was just north of the Route 9 crossing.

We were driven into the compound which served as the headquarters of the province. We were to have lunch with our hosts who had proposed the project. The temperature was about 80 degrees and our group consisted of Richard Hensel, our President, me and an interpreter. Our Vietnamese partner, who had worked for the Americans, did not come. I was soon to find out why, as we stepped in the room. Our hosts were mostly in uniform. Impossible to miss was Major Kwan, who had on a full fur cap with a bright red Russian star embossed on the front. The others were dressed in full military uniforms, which I recognized as North Vietnamese. It appeared this would be their occasion to celebrate their victory over the Americans. We were introduced and after hearing several speeches about their great progress under the communist leadership (which none of us had observed in this impoverished country) the mood abruptly changed.

A large bottle of premium Russian Vodka was produced and poured directly into water-sized glasses. "We now drink to a new era of American friendship," the interpreter beamed. I cast a panic-stricken glance at Richard Hensel, our ostensible leader. He was quicker than me. "As an Adventist we are not allowed to drink….., Jerry will be honored," he said, smiling profusely. "Oh no," I said, but was too late. Major Kwan was facing me with his glass extended. While I was no longer a Mormon, I very rarely drank and never at lunch. Trapped, I raised the glass thrust in my hand and felt the Vodka burn down my throat, as I closed my eyes. When I opened them, everyone magically had another filled glass, including me. "To America!" What was I to do, appear to be a wimp to our former enemies and not pay tribute to America? I lost count after the third toast, but my head was spinning and I could feel tingling all the way to my toes. I was completely drunk as the lunch ended and I was led to the river to see the hotel site.

I was horrified to see I was about to embark on a rough handmade barge, with a small two-cycle engine emitting a thick black cloud in the back while we sat on two wooden benches in front of the engine. We proceeded down the river as my head seemed to be hit by the pop-pop of each cycle of that engine and I vowed not to vomit in front of them. Even in my drunken state I could see the villages along the river were all on stilts, and far in among the mangroves the high water marks from the rainy season were six feet above our boat. If you build a river front hotel here, it had better be able to float. At some point I got them to turn the boat around and I completed my mission of not barfing their lunch back at them. As I mercifully arrived on shore my head was still splitting from the pop-pop of that engine. I saluted and thanked my captors, gave a one-fingered salute to Hensel, who despite being an Adventist, would drink a beer in Hue that night, and escaped in the car.

We did design a hotel in Vietnam. It is on the Perfume River in Hue, where the brightly decorated dragon boats line the grassy banks. We tried to complement the beautiful but aging French colonial buildings along the shore. After submitting the plans, we were told environmental restrictions prevented our getting the permit. Getting any approvals can be a murky process in Vietnam, since most businesses are owned by government agencies or military units and the final authority is always the province's Communist Party Chairman. Similar to the situation in China, I call it the "new Asian fascism." But, if you go to Hue today, you will see the hotel, just to the west of the main bridge. It was built by a Thailand partnership with the official Tourist Bureau of Hue.

Imogene Boring, Where Are You?

By Phyllis Findley (Phyllis Anderson)

My 86 year old Dad wrote this poem about my life beginning at age five:

When I was just a little girl before the age of five

My Mom was called to Heaven and taken from my side

She taught me about Jesus the time she had before she died

My Dad and me were left alone except for Grandma by our side

Grandma's hands reached out to me and pulled me to her side

She held me close and brushed away the bitter tears I cried

She let me know I had some one who would understand

And from that moment I held on to Grandma's hand

She didn't have much money, wasn't rich in earthly things

But what she had you couldn't find in palaces of kings

She had a heart so full of love and gave it all to me

That meant more than any thing on earth could ever mean

She took me off to Sunday school and taught me right from wrong

She taught me all the things I'd need to know to get along

And some times when I'd misbehave or stubbornly I'd stand

I'd get a real good lesson, right straight from Grandma's hand

Now I've grown to womanhood and she has gone away from me

But without the touch of Grandma's hand I wonder where I'd be

But only those who've gone this way can really understand

Just what I mean when I say, thank God for Grandma's hands

Grandma's hands did things for me that no one else could do

She always seemed to understand what I was going through

At night she'd take her Bible down and read the word to me

And I learned more about Jesus at Grandma's knee.

Then, my Dad remarried and things got really bad for me. That is when we moved to Wheat Ridge on 32nd and Benton, next to John Bandimere, my first crush. I started school at Columbia Heights, then went on to Wheat Ridge Jr. High and High School.

I have very few memories about my high school years, because that period of my life was horrible, and I blocked it out. I tried to melt into the walls and not be noticed. I was not allowed to participate in any school activities. I was not allowed to have any friends. I never went to a football, or basketball game. I never had my picture in the annual. I am not sure that I really existed during those years. I was taken out of the home in my sophomore year and went to live with an aunt in Missouri. In my senior year I came back to Wheat Ridge. I walked across the stage at graduation as part of the Wheat Ridge class, but my actual diploma came from Missouri. So, I guess that is why I was never invited to a class reunion. But, thanks to the internet and "www.classmates.com" I was able to find some of my old classmates. During my senior year I finally got up the nerve to make a friend, Imogene Boring. We stayed in touch for a while, after graduation, then lost track of each other. I would sure like to find her now. She is my only good memory of high school.

Things Worth Waiting For...
Happy Endings
By Phyllis Findley (Phyllis Anderson)

After high school, leaving home and marrying, I spent many years rebelling against my religious upbringing. I had a terrible childhood. But, the time came in my life, when I finally said, "ENOUGH!" Enough fighting and crying and struggling to just hold on. I began to see the world through new eyes. I realized that it was time to stop waiting for something to change. "He" was not prince charming, and "I" was not "Cinderella," and this was the real world, not a fairy tale. I finally stopped blaming other people for things they had done to me and decided the only one I could count on was "ME." I learned to stand on my own two feet and take care of myself. Life's trek took me through many states before I finally found happiness and contentment in Texas. There, I met my husband, and I found in him something I never had before - a man who cherishes me and treats me with more love, kindness, respect and sensitivity than I knew was possible.

For the first time in my life I was able to pursue things that made me happy. I started doing a wood art called, "Intarsia." I was involved with it for many years until the sawdust got to me and I developed allergies. During this time I reached way back to my roots and found The Lord. He had never left, nor forsaken me, as I had Him. I like to say I am like Moses - I spent 40 years wandering in the wilderness.

I started spending a lot of time on my computers; we have four. My husband, John, has one just for his games. We have one that I keep for the thirteen grandkids to play games on, and we have a laptop for traveling. And, there's mine that I use to surf the net, play scrabble, send e-mail and write stories for this book.

John retired from a chemical plant three years ago. We bought an RV and have been traveling ever since. All three of my children live in North Carolina; the two older girls by choice, and my son because of the Marines. We just returned from two and one half months in the Northwest. We started in Denver and gave a 50th wedding anniversary party for my dad and stepmother. I had visited Marble, Colorado in the 50's, and was able to make a lifelong dream come true by visiting it again. The old marble quarry was not working the first time I was there. In those days we were able to travel in jeeps; however, today the area is operational and you cannot drive the road. So, Johnnie and I climbed a very narrow, steep trail up to view the new quarry. They said it was ¼ of a mile, but it felt like 1 ¼ mile. Needless to say, I stopped and prayed a lot for oxygen before finally reaching the top. And, it was just as awesome as I remembered.

Being raised in Colorado, I never had a fear of heights, until this trip. We crossed pass, after pass, and every day my fear got worse. I finally reached the point where I became sick and was so terrified I covered my head with a blanket and cried all the way down every hill. Johnnie, being the sweetheart he is, said, "OK, no more passes." So, we didn't go to several places we looked forward to visiting. On that trip I learned I am a "flatlander." I belong in Texas, and I also learned a blanket is useful for something besides bedclothes - it makes a wonderful shield between me and the drop offs.

I love to salt water fish. Johnnie doesn't like to fish, but he goes with me and uses the computer. So, we spend as much time as possible on the Gulf of Mexico. I even learned to use a cast net and I always catch my own bait.

It seems ironic that my first love was a fellow named, "John" Bandimere, and my last and true love is also named, "John." I feel as though I have come full circle - back to my early teachings from the Bible:

"Give a man a fish and you feed him for a day. Teach him to use "the Net" and he won't bother you for week…"

All my adult life I feared getting cancer. Just hearing the word was traumatic. Then one evening in October 2007 after a routine Mammogram, I got a phone call and a very sympathetic nurse told me my lump in my breast was malignant. After that really sunk-in, I began to pray. God gave me such a peace about it that until this day, I never lost even one minute of sleep over it. The Peace was just so awesome, and not in my nature to not worry, but worry I did not. He sent Dr. Scott Kacy, the best doctor ever, to do my surgery. Dr. Kacy has such a wonderful bedside manner and took such good care of me, he remains my friend and email buddy. Then when his part was done, he sent me to the best Cancer Doctor, Dr. Birdwell, to follow-up with the treatment. Dr. Birdwell is also a wonderful, caring doctor. I tell anyone that getting cancer was one of the best things that has happened to me and I really get some strange looks until I tell them about the peace God gave me and the things I learned that have made my life better. I have learned compassion and have been able to witness to others and to be there when they need someone. It also taught me humility, and most of all, I learned to give it all to God and leave it with him. I shutter to think of how it would have played out if it wasn't, first of all for my God, my husband Johnnie and these two great doctors.

There are things worth waiting for in life…like happy endings.

Marianne and Me
By Bill Ehrich

We would meet at Wheat Ridge High School at about 8:00 on Saturday mornings and then drive across Denver to other high schools to compete in speech contests. The Saturday morning I still remember was in mid-November, with frost on the ground and slate gray clouds keeping the mountains from view.

We each had small, green steel boxes with hand-written note cards, yellow legal tablets and notebooks crammed with information related to the year's national debate topic. Wheat Ridge fielded two debate teams. Two young men were juniors. We were seniors.

When the fall semester started, I hadn't chosen a debate team partner. Then Marianne MacDonald showed up at the first organizational meeting. Knowing the kind of student who usually appeared at statewide debate meets, I felt sure we could win and win often. Marianne was my secret weapon.

By mid-November, we were very familiar with the national topic and had won our first few matches. That Saturday morning, we drove to Denver South High School. Our first opponents never stood a chance, two sophomores from Mullen High School. These boys wore ties their fathers had bought soon after World War II and clopped around in comfortable black wing tip shoes. Their sport coats were much too large for them. They had never had to compete against a tall, good-looking young woman in a red dress who looked anything like Marianne. As soon as she walked in the room, the two boys forgot everything they had learned about debate, about the topic for the year, and about how they were supposed to breathe.

Marianne swept by their table, smiled at both of them, looked each one in the eyes, and said, "Hi, boys." They whimpered and mumbled something in return. The boys from Mullen had been unbeaten until they faced the terror of Marianne in her red dress. Later that year, a young man from another high school fell out of his chair trying to pick up a pencil Marianne had dropped. She smiled at him when he finally handed her the pencil. His brain turned to mush before our eyes.

Most of the young men involved in debate in Colorado high schools in the late 1950s looked a lot like me. They had short haircuts, plastic rimmed glasses and wore suits picked out by their mothers. The few young ladies who competed in tournaments squinted, wore cardigan sweaters, and only occasionally washed their hair.

Then, there was Marianne. She was almost six feet tall with black hair, a great smile and dresses that clung to her. Other schools didn't want their students to face us. Boys knew instinctively they couldn't keep their minds on the debate subject and the few other girls felt inadequate in Marianne's presence.

Long before people talked about it, we used physical looks and implied sexuality to our advantage. For a kid who could have passed for 15 with ill-fitting glasses and saddle shoes, this was a revelation. It was fun to have an "edge" that we could exploit.

Very soon, we could walk into rooms and determine quickly how much effort we had to put into matches to come out winners. We knew when we could cruise and when we had to work hard. The one team that gave us the most problems was one from South High School with a young woman almost as pretty as Marianne.

Marianne and I went to different universities after our senior year. I went to the University of Denver and having learned my lessons on how to work the system, immediately teamed up for college debate meets with the pretty young woman who had graduated from South High School.

Since our senior year, never have I walked into a room and known that, whatever the contest was, victory was mine because I had an edge: a smart young woman who knew how to think and how to bend others to her will through the power of her smile and delightful way she walked. At least it happened to me once. For most people it's just a dream. I got to live the dream.

Hoosiers
By Bill Ehrich

I remember sitting in church one spring day in 1954, reading one of the many "uplifting" stories that were thrust upon us by well-meaning adults in a vain effort to get us to want to live "better lives." The story was about a group of high school students who did something that had never been done before. The majority of the boys in a small rural Indiana high school were on the varsity basketball team.

The regular season ended and the team, like all Indiana teams at that time, went into the single-division playoffs. They kept winning and got all the way to the state title game played at Butler Fieldhouse in Indianapolis. The famous "Miracle of Milan" happened when Milan beat the highly-regarded Muncie Central Bearcats for the Indiana State Title. The article tried to impress on us that, every now and then, David does beat Goliath, if he tries hard and his heart is pure. The high-minded stuff left me cold, but the desire to watch a lot of basketball games stuck.

In the 1950s, Denver was a wonderful place for a basketball junkie to grow up. Each spring, after high school tournaments and college tournaments ended, a large group of teams from all around the country came to Denver for a week and the national AAU championships. My dad and I would take a vacation from work and school and go to the various arenas around the city where the games were played. In 1960, it even got better: the week after the AAU tournament ended, the Olympic trials were held in Denver.

One of the reasons I moved to Indiana in the mid-1960s was so I could watch Indiana high school basketball. There are still small Indiana towns where the entire population attends the games on Friday evenings. Only Indiana has a significant number of high school arenas that seat the entire town population.

In the 1970s, I was an administrator at Earlham College in Richmond, Indiana. The basketball coach was Del Harris, who would later coach the Houston Rockets and the Los Angeles Lakers of the NBA. I started announcing games while at Earlham and then for a branch campus of Indiana University.

A few years later, while working for two different schools in the Chicago area, I was the arena announcer for the Schlitz Malt Liquor Summer Pro Basketball League. I met a number of pro athletes who played on league teams. Before each game, I talked with them to see what they wanted me to say about them when their names were announced. It was somewhat disconcerting to be standing while they were sitting and we were about the same height.

Times have changed. On Thursday evening I'm driving to a small town near here to see a young woman play (she's a junior) who is being recruited by most of the major college programs in the country. All of this started when I was in high school and found out about a place where high school basketball was considered the sport of kings.

Memories – The Way We Were
By Patti Knipp (Patti Glenski)

"Memories, in the corner of my mind
Could it have been so simple then..."

Moving to Wheat Ridge in the summer of 1949 into a new house on a hill was so exciting to me. I was nine years old. After living in Denver in a very ethnic, almost inner-city neighborhood, moving to Wheat Ridge, a suburb of Denver, was like moving to the country. We had an orchard up the street with fruit trees, an irrigation ditch behind our house and wheat fields on a nearby farm with wheat so high we made tunnels through it. Every tree in the orchard had a name. A huge old gnarled apple tree was named, "the airplane tree." It was my favorite. I used to pretend to fly everywhere in that tree. Being the pilot in the highest most point of that tree, I would fly my passengers on the lower branches to the destination of their choice. The irrigation ditch behind our house created our play world of docks and wooden boats.

Saturday mornings were spent listening to a series called, "Sky King," on the radio. Sky King, my hero, was a rescue pilot with a small plane. My childhood dream was to be a pilot and to fly around the world - that I did at least accomplish in my "airplane tree." A family vacation to California that year on a United Airlines airplane was a highlight that did influence my decision to become a flight attendant later in life for United. The "stewardess" on the flight let me help her pass out gum to the passengers, and it was indeed an honor. When we landed, the pilot allowed me come into the cockpit. I was in awe and wonder on my first real flight.

In the summer, the neighborhood gang had "dirt clod fights" with the other "intruders" in our play world. Dirt clods were formed from the mounds of dirt pushed up by machines for the construction of new houses in our neighborhood. We defended our turf until the other "dirt clod gang" ran off crying. Our gang consisted of Byron and Warren Cook, Bobby Carlson, (where are you, Bobby?), Richard Garramone and myself. We also played a continuing Monopoly game for days in my garage with an occasional bike ride to the A&W Root Beer drive-in on 38th Avenue for Root Beer floats.

Many hours were spent in our fantasy play world in the outdoors with lots of Colorado sunshine. The beautiful fragrance from apple blossoms in the orchard, the pungent odor of wheat in the fields and the smells of fresh earth and water in the ditch were such a part of those memories. Colorado has the bluest of all skies and fabulous formations of puffy white clouds. The climate is dry with four very definite seasons. Wintertime brought sledding, snow ball fights, making angels while lying in the snow and building snowmen. Being outdoors playing, was what we did then.

Entering a new school in the fourth grade that fall with a soft-spoken teacher named, Miss Boland, who made me feel so welcome, was also a turning point among my memories. There were lots of new friends to meet. Gary Stites was my handsome new boyfriend. In fact we were "married" on the playground in the "high jump pit." Gale Taylor was the "preacher." My bridesmaids were Nancy Quante, Linda Fitting and Cynthia Chaney. Gary's parents even took us on a date (my first) to a movie with ice cream afterwards. My new school was going to be great and everyone there was friendly and fun. Life was grand! This all set the basis of my enthusiasm for school and the social scene that continued on through high school.

Sixth grade was a highlight in my book of memories. Our wonderful teacher, Miss Lynen, was one of those rare, dedicated teachers who made an indelible impression on many students. One of our projects was building a paper mache volcano about four feet tall with a tin can on the top where we put dry ice to simulate the smoking volcano. Why that project sticks out in my mind, I have no idea, other than it actually worked, it was big and impressive or that we received an "A" on it.

It seems to me that about then in sixth grade, my group of friends became like an extended family. That peer group influence was very strong then and gained strength each year as the years went by. We thought we were so cool, laughed a lot and shared so much growing up.

With sixth grade came a new boyfriend, Don Shepperd, who was actually going to influence my future, but we did not know it at the time. He was the smartest, cutest and nicest boyfriend, and actually walked me home from school carrying my books. Being romantic then, involved eye contact and maybe handholding, never any kissing, but it was enough to cause palpitations of the heart. He gave me a bracelet with a seashell attached to it. You would have thought he gave me a diamond ring, it was very special.

Don was on a little league baseball team that Don's dad coached. I attended many a game, cheering. Cheering for the team must have created one my newly acquired skills, and it all started at those little league games, as I became a cheerleader in junior high, high school and college.

Don later went on to the Air Force Academy to become a pilot and introduced me to my ex-husband at the Academy, who was also to become a pilot. They went to Vietnam at the same time. R&R was spent in Hawaii together. My husband and I, Don and his wife, Rose, all had dinner together under the palm trees near the ocean. Our lives were meant to cross once again.

"They were the best of times and they were the worst of times."

Junior High arrived soon enough and it was a trying time, even traumatic for a few. Why? Because puberty is just that. We were leaving childhood behind and life became very serious and complicated.

Girls were having "periods". Boys were getting taller and had crackling voices. Feelings were so sensitive and it was easy to become embarrassed over the slightest incident.

Thinking independently was put aside, as conformity took over, and as I learned from an embarrassing incident. A teacher took a poll in our eighth grade class on how many of us thought that 18 year-olds should have the right to vote. One person thought not. Yes, I had to defend myself in front of the whole class on why I felt 18 year olds should not vote. One of those dying, frozen moments in your life. How ever did we survive those trying times? If we had a choice to live our lives over again, I would say, yes, but definitely skip the junior high years.

Ninth grade was part of high school at Wheat Ridge, and if we made it through junior high, it just had to get better. And, indeed it was. Life was grand again. Going through puberty proved to be successful as feelings towards boyfriends did change tremendously. I was in love for the first time with the most handsome blue-eyed, dark-haired, athletic, young man named, Dick Leebrick, oh, my! A term back then was "going steady," which meant that the guy would give you his class ring to wear on a chain around your neck to signify commitment. The girl would give him her class ring to wear on his pinkie finger. Dick was my first "steady". He used to ride his bike over to my house to visit. We watched TV on my parents' first-ever, black and white television. Dates were to the local movie theaters; the Federal, the Oriental and the Coronet. We always sat in the last row of the theater, holding hands. Then, the big move was for the guy to put his arm around the back of the theater seat, gradually slipping it onto the girl's shoulders, heads together, and an occasional kiss that actually made it difficult to watch the movie. But did we care, not in the least, and that was the extent of "sex" at that age. First loves are never forgotten, nor are seconds, thirds, and fourths! Yes, there were quite a few. Academics took a back seat to those young men at that high hormonal age.

We wrote "notes" in class as one way of communicating with our friends during school. The notes were then passed on in the hallways while changing classes. They had to be folded palm-size in order to discretely slip the note into our friend's hand. To have a teacher find us writing a note and have it read in front of the class was indescribably embarrassing.

Study Hall was an extra class period slipped into our schedules that was supposed to help us take time to study and do homework. It was also a time to write notes and catch up on the latest gossip. I remember being with Gary Taylor, one of my unforgettable friends, who was very smart and helped me with my homework in study hall. He also gave me lots of needed advice on my love life. He became a dentist later in life and I was one of his patients. We went out to dinner many times to discuss our lives once again. I was asked to do his eulogy when he passed on. His death in 1993 came way too early in life. He is missed a lot and I think of him often.

Then, came driver's licenses, drive-in movies and drive-in hamburger/ malt places. A new independent age with freedom to do what we wanted, go where we wanted, and with whom we wanted, with the major exception - a whole new set of parents' rules - curfews, being grounded, report card stipulations and many a lecture on a variety of subjects. I was not allowed to watch Elvis Presley's first TV performance on the Ed Sullivan show. My mother heard it was risqué and not to be viewed. Parents were not prepared for the new "Rebellious Beat Generation" as we became known as later.

A date to the Wheat Ridge Letterman's Banquet with Dean Reed, a senior with a car, when I was only a sophomore, took lots of parental persuasion with the new rules. Finally, they gave in. On the way to the banquet, we were in an accident; hit by an old man who ran a red light. I was sitting next to Dean and was thrown forward into the rear view mirror. Seat belts back then were non-existent. The impact of my face hitting the mirror shattered tiny fragments of glass that imbedded my face. The car behind us just happened to be the wrestling coach, Mr. Brockman, who also taught first aid in school. He had a first aid kit in his car and proceeded to pick out all the pieces of glass in my face, swabbed off the blood and we were off again to the banquet. Cars in the 50's were like army tanks and it took quite a lot of impact to really damage them. We proceeded on to the banquet and later to Lakeside Amusement Park to avoid going home too early to face my parents. The next morning, the inevitable had to happen. Dean had to come over and tell my parents what had happened. Fortunately, my father felt sorry for him. Most young men back then had to work very hard to buy their first car. They took a lot of pride in the way their cars looked and how fast they could go, a symbol of their young manhood. My father thought it took a lot of courage for Dean to face him. All was forgiven.

Dean later became an international singer in South America and Russia. He was the "Elvis Presley of Russia" as stated in People magazine. He married an East German actress and had two children. I saw Dean about 30 years after high school. Neil Good, Dean's Wheat Ridge classmate, brought him up to the office where I worked. We had a nice visit and reminisced about the accident. He said he missed Colorado so much, especially the blue skies and puffy white clouds. He wanted to bring his children to this country to see Colorado, but his wife was objecting. Two years after our visit he was mysteriously found dead in a lake in East Germany.

At that Letterman's Banquet, Dean and I sat across from John Bandimere and his date. It was the first time I had met John. He too was a senior and an outstanding athlete, who won many awards that evening. Being about the only sophomore at the banquet, just coming from an accident, and being patched up by one of the coaches, I received a lot of attention, especially from John. We met again at the "Grand Opening" of one of the first suburban shopping centers that summer. I had a job handing out coupons at the door of Woolworth's. He and his friends came through the doors many times that day and received my attention. We began dating, going steady and attended my Junior and Senior proms with him. John had one of the fastest, if not the fastest car, in the area. Berry's drive in on Colfax Avenue was a local gathering spot for several schools. He was challenged many times, cruising that drive-in on a Saturday night. His father developed the first drag strip in the area, with the intention of getting high school kids off of the street - a safe place to challenge and drag their cars.

I must mention another classmate, David Sutcliffe. He and I were good friends, never really dated, but he was always there for me when I needed a shoulder to cry on. A true rebel and non-conformist, he challenged and debated many a teacher. I blame him on some of my attitudes towards society. He taught me not to be fearful about challenging and questioning religion, politics, laws and life in general. He went to C.S.U. also. Later in life, David was the first high school teacher in a Wisconsin school district to wear a full beard and get away with it against their rules. The ruling was changed after he battled them and won. The beard was started after being a pilot in Vietnam. His mission was to fly dead bodies, causalities from a senseless war, from Saigon to Honolulu. Yes, it did affect him considerably as it did many others. He developed cancer later in life and was given six months to live. He and his two children drove from Wisconsin to be in Colorado once more and then on to see other friends and relatives. He stayed at my home during his visit and I threw a "goodbye" party for him with classmates from Wheat Ridge, who found it difficult to believe that he really was dying. He knew he would not make it to our 30th reunion in 1988 so he gave me money for a champagne toast to him on that Friday night in Winter Park at the reunion. I loved David, think of him often and he is missed very much. He is mentioned in many a conversations about the good old days.

The mountains have always been my solace. My dad leased 1700 acres in the mountains with several cabins on the property. No running water, only natural springs and no electricity. We used Coleman lanterns. It was homesteaded by a Dr. Staunton in the 1800s and became a lumber camp operation for many years. When his only unmarried daughter died, she gave the property to the state of Colorado to become a park. It is now known as Staunton Park and is still unopened pending funds.

Actually, politics being as they are, when the property was turned over to the state, it was devastated by greedy officials that chopped down the majority of trees and stripped the cabins of all the antiques. It was pristine and untouched with every imaginable wild flower growing there when my father had it. I was taught at an early age there to respect and appreciate nature. A herd of elk and many coyotes claimed ownership there also. My father would take us on hikes up to the tops of those mountains and if anyone would falter or slow up, you would hear a word or two from him about "pushing yourself to the limit builds character." Those words still echo in my mind.

I received a card in the mail from a classmate that said, "old cheerleaders never die, they just plan reunions." And, indeed I have, along with a great committee. We have thoroughly enjoyed all of the planning. Many of our reunions have been in the mountains. There were 222 graduating members of the class of 1958, 29 are deceased now and many are missing, or unable to locate. Our 30th reunion was held in the mountains at a resort in Winter Park with a video made of the entire weekend. The 40th found us in Vail for another weekend of renewing friendships and bonding as we once had done during those "wonder years" in Wheat Ridge. Our 45th was held at the Lake Shore Lodge in Estes Park.

I have often wondered why some never attend reunions. Did they not feel the ties that held us together during those formative years, or do they not want to look back and remember, because of painful memories? A commonality I have observed working on all the reunions was that we all had some painful experiences growing up, some more than others. Growing up wasn't easy, but those supportive friendships made it bearable. Those friendships have endured all these years and will continue throughout the remainder of our lives.

Wheat Ridge was a wonderful place to grow up in and the school did prepare us in a good way. A tribute to the teachers for all their hard work and especially their patience for putting up with us.

After Wheat Ridge High School
By Patti Knipp (Patti Glenski)

...attended Colorado State University, majoring in Piano...yes, I wanted to be a concert pianist...at least that year...pledged Pi Beta Phi sorority and adjusted to life after Wheat Ridge. I loved the freedom and independence of college life, although academics were still not a priority. A counselor at C.S.U., who was a very old man that should have retired many years before, told me that I should just get married and have babies like he felt all women should. That piece of advice in 1959, shifted my priorities so much that I left college to be a Flight Attendant for United Airlines. I was off to see the world and fulfill my desire to fly. Based in New York City was not only a huge adjustment, but a cultural shock besides. It was curiously exciting and intellectually stimulating. I loved it!

But in 1962, a cadet at the Air Force Academy that I had been dating popped the question. "Come travel with me in the Air Force and see the world"... and travel we did. Our song was Moon River, "...we're off to see the world...there's such of lot of world to see."

The Air Force had so many rules and regulations...even for officer's wives. We were not allowed to socialize with two ranks above, or below, our husband's rank. Yea, right. It definitely was not my style. I was in a bridge club with the general's wives and a book club with non-commissioned wives. After my husband's tour in Vietnam, he left the Air Force and became a pilot for Continental Airlines. My husband had been gone so much in the Air Force and now was traveling again. Meanwhile, I was raising our two children and keeping the home fires burning again. The obvious happened. After 23 years of marriage, and leading separate lives, I filed for divorce.

Divorce was not even in my parents' vocabulary, but they and several of my friends were very supportive during that time. The temporary insanity caused by divorce lasted about a year. My self-esteem was at an all time low, the big money was gone and it became necessary to obtain a full time job.

The business world had changed, and even though I had Flight Attendant experience and tons of voluntary time listed on my resume, employers had their doubts. So, I took a government test, scored a 95 on it and was offered several jobs. I chose the Department of Energy's nuclear plant at Rocky Flats pending a "Q" clearance needed for the job. After going through the late 60s as somewhat of a "hippie," long hair, head band, peace necklace, which was the attire on the beach in California at that time, my clearance was granted on the condition that I would not donate to, or participate in Green Peace. The whales and seals were going to have to wait for awhile.

It was actually the most "down, dead time" of my life. It was a job, it paid the bills, but left an awful lot to be desired as far as "personal growth." I was bored beyond boring and was thinking about how to make the break, after working there for 8 years, when I was caught in their big layoff of 2400 people.

Meanwhile, I found a new "religion," a new "old" high school love, Dick English, at the 30th reunion, a new job, and purchased my first home, all on my own. I am now retired after working at Coors Brewing Company in the Sales Department. I do volunteer work at the Democratic headquarters and am a delegate at the convention. I am finishing my degree at Regis U. at nights maintaining a four-point average. Academics are now important as I plan on getting a master's degree and perhaps a PHD! Don't you just love it!

My father passed away not too long ago and I miss him tremendously. We used to talk twice a day discussing politics, the cattle business, etc. He always used to say, "There is something wrong with your mother.

Take care of her when I go." She was diagnosed with Alzheimer's disease which was devastating to her. It took her life a few years ago.

My two wonderful children are not only my son and daughter, but they are my friends now, and live near by. My son has given me two beautiful grandchildren. My daughter has a very successful career, and I have never told her to "get married and have babies like all women should." But, perhaps that old counselor at C.S.U. had "some" insight, in that marriage, children and grandchildren have brought me many of life's rewards and gifts.

A Little Bit Crazy
By Phil Nichols

Background – My family moved to Wheat Ridge about halfway through my junior year from Evanston, Illinois. I had only spent one and a half years in Evanston having moved there at the end of my freshman year from Barrington, Illinois which is located about 15 miles northwest of Chicago.

As a newcomer to Wheat Ridge and not having grown up with the rest of the class I had a slightly different background: I was born in Cairo, Egypt. My mother was French, born in Paris, but spent most of her life as part of the European society living in Cairo where my grandfather, who was French but also born in Egypt, was a surveyor for the Bank of Cairo. His job was to survey the property lines after the Nile river flooded each year (this was before the Aswan dam). My father was an American born in Toppenish, Washington and a graduate of Syracuse University. As part of a grant with the Congregational Church, he was sent to Egypt to be a journalism professor at the American University in Cairo. As German General Erwin Rommel, the Desert Fox, closed in on Egypt during WWII, my mother, sister and I became war refugees and were sent south to Khartoum in the Sudan. Once the Germans were defeated and it was deemed safe to bring the women and children back to Cairo, my father became a war correspondent and removed us to safety to live with my American grandparents in Yakima, Washington. At the end of WWII we made a series of moves, Yakima, to NY to Barrington, IL and then to Wheat Ridge.

With that said, many classmates probably do not remember me at all. However, some might remember the "explosion" in the central courtyard of the old Wheat Ridge High School one day, actually the sound of a cherry bomb going off. Another boy and I, can't remember his name, were caught and were to be expelled or suspended from school and, of course, our parents were to be notified. I pled with the principal, Dr. Romine, that instead of being expelled, we be permitted to come up with our own punishment and to write a letter of apology. He bought it, and I wrote a masterful document that indicated we would not be allowed to hold any sort of office in the school or participate in any school activities, i.e. sports, etc. Ah well, that worked and that was our punishment and I escaped the wrath of my father.

Being full of energy and short on brains and common sense, I began to break the agreement I made with the principal. Some might remember being required to sit in the physics classroom while little "explosions" went off. To all of you, it was my doing and I apologize. I got along with the chemistry teacher, I've forgotten her name, but somehow I impressed her and showed a flair for chemistry and out of trust she gave me the responsibility for and the key to the chemistry supplies, ah trust. No wonder I never finished being a Boy Scout. I was not trustworthy! I had learned that if you mixed iodine crystals with ammonia and stirred it up and then filtered the ammonia out of the mixture, you could put small amounts of the residue, about the size of a B-B on the floor, or under desks, or on the counter below the window. When this stuff dried, it became very sensitive and eventually would explode on its own accord with the sound much like that of a cap gun. All very mysterious, and several teachers were adamant and bent on finding the culprit. Well, since we were all sitting there with hands on our desks and no one moving and with three teachers watching us, and no one admitting to be the perpetrator, they finally had to let us go when the bell went off and we had to go to our next class. Whew, I just about peed in my pants on that one.

Of course, that wasn't enough. Two more incidents had me very anxious and would find me in violation of the terms of my punishment. One involved the Senior Play (remember – no participation in school activities!). I let myself get talked into playing the part of Bert Jefferson in "The Man Who Came to Dinner." I was sure that Dr. Romine would call me down on that one and yank me out of the play which would mean that I let all the members of the cast down. Although on second thought, the play would probably not have suffered much without my presence.

The second incident demonstrates that I am sucker for causing myself to suffer anxieties that would haunt me for weeks. Not learning from one episode, I allowed myself to be talked into standing-in for someone and reading his lines for the school's entry in the statewide contest play, "The Death of a Salesman." Day after day, I stood-in for this missing boy until it was obvious there would be no time for the other fellow to learn the lines and be ready for the competition. There were only four of us, Keith Thomas, Marie West, Dick Bishop or Bill Erich and me. So, there I was again, standing up in the line of fire, practically waving a flag to draw attention to myself. How could Dr. Romine miss me now?

Well, we won the county, then the region and then we competed in the state-wide run-off and good God, we kept winning and our names and pictures were shown again and again. I was sweating up a storm. We won, we received our accolades and recognition from Dr. Romine and others, except for the "REMRAF" yearbook, which failed to recognize our outstanding and superlative achievement especially as Keith Thomas forgot one of his lines and for a small period of time the four of us froze and looked at each other for what seemed like an interminable amount of time. All I remember of that incident was skipping ahead to one of my next lines and reciting a line that got me off stage but which I guess spurred the others on. We all felt we had blown our chances, but even with that one slip we took 1st place. Disbelief! We were so happy!

The day of our graduation from Wheat Ridge High, I presented myself in Dr. Romine's office and asked him to remove the mention of my cherry bomb incident from my high school transcript. I didn't want to be forever branded with the scarlet letter as "the mad-bomber of Wheat Ridge." Talk about Chutzpah! At first, Dr. Romine didn't know what I was talking about. Had he forgotten me and what I had done? He got my records and tore up my letter of apology and my letter of proposed punishment, all without a word of recognition of my transgressions. Whatta guy! Perhaps he knew all along and this was just the way he meted out my punishment. The fear, the sweating, the not knowing if and when the other shoe was going to drop, was punishment enough. And believe me it weighed heavily on my mind day after day until after graduation. Thank you Dr. Romine.

The Slacker Moves On
By Phil Nichols

After getting through high school at Wheat Ridge by the skin of my teeth, I found myself headed northwest to Yakima, Washington to attend school at Yakima Valley Junior College. I was supposed to live with my grandparents, find a job to pay for the tuition and not be a burden to them. You'd think that I would have learned something after my year and a half at Wheat Ridge High, but sadly, I couldn't shake my immaturity. Wheat Ridge was not a complete bust. I managed to get A's in history and B's in chemistry and math but I was terrible at English. I won, or placed, in the math contest, my prize being a slide ruler. Other than that, I had not found myself. I had no real focus and this continued in Yakima. The sad thing was, I was aware of all this. I participated in several plays, even had the lead role in one or two. My junior college grades were spotty and so, after two years in Yakima basically wasting everyone's time, I had an inward face-off and decided that I really needed someone to kick my ass and wake me up. Ergo, I joined the United States Marine Corps.

Why the Marines? I really don't know except that I'd heard that they were tough. I remember as a youngster having a picture of the Marines raising the flag at Iwo Jima in WWII pinned to my wall. I don't recall any big discussion regarding Iwo or the Marine Corps with my family or friends. It must have been just collective bits here and there, sort of a subconscious acknowledgement that they were TOUGH. So, in my slightly demented way, I decided that if anyone was going to kick some sense into me, it would be the Marines.

Looking back, I have to say - it was the best decision I ever made. There was a little discomfort when I signed and realized my ass was theirs; a little fear of the unknown, coupled with the realization that I now had no wiggle room. I was committed and that was it. But, as I said before, for once I had "chosen wisely."

Being a little older than most of the other recruits, I soon recognized what it was all about, the hazing, the punishments, "Give me 10!" every time you turned around. They were stripping away the silliness and immaturity of youth. If there ever is a group that can "clean up your act," it's the Marines. To this day I look back fondly on my Marine Corps experiences. They can take immature and empty-headed young men (or boys) and mold them into something better. For the young men who join there are very few decisions that have to be made. The Corps makes them all for you. But, for those young men with half a brain, "Raise your right hand, Phil. No, Phil, your RIGHT hand," they can help people develop and use their intelligence more wisely. And, as the Marines say, "We build men."

After boot camp, they shipped me off to Marine Corps Air Station Kaneohe, Hawaii. While back in Staging Battalion in Camp Pendleton, CA, I volunteered to assist in the Battalion Admin Office preparing the documentation to send us to Hawaii. Horrors! They found out I could type! I had kept that information to myself when joining the Marines. I figured that Staging Battalion was just a temporary assignment and I would still join the Engineers. Ha! The good folks in the Battalion Office sent a "Letter of Commendation" forward to the processing office at MCAS Kaneohe and I was sent off to Headquarters and Maintenance Squadron-13, Marine Aircraft Group-13, 1st Marine Brigade to work in the office. So, no Marine "grunt" duty for me; no running around throwing grenades, skipping over land mines, using flame throwers and such. I was a United States Marine Corps "killer typist," a heart breaker, since as you all know from my first story I liked things that go "bang.".

After two years of hard duty water skiing, sun-bathing, typing and getting promoted, I was selected to take the "Service Record Books" (SRBs) back to the States, to Treasure Island, San Francisco, for in-processing all of us who had finished our tours in Hawaii. I was again assigned to an office job at Marine Barracks, Treasure Island, blah. However, in a way I was fortunate as I made another wise decision. While at the Marine Barracks, I was given the task of finding some Marines who would be willing to go to Marine Security Guard School in Arlington, VA. This sounded interesting. Maybe I could travel? Maybe even get assigned to Cairo, Egypt a dream of mine for a long time since I was born there. Who knows? I went, became a Master Sergeant and began to see the world.

My first tour as a Security Guard was the American Embassy in Mogadishu, Somali Republic. This is way before, "Black Hawk Down". While traveling to Mogadishu I had a layover in Cairo (wonders never cease). Having been born in Cairo, this was the greatest thing that could have happened to me. However, while I was there on a three-day layover, the world learned that President Kennedy had been assassinated. Surreal! There were no radios or TVs at that time carrying non-stop coverage of what happened. The greatest impact on me, was walking the streets of Cairo and having poor farmers "fellahin," who until that morning probably didn't know more than two words of English, walking up to me and asking, "You American? You American?" And, when I acknowledged that I was, they said, "So sorry. So sorry," with tears in their eyes. It was astounding! What an impact Kennedy had on the world. His charisma reached across oceans and into farmers' fields and touched some of the poorest regions of the world. I will always remember those tears and those poor Arab farmers.

From Mogadishu I was sent to Cairo for a nine-month tour. How happy did that make me? I was ecstatic! It was an opportunity to really spend time seeing the sights of Cairo, my birthplace where I had roamed as a youth during WW II. The nine months went by all too quickly and I was once again headed back to the good ole U.S. and my next duty post, Quantico, VA. Nine months later I left the Corps and accepted a job with the U.S. State Department in Washington, D.C. I was sorely tempted to stay in the Corps but I was determined to finish college and with help from the G.I. bill I started classes at American University, taking a couple of courses each semester, attending during the day, then working at State from 4:00 p.m. to 12:00 midnight. It wasn't much fun. The "light at the end of the tunnel" wasn't getting any brighter because tuition at American University was very high and the VA didn't cover everything.

I decided to look for a better solution and found George Mason College of the University of Virginia only five or six miles from where I lived. Tuition there was much more reasonable, but it still wasn't fun. As I got more courses under my belt, the light began to get brighter. On the 6th of June 1971 I received my diploma and gave a big sigh of relief.

I worked in the Operations Center at State, basically a clerk-typist job, but again, fate intervened. I was given the opportunity to take an aptitude test to see if I could find my ass in the dark with both hands; actually a test to see if I had the qualifications for the computer field which was in its infancy. I scored high enough and began a great career in computers. Eventually, the Department got involved with Wang computers and I was put in charge of developing applications for our consulates and embassies around the world installing Wangs and training the individuals who used them. This provided the opportunity to travel in conjunction with the automation programs. I visited Mexico City, Buenos Aires, Rio De Janeiro and Brasília in Brazil; Pretoria and Johannesburg in South Africa; Nairobi, Kenya, Addis Ababa and Asmara, Ethiopia; Aden, Yemen; Jeddah and Riyadh, Saudi Arabia; Tel Aviv, Rome, Paris, Bonn, London, Vienna, Prague, Budapest, Brussels, Stockholm, Copenhagen, Tokyo, Hong Kong, Bangkok, Singapore, Malaysia, Wellington in New Zealand, Jakarta, New Delhi and Abidjan, Ivory Coast. Most of these visits were for a week or two, but some went for as long as a month.

Five years before retiring, I became a GM-13, a management job and believe me, except for the pay, I would much rather be doing something more productive. I retired in 1999 and was asked to return to duty with full pay (to also include my retired pay) assisting with the Y2K project. A year and a half later I retired only to return for five more years as a contractor working at State. In June of 2005 I had a stroke and called it quits. My wife, Joyce, retired in June 2007. The house is paid off, the kids are grown up and we'll be going to see our son, Marc, graduate from the Air Force Academy in May of 2008. Now we can have fun! I guess the one thing I reflect on is that I owe it all to taking a typing class in my sophomore year of high school and deciding to join the Marine Corps. If any organization can help you get your shit together, it's the U.S. Marine Corps. Semper Fi!

A Tribute to My Folks – Role Models

By Beth Dougherty (Beth Barbich)

When I was in the fifth grade, my folks decided to move the family way out into the country to a place called, "Wheat Ridge". My observation was, "Good Lord, there's nothing around!" We had an apple orchard across the street and a cornfield behind us. We also had a cornfield to the north of us across 44th Ave. My brothers and I were not very happy about the situation. We moved during January in the middle of winter on my birthday. When I went to school, I ended up in a mixed 5th and 6th grade class - bummer. I quickly got to know some of the kids, and then it didn't seem too bad.

Most of the time there was a lot of work to do around home because there were five kids, and my mother didn't work. It wasn't easy feeding five children. We had a large garden in our yard because we needed it. Every spring my dad rented a tractor and plowed up our yard for the garden. We all had to help. We were never allowed to play on Saturdays and Sundays if Dad had chores for us. One year, the tractor my dad always rented was broken, so we had to dig up the yard by hand. Our friends wanted us to play, but we couldn't because we had to help dig the yard for the garden. The other neighborhood kids, about six in all, thought it would be fun to join. They went home and got their Dads' shovels and came back to help. We played a game to see who could get to the end of the row first. We had the whole yard dug up it no time. There were no child labor laws back then and my dad, being the good guy he was, treated all of us to a malted milk from Wheat Ridge Dairy with the money he would have used to rent the tractor.

My folks were always the parents with whom the neighborhood kids wanted to hang out. They were always there and always treated everyone the same - with kindness, concern and humor . We would be doing clean up on a hot Saturday afternoon, and all of a sudden someone would get squirted with the hose, and the war was on. The whole neighborhood would show up to join in, and right in the middle of it were my Mom and Dad. Our whole family always worked and played together because the chores weren't nearly as hard, when we all pitched in.

My dad built a two and a half stall garage behind our house out of brick and cinderblock. We all "got" to help. As a young girl, I learned how to mix mortar and lay bricks. I can still do it. We built a pump house behind the garage for the well that to this day still waters my dad's yard. My dad let my brothers and I build one side pretty much by ourselves. It all matched the house. My two younger brothers were too young to help on those early projects, so about ten years ago my dad and my younger brother Wayne built an outdoor barbeque for my patio - the youngsters finally got to help. Yes, I mixed the mortar. I hadn't forgotten how.

One year, we had a terrible snowstorm that dumped about two feet of snow in heavy drifts on the roof. My dad was afraid the snow on the garage might slide off, when it started melting, and bury someone. So, my brothers were sent to shovel the roof. The pile of snow on the ground got so high they were able to slide right off the roof on their shovels while my dad took pictures. We always made work fun.

We did not get to go to the movies much, when I was a kid, because there were too many of us, and we didn't have the money. But, one Saturday my Dad and Mom took us and a few of our friends "downtown" to a movie. There were two older women sitting in the row behind us, and as we filed into the theatre taking up almost an entire row, my Dad said to my Mom, "Aren't you glad we left the rest of them home?" The ladies sitting behind us couldn't stand it. They had to ask if all the kids really belonged to my parents. We all had a good laugh.

The two things I remember most about growing up in Wheat Ridge are - it seemed like we were so far out in the country and now it seems like it is all in the middle of town. AND - my mother and father's love. I have always wanted to be as good a parent as my Mom and Dad. I don't think I ever quite made it, but I tried. . They were poor in money, but rich in love. They were terrific role models.

What a Wonderful Life
By Beth Dougherty (Beth Barbich)

As a kid I always wanted to travel. When I graduated from Wheat Ridge High School I applied to become an airline stewardess. I dreamed of traveling the world – no such luck. I was too short to qualify.

I went back to work at the First National Bank of Denver where I had worked summers during high school, terribly disappointed. I attended Colorado State University for one year and then met and married my husband, Ray, a Cold War veteran. We just celebrated our 48th wedding anniversary.

I continued to work at the bank until I had my second child and then became a stay at home mom. We were doing pretty well but not making a lot of money. I then started working as a temporary at the bank. The kids were in school all day so I only worked the hours the kids were gone. I never got to travel much. We did go to California because Ray's folks had moved there. Every other year we went there for vacation.

When the kids were teenagers I started working full time and that's when we started traveling. We have been to just about every state in the union including Hawaii and Alaska. We have been from one end of Canada to the other and the same of Mexico. We have been on about 20 cruises in the Caribbean and this fall we are going to the Northeastern US and Nova Scotia, Prince Edward Island and down the St. Lawrence River to Quebec City, Canada and flying home.

As I look back, my dreams have been fulfilled. We have two wonderful children, four grandchildren, and two great grandchildren, and I finally got to travel. I don't think you can ask for much more than that – what a wonderful life.

Dinner Table Remembrances
By Bill Weiss

When we were teenage boys we liked to eat and looked forward to invites to our friends' homes. Dick English's mother was well known for her spaghetti and occasionally fed five or six of us at a time. In addition to her ability to make a perfect red sauce, she recognized that she could never make too much.

My mother, Vera, also enjoyed having my friends join us for dinner. She too prepared big meals since there were seven of us in the family. She always cooked enough to insure plenty of leftovers for the following day. We ate at a round dinner table which limited seating to a maximum of eight, or nine.

Danny Hershberger and Dick Leebrick were two of my friends who I recall frequently seemed to be at the Weiss house around dinnertime. Both, along with me, were hungry boys. I'm sure the reason I remember them among my dinnertime friends was due to their ability to eat, and I have since come to appreciate big eaters. But, I remember Danny being clearly the champion. Vera had prepared a large ham, big enough to insure school lunch sandwiches for my brother, three sisters, and me for several days. She had all the trimmings: sweet potatoes, mashed potatoes, vegetables and salad to go with the ham. Danny sat next to my dad, Oscar, who sliced the ham. Oscar kept slicing and Danny kept eating until there was nothing but bone. It was a marvelous feat.

While attending The University of Colorado I always went home on weekends. I had a weekend job at Stites' service station, but really went home to eat. I'd met some Arabs who lived in the dormitory and mentioned it to Vera. Having never met an Arab, she insisted that I invite them to Sunday dinner. The Arabs were from Saudi

Arabia, Yemen and Iraq. Vera prepared a large lamb roast and all the trimmings including black tea. The Arabs were all very polite wearing coats and ties. I recall that only two of my sisters were there that day. Somehow the conversation turned to politics and the possibility of a war somewhere. Oscar volunteered that we should "...nuke the SOBs!" One of the Arab students, an excitable socialist, stopped eating and stood up to address Oscar's remarks. The guy from Iraq grabbed him by the coattail to pull him back into his chair. Oscar sat there smiling and agreeing with the guy. Of course Oscar had no idea what the socialist was saying since he had a heavy accent or perhaps was speaking Arabic. No blows were struck.

Later, while working for Sun Oil Company at The Dallas Research Center I got to know Big Ed and Don. Both were college football players who enjoyed a good meal. We got in the habit of going to Jimmy's Chinese lunch buffet about once a week. I thought I saw Jimmy shudder when he saw us approaching. I finally asked him if he lost money on us. Jimmy replied that we were light weights compared to some of the prodigious feeders that really hurt him. He said he finally had to chase them away. I guess I wasn't the glutton I thought I was.

Background and the Story
By Bill Weiss

Background

After graduation from Western State College in Gunnison, I went to work for Calgon Corporation, a water treatment company. In 1968 I was transferred from Evansville IN to Denver to sell chemicals throughout the Rocky Mountains for the oilfield division.

The National Supply Company served as Calgon's oilfield distributor. National had stores in all the domestic oilfield areas. They sold pipe, pumps, drilling rigs, supplies, chemicals and anything else needed to operate an oilfield. In those days they had field salesmen who knew the local area such as where the rigs were drilling and where the fields were located. Calgon provided technical support to these salesmen and serviced the larger accounts. I made monthly trips to D-J Basin, the Powder River Basin as well as occasional trips to Williston ND and Cut Bank MT.

In early 1970s the oilfield was booming in the Powder River Basin of Wyoming. National had a store in Gillette that serviced north and south of highway 90, halfway to Powell toward the west and over to Newcastle toward the east. There were three or four salesmen who worked out of the store, one of whom was Jim Hochnadle. Probably it is not well known that wells produce water along with oil and gas. Depending on the chemistry of the water it can cause scale or corrosion problems that damage the well's pump or pipes or possibly plug the formation. Jim had been through the Calgon schools and knew which products to apply to solve specific water treatment problems. Jim had a customer named Joe Stewart who had some Minnilusa wells north of Moorcroft that he considered to be a waterflood prospect. Waterflooding is a recovery technique where water is pumped into a well to displace oil from nearby wells. It is important that the water used to displace the oil be compatible with the oil-formation water. Incompatible waters can plug up the formation.

Jim had suggested to Joe that he have a compatibility test run with the formation water and a shallow water zone that was a potential source water. I was in Gillette in December when Jim was discussing this matter with Joe. Having met Joe a few years earlier in Kentucky I agreed to go with Jim to obtain samples of the produced water and the potential source water. I drove a company station wagon with the necessary equipment to run tests for dissolved gases, pH, and bacteria. Jim and I left Gillette early to go do the field work. Knowing that the fields in the Moorcroft-Newcastle area were small, remote, and in the foothills of the Blackhills I asked Jim if he had a map to follow. He said not to worry because it would only take two or three hours and he had an "uncanny sense of direction." Eight hours later we found the wells and spent an hour testing and gathering the samples for later work in the laboratory. It was four o'clock, we'd had no lunch, and faced an eight drive back to Gillette in cold and blowing snow. Jim said he knew a short cut to Newcastle where we could get gasoline and something. And he did!

We arrived in Newcastle about six, gassed up the car, and Jim suggested we stop in the Cowboy Bar for a beer. I advised him that I had stopped there a few months earlier, but had been dissuaded from entering by two cowboys on horseback trying to ride through the front door. Jim said not to worry because that seldom happened.

The story

He was right again; not one horse on the Cowboy Bar. We sat at a table, had a couple of drinks and noticed that were about an equal number cowboys and drilling rig hands, plus a table of volunteer firemen. Except for the firemen, these folks regularly meet in Rocky Mountain oilfield bars for refreshments and fistfights. Additionally

Jim noticed that Yale Lewis, a successful Denver landman and Bill Coats, the owner of a fleet of water trucks were standing at the bar. They had attracted a half dozen of their friends who provide services to the oilfield because they were buying drinks for everybody in their group. Jim knew them all and suggested we join them for an evening of free whisky.

As the night progressed the music got louder and the go-go girl was dancing for the firemen. I was standing in line behind an older rig-hand who was using the urinal. A young volunteer fireman was puking in the wash basin and splashing water on his face to get in shape to go back to trying to impress the go-go dancer. The rig-hand turned to me commenting on the disgusting vulgarity of the kid puking in the sink. As he did so he lost track of the urinal and pissed in his own galoshes. He never even noticed.

Later back at the bar, our crowd had remained fairly constant at six to eight who were by then all good friends of Bill and Yale who were still buying about as fast as we could drink them. There was only a single waitress serving the seated customers, but eventually she noticed that the money was at the bar. She was dressed in a black sequin pants suit and pushed her way into the moneyed crowd telling us one and all that she was the Saturday night go-go dancer. I thought I'd pat her butt for being so friendly, but there were six hands already there.

The landman and the fleet owner were older than rest of the group and tired easily so they left when the bar closed. The rest of us went to the Halliburton station mangers house for an after hours drink. The go-go dancer had taken a shine to him so she came along. I had fallen asleep in a chair when Jim kicked me awake saying we had to drive to Gillette to be at work in the morning. We left and had one interruption on the drive to Gillette; a driver had lost control on the ice and rolled his pickup though a fence along side the road. Jim and I stopped, crawled through the fence to see if we could help. We couldn't since there was no one in the pickup. We arrived in Gillette in time for Jim to report for work. His boss made a snide comment about drinking scotch was bad enough, but bathing in it was uncalled-for.

Nights like the evening at the Cowboy Bar did not occur often, probably every other month and occasionally during the day, like the Sunday afternoon the high school wrestling coach came into the Vets Club with the claim he could lick anybody in the house. Me, Jim and Kosmicki were drinking beer watching the ball game. Jim thought he could certainly take that little guy. The wrestling coach had Jim pinned on the floor in less than a minute. We bought him and his group a round and went back to drinking beer. An hour or two later Kosmicki convinced Jim that the coach had used an illegal hold on him and that was the only reason he had lost. Jim asked the wrestler if was willing to give him a second try. The coach threw him faster than the first time and it made Jim mad, so he grabbed the coach by the nuts. The coach went crazy. His friends pulled him off. We had to take Jim home.

I can probably recall fifty more bar room stories, but those involving Jim were among the best. His girlfriend found him dead on his living room floor one morning in 2006.

Growing Up in Wheat Ridge and a Little Beyond

By Devona Spykstra (Devona Hubka)

I was born 04-04-40, after a sister died of leukemia at age nine. My brother was four years older. My parents were older than those of most of my friends' parents, but, what wonderful parents they were! We lived at 32nd and Depew, across the street from the famous Babe Zaharius, who lived in a huge house! Babe was recently voted "the greatest female athlete of the 20th century!" Neighborhood kids were invited to her home on Saturday mornings to watch film clips of her Olympics events. She loved the climbing red roses on our front fence. She frequently stopped to pick a bouquet and raved about how she loved them! When she died of cancer years later in Texas, I sent a huge bouquet of those roses, in full bloom, to her funeral in memory of a great neighbor, a good person and a world class athlete. Her husband, George, was a professional wrestler at Mammoth Gardens in Denver. I never imagined that later in life my son-in-law would also be a world class professional wrestler. As it turns out, he became the #1 mixed martial arts contender in the world, but after 20 years of marriage and 2 children, he and our daughter just divorced.

Memories? - I remember Agnes Carter, Mariel's mother, as a wonderful woman, who was our 4-H leader. She demanded perfection in cooking, sewing and gardening. I learned much from her expert guidance that I used later in life. Gerry Heaston and I were "quarantined" from a polio outbreak at one of the camps we attended. I remember two members of the Carol Holt family died from that polio epidemic.

Memories of my classmates from Columbia Heights? - Tom Hoff, Dale Sprinkle, Cliff Miercort, Bob Brown, Lois Andrews, Shirley

Eroddy, Marianne MacDonald, Kathie Krebs, Mariel Carter, and Bonnie Stebbins often surround me. Bonnie and I practiced "high-jumping" for endless hours in her sawdust pit. And, all that practice paid off - I finally beat Loa Wilson in the high jump one high school Blue and Gold Day! Hanne Jensen's black Pontiac that honked, when we turned corners, is a warm memory. I remember the drill team practices and the Pep Club events at Marilyn Newton's house. Two years as Majorette was a highlight in my life at that time – even better than beating Loa at high jump! I loved doing the twirling routines and marching with the band.

I wanted to be "head twirler" at the University of Colorado. I applied and was accepted, but instead I chose to be a "Golden Jet Girl" for a year. I was one of three girls selected by Continental Airlines for a publicity tour. We traveled with the "Six-guns" - Continental President Robert Six and his five vice-presidents. Mr. Six was married to the Broadway legend, Ethel Merman, and we went to meetings at their Cherry Hills Estate. We traveled to all the destinations that Continental Airlines served to promote the new "Golden Jet Airliner" they put into service in Denver. Continental even designed special outfits for us - white cowgirl hats; white western jackets with gold trim; gold pants; white cowgirl boots and toy guns. We held "fast-draw" competitions with movie stars and entertainers wherever we traveled. We met many of the stars of the times. It was a special year; one that I felt was well worth exchanging for a year of college.

Instead of college, my education continued with years of free education earned during "beauty contests." I wanted to travel. My brother, Arlin, earned a four-year athletic scholarship to C.U. and traveled extensively with the football team. He even went to Cuba where they celebrated their Orange Bowl victory over Clemson. A special memory was spending time at our house with Arlin and his fraternity brother, Robert Redford - little did I know I was in the presence of a future movie star legend!!!

When I found out the 1958 "Miss Universe" contest was to be held in Long Beach, California, I decided to enter for the chance to travel! Of course, I had to win the local contest first. I won Miss Colorado, but I didn't win Miss Universe. I did win two years of professional training at Morganti's, the top-modeling agency at the time. The national "Miss Press Photographers" contest was held in Hollywood, Florida. I did not win the national, but as Miss Colorado Press Photographer, one of my prizes was two years training at the Powers Modeling Agency. The contest also landed me a job at the Agency. Powers had just opened their Denver Agency, and I became one of the eight original "Power's Girls" that had to first be approved through the NY Agency. That was the beginning of what my life would entail after high school. My final contest was winning the "Miss Broadmoor" contest in Colorado Springs. One of the prizes was a vacation at the Broadmoor Hotel. My contest career came to an end - I married and used the prize for my honeymoon - and my real life began.

Professional Life and Real Life
By Devona Spykstra (Devona Hubka)

I took extensive training preparing to be a professional fashion model. My career started with a bang. In 1962 I landed two national commercials for Chevrolet. The commercials were shown for a year on the popular television programs, Route 66, My Three Sons and Bonanza. I took part in large runway shows at the Denver Hilton for May D&F and did photo shoots in Vale for Ski Magazine. It was all work and no play, most of the time. But, the popular song, "Unchained Melody," strummed on my heart strings and I fell in love with a great guy, Joe Spykstra, from Lakewood. We were married and it wasn't long after, when President Kennedy began drafting married men without children. Joe got his draft notice in the mail. I was so proud - he wanted to serve his country! I wanted to join him, when he went to Germany during the Berlin Crisis, and I sold our 1958 Corvette to pay my way. We lived on the German economy in Idar Oberstein. Pres. Kennedy was assassinated the next year. I then went back to Denver and had our first child at Fitzsimons Army Hospital while Joe was being sent to Georgia for the Cuban Crisis.

I enjoyed a 16 1/2 year modeling career, and then, Joe and I started our own printing business. We worked hard together for 28 years. We played hard as well - went on three cruises, vacationed at Sanibel Island in Florida and Cabo San Lucas in Mexico. I remember when our daughter graduated from UNC, our son graduated from high school and we celebrated our 25th wedding anniversary, all the same year. We celebrated with a trip to Hawaii. We were still so much in love. Life was wonderful. We were on top of the world. Everything was going our way.

Our son, Dan, graduated from C.S.U., got married and became a project manager in Ft. Collins. His first project was a 32 million-dollar tech building. He now owns his own custom building business in Windsor, CO and is a basketball coach. His wife, Stacey, is an awesome interior designer and a volleyball coach. Our daughter, Jody, is a global executive and Senior Mary Kay Director in Greeley and a track coach. She won the "Miss Figure" Fitness contest in Boulder last year. We bought a home on Horseshoe Lake in Loveland, where we plan to retire. We have four outstanding grandchildren, Justin, is a two-time Wrestling 4A State Placer, Austin, is the State Slalom Ski Champion, Mitch, played on the Team USA Basketball team in Holland last summer and, Lexie, is a 1 and 3 meter diver ranked nationally.... all who started water-skiing when they were three!

On my 60th birthday - we got the paralyzing news – Joe had cancer! How could it be? It can't happen to us. Our life has gone so well. What are we going to do? We were so frightened! After a second opinion, it was obvious it was true. Final tests were taken and Joe was prepared for surgery. We talked to Pastor Steve and Pastor John. We prayed. I asked other people to pray for us. Our children and friends had their churches pray for us. Jody was in the Philippines opening up a world market for Mary Kay the day Joe had surgery while Dan and Stacey were by his side. She had over 2000 Filipino women praying for her dad. Thousands of Mary Kay directors and consultants formed a prayer chain for Joe. I believed that God can heal but were we deserving of a miracle? Suddenly, nothing else in life mattered. Life and health suddenly became of ultimate importance! I don't want to live if Joe doesn't! We have loved and been devoted to each other for so many years. **God answered our prayers!** Joe survived one of the worst eight-hour operations – an esophagogastrectomy. He actually died two times during the surgery. But, they got it all! – Joe is CANCER-FREE! We are certain God has a plan for Joe - He let him live!

I continued to run our printing business for three months by myself, with our five employees. Joe tried working part-time; however, it takes a long time to heal from major surgery and he wasn't healing. He was losing weight fast. He lost over one quarter of his total body weight. His doctor told him to think about retiring. Out of the blue, an old friend came by to see us. He was plant manager of a large printing company that was looking to buy a smaller print shop. He didn't even know Joe was sick, but he came to find out if we were interested in selling. It was meant to be - God's plan for us - the sale went through and Joe was able to retire the end of November 2000. I retired the end of January after working three months for the company that bought ours.

Our story has a happy ending. Joe started to gain weight - 20 pounds to be exact! We can now enjoy our home, our family, each other and do all the things we have never had time to do. We now know what is important in life. Everyone should take this lesson from us - life is precious - enjoy it - love someone. It can all be taken away from you in a heartbeat. Have faith and believe God has a plan for you.

Depew Street
By Dale Sprinkle

Depew Street, which runs behind Columbia Heights Elementary School, was a special place to grow up. The length of Depew between 29th and 32nd streets was a focal point of great winter, and yes year round activities. Certainly foremost was the sledding. On a snowy Saturday morning, it looked like a convention of Radio Flyers. There were so many kids sledding that the street got so slick a car could not possibly run up it. My Dad frequently grumbled that coming home from work he had to go up to 32nd street and drive down; coming up from 29th was impossible. The primary culprits from our grade were Tom Hoff, Cliff Miercort, Devona Hubka, and Bob Brown.

And Halloween…who didn't enjoy those days? Everyone on the block participated except for old man "what's his name" next to Don Nimtz. He would yell at kids crossing his lawn, threatening to "tie them up by their thumbs." Then of course, there were the older kids who had a tree house in front of our (Sprinkle's) house. They would scare younger kids who weren't escorted, then grab their dropped bags of candy (I can't believe I'm related to one of them).

Here's a little known part: You know Devona. We now remember her as a pretty, urbane, classy lady. Well, let me tell you…our front lawn was the scene of many "pickup" football/dodgeball games. The rules of what we were playing got pretty muddled, but we had fun. Some of the girls would be on the sidelines developing their cheerleading skills. There was one girl though, who was in the thick of action. She held her own. 'Nuff said.

Our side lot developed into a bit of a menagerie during grade school years. People finding stray animals or having pets they couldn't keep would bring them by, knowing they would be taken care of. There were magpies, turtles, snakes, and my favorite, a skunk.

Deodorized skunks make great pets. Though they are generally friendly, one of their characteristics is that they become attached to one person. My skunk, Flower, was no exception. He would follow me anywhere.

My Mother was involved with the Wheat Ridge PTA. One spring morning she had a group of ladies at our house for some sort of meeting. My Dad was home and seeing me with Flower in the back yard, called me over. He suggested that I simply walk through the house with my pet. I immediately recognized the devilish nature of his suggestion.

With a forced straight face, I did simply walked through the house, by the ladies, and out the front door. There were a variety of reactions from the PTA ladies to the skunk. They ranged from jumping and shrieking to, "Oh, isn't that cute?" My Dad talked about that for a long time. Unfortunately, so did my Mom.

Damn That Tom
By Dale Sprinkle

Tom Hoff and I grew up just a few doors apart on the same street. We were classmates through grade school and high school. After graduation we independently enlisted in the Marine Corps. Though never stationed together, through the next few years we did see each other from time to time.

Following the service, we both drifted back to Wheat Ridge. Our stay there was short lived though, as Tom was accepted by the Los Angeles Police Department to enter their academy. We sort of carpooled out to Southern California, where Tom worked into his new career, and I took a job with the Federal Reserve Bank in Los Angeles.

Whenever we got together, Tom regaled me with recounts of his latest adventures on the streets of Los Angeles; the whackos, the car pursuits, arresting bad guys; it was all too much. I just had to become a cop, and that I did.

Upon successful completion of the Police Academy, new officers were assigned to street duty in one of 17 geographic Divisions. So, what are the chances that two boys from Wheat Ridge would both be assigned to the same Division in Watts? Yes, "Shootin' Newton" Division number 13 was our new home. Tom and I worked different shifts, though, so we only saw each other once in a while.

Fast-forward about one year. I am in my apartment packing my bags. I have a few days off and am getting ready to drive to San Diego to visit my brother, Bob, (Wheat Ridge class of '53). I'm listening to music on the radio, which is interrupted by a news bulletin telling of the developing Watts riot. Part of that story was that the Police Department was fully mobilizing, with all leaves and days off canceled.

Well! Now I do entertain a sense of loyalty and duty? But then again I reasoned that the riot would go on whether or not I'm there to participate. Certainly, one more body on the police lines won't bring the event to a quicker end. Plus, the San Diego beaches are beautiful, as are the ladies who frequent them, and who deserves a little time off more than me? The decision was set. I would not answer my phone. If they don't contact me, I cannot be charged with desertion, or whatever that might be called.

Clicking my bag closed and preparing to leave, I heard a knock at my door. Carefully, I looked through the peephole. There stood Tom Hoff. No sweat, I thought, as I opened the door. Tom greeted me and we engaged in some small talk. Tom added, "Oh, the Watch Commander wanted me to come by to tell you we're going to 12 hour shifts, and your first one is tonight."

Wonderful! Now the idea of leaving town took on a whole new "career ending" aspect. I tried to reason that facing a bunch of angry mobsters would be just as interesting as checking out the bikinis.... maybe not, but that's how it's got to be.

That first night was a unique experience. Working with my partner, we joined a caravan of police units circling the main area of the rioting. This involved about a dozen square blocks. We looked like one of those booths in the fair midway with the ducks floating by while contestants shoot at them, hoping to win a stuffed animal. Truth is, no one was actually shooting at us, but the rocks and bottles were flying off and into the police cruiser with some regularity. We noted in our official shift log that we "played target for people throwing various objects."

The point was that we were just supposed to contain the crowds, not engage them in any way. This would quiet the folks and the hostilities would end. The wisdom of that decision was evidenced the next day when the riot spread to an area ten times what it had been. I thought: Damn the Police administrators! Damn the rioters! And, damn that Tom!

After those first couple of days, the tactics changed. We were now supposed to engage rioters, and make arrests as appropriate. Officers were assigned four to a car.

Reporting for work, I found the car to which I was assigned. I started to get into the rear seat area, behind the driver. I looked around to see whom I would be working with. The fellow in the right front passenger seat turned around, smiling. Yes, it was Tom. He politely welcomed me to the car. Thoughts of the San Diego beaches entered my head. I muttered, "Damn that Tom."

Though the streets of Watts became eerily quiet, you could cut the tension with a knife. The night was dark and we were slowly cruising down a deserted commercial street. About a block ahead of us was a National Guard roadblock. We heard that those guys were tending to be a little trigger happy, so we approached very slowly. Then, we saw car lights approaching the roadblock from the other side. As that vehicle got to the barricades, it sped up, blowing by the troopers and coming straight at us. Our driver immediately stopped the police car, and all four cops dove out of the vehicle scrambling for cover. Simultaneously, we had realized that the Guardsmen would open fire on the fleeing vehicle, with us directly in the line of fire. Sure enough, with a barrage of fire that filled the street, they managed to kill that car and its two occupants. The car came to a stop just in front of our cruiser, which was sitting in the middle of the street with all four doors wide open. I was hiding behind a parked car, muttering, yes, "Damn that Tom."

The truth is I fully realized that Tom had no way of knowing that I was planning a trip, nor that I was starting a series of days off. We did in fact work well together and remained friends. But I just couldn't get that refrain out of my head.

Idyllic Summers
By Carol Greenwood (Carol Combs)

I grew up in a typical white, frame, two-story house in a small Ohio town on a street paved in red bricks. Each spring the huge maples lining both sides of the street leafed into a wonderful arch. Even as a young girl I was aware of the unique beauty of this arch as I rode my bicycle through what seemed to be the most beautiful tunnel in the world.

Summer brought more beauty with the abundant flowers, vegetable gardens and a fruit tree or two in every yard. From neighboring trees, my friends and I ate apples, cherries, and pears. We spent leisurely, hot sticky days reading comic books and eating grapes under the cool shade of our grape arbor. One neighbor's berry bushes produced the most coveted edible prizes, black raspberries. We were admonished not to pillage from that garden, but occasionally the temptation was so great we crawled under a fence through dirt the length of long garden before reaching the plump, juicy delicacies.

In those days of non-working moms, the house interiors were their fiefdoms and they were kept clean and in order. Children were expected to play outside. And what a perfect neighborhood in which to find all kinds of play! Because we were at the end of town, our street was edged by corn fields, a huge wooded pasture with a creek where horses were boarded and a new neighborhood with residential construction.

Our first summer there I was told that children were forbidden to play in the wooded area because everyone knew the creek there could cause little children to drown. Frightened at age nine by the threat of drowning, I avoided the area. By the next summer, being much older, the lure of the area was too great for my best friend, Barb, and I to ignore. Separately, we headed in opposite directions, circling around through yards to fool all who might care, finally crawling under a barbed wire fence that surrounded the large, treed pasture. It was our delicious secret. "The Creek," as we called the area, was lovely, leafy and cool during the hot muggy Ohio summers. We waded and played in the water and created houses in the big roots of trees that grew alongside. We read The Bobbsey Twins and Nancy Drew mysteries. We reveled in having this wonderful haven to ourselves.

The next summer we decided to become cowboys. Barb, less adventurous, watched as I coaxed a horse to the fence with an apple, and then flopped onto the horse and held onto the mane for dear life. I rode this way several times until eventually one horse realized that by going under a low hanging branch it could scrape me off. Other than bumps and bruises I wasn't hurt but I was irritated that the horse had made the decision that our cowboy days were over.

After seeing a movie where Tarzan jumped from one tree to another, I decided that I too wanted to jump from treetop to treetop. After carefully considering the various trees at The Creek, I picked a couple of young ones. With Barb watching, I almost killed myself when I jumped from one small tree to another and slid down through the branches, being scraped by limbs and branches on the way down. I guess they have a different kind of tree in Africa, or more probably my skinny little arms weren't strong enough to grasp and hold onto a branch.

Although The Creek was always the favorite place, there were other favorite activities involving the sixteen kids in our two blocks. There were clubs and more clubs, girls only, boys only, and mixed-gender clubs. There was the Fallen Tree Club, the Comic Book Club and the Grape Arbor Club. But our pride and joy was the Chicken Coop Club.

There was an old chicken coop at the rear of one of the deep back yards. The parents gave permission for us to use it if we would clean it. (shades of Tom Sawyer). We shoveled, swept, and white washed. We hung curtains made of old sheets and brought in castoff furniture. We were ready – well almost. There had to be an initiation for the privileged members of the Chicken Coop Club.

After much discussion, it was decided each potential member had to jump from the roof where directly below grew a large, stickery rose bush. In those days I was known for my lack of fear so heart in throat I leaped and lived. One by one each kid gathered courage and jumped over the rose bush, young and old, boys and girls. Finally there was only one potential member left, my wimpy, 18 month younger sister, Suzy. We pleaded and threatened. We begged and waited. She just wouldn't jump. Finally, craftily I cajoled her to the edge so I could show her how easy it would be. Then I pushed her off. Oh, yes, she cried. Oh yes, she tattled. And, oh yes, did I ever get into trouble! But, it was worth it! Our club was up and running. From the first moment of cleaning to the day school started it was the place to be.

Although the Chicken Coop Club was the place to be that summer, other idyllic days brought other places in which to hang out. In the back of another yard was an old stable with a large, open second story room above it. The kids in the neighborhood with a minimum of direction from parents formed an actual working library. First we collected books, carefully putting each family's name in the front. We glued in pockets for cards and set up a card catalog system. There were regular hours every afternoon with the older kids acting as librarians. Everyone read books that summer, lazing away hot afternoons on the stacked mattresses and chairs of every size to fit a child of every size. And as it was the 50's, not one parent had to monitor the books. I don't think it would have occurred to any family to offer a book that wasn't acceptable to every family.

One lovely summer afternoon we held a mock wedding in our back yard with 15 children participating. We spent weeks preparing. First, each wedding party member and the appropriate child to play the part had to be decided. We wrangled and negotiated over bridesmaids, best men, and ring bearer. We ended up with the youngest boy and girl, aged four and five, being the bride and groom. The daughters of the minister who lived across the street were picked to sing hymns. We practiced and practiced. It absorbed every waking moment for days.

Each of the older children had an assignment. One baked the wedding cake, one gathered chairs, and one arranged flowers. Men were away at their jobs, so all of the attendees were women (mothers). Children were impressed that the women had put away their pedal pushers and wore dresses just as if they were attending a real wedding. The procession was lovely with the groom in his tuxedo and the bride in her long, white, dress and veil. Vows were recited and hymns were beautifully sung. The white wedding cake and ice cream were enjoyed by all. It was a delightful, creative event.

Various activities claimed our time during the day, jump rope, jacks, high water, marbles and always, comic books. Boys favored cowboys and Indians or cops and robbers, and sometimes I joined in while most girls favored dolls whose company I rarely sought. I was the quintessential tomboy. Summer nights were reserved for hide-n-seek. Year after year the big tree in front of our house was home base. Hot nights were filled with the tiny sparkle of lightening bugs and lush smells. First, came, "One Potato -Two Potato…" to decide who was "It," and then nights were filled with the sounds of children's voices yelling, "Free!" or, "Ollie, ollie oxen free!" It was always my favorite part of the day.

Fall brought Halloween and time for a little mischief by older children, usually throwing dried corn at windows or pinning car horns. Of course no one ever locked a car then, so to pin a horn, a stick was inserted under the steering wheel rim and over the center horn button and back under the opposite rim. The result was the horn would blare until the stick was removed. The reward to the fifties version of a juvenile delinquent was in watching a very irritated dad come out of his nice, warm house into the cold fall air to stop the blaring horn by removing the stick.

One dark October evening I finally gathered the courage to indulge in my first nefarious activity. All I needed was one stout stick. While

Mom was watching TV, I snuck to The Creek and climbed over the barbed wire fence. I was trying to find a stick in the dark when the sudden noise of a horse scared me. I ran and tried to jump the barbed wire fence. Unfortunately, I landed in the middle of it instead. I could feel the blood running down my leg and I knew that my jeans were ripped. Now I was really in trouble. Not only had I been in a forbidden area but I had destroyed my clothing.

The situation called for a stealthy strategy to get to the one and only bathroom in the upstairs of our house without my wound and ripped jeans being noticed. There was an old overcoat of my Dad's hanging in the garage. Aha, the solution. I was saved. Overcoat dragging on the ground, I passed Mom who glanced at the overcoat and asked what I was doing. Quickly I replied that I was just thinking about Halloween costumes. Moments later I was busted after she followed the trail of blood through the house, up the stairs to the bathroom where I was frantically trying to bandage my leg. I still have the scar on my thigh from the leap over that barb wire fence.

During ninth grade, I headed for Wheat Ridge High School where sports, high school dances, new friends, cheerleading and a driver's license replaced forts and clubs. The Creek didn't seem quite so alluring any more. "Big girls" didn't play hide-n-seek with little kids. It was called growing up. I have never forgotten the deep feelings of joy brought on by those magical summers. Do kids today experience the same depth of happiness from computer games and organized sports? I don't know. But thinking back, it is idyllic summers filled with good friends sharing creativity, initiative, and independence that I wish for all children.

"Daddy! Daddy!"
By Carol Greenwood (Carol Combs)

It is often said that one's high school years are complicated years because of peer pressure. It is the age when friends, clothes, cars and one's appearance become increasingly important. Add to those pressures a move from across country, a parent's death and the poor adjustment to widowhood by the surviving parent and a picture of my high school years emerges.

For many years of my childhood in Ohio, my Dad traveled the state for a living. Each of his returns on a Friday evening was a cause for joy. We children would run out to the car yelling, "Daddy! Daddy!" Growing up I always thought our joy was because we were glad to see him return home. Many years later I realized that happiness was also because we children were no longer alone with just our Mom.

During Christmas vacation of my freshman year we moved to Wheat Ridge. Having left a big, two-story house, it was discouraging to be moved into a duplex where I shared one bedroom with my three other siblings ages 12, 9 and 4. My parents were going to build a new house and this was only temporary. Nevertheless, I wasn't about to admit to any new friends the new living arrangements-- that is, if I was going to have new friends. During that semester I was an intense observer. The Wheat Ridge girls were more sophisticated than were my old girlfriends at my Ohio junior high. I made attempts at imitating their hair styles and their classy ways of dressing. It was difficult as there was no extra money for me to have new clothes or shoes while the new house was being built. I suffered and watched. I wanted to be one of those stylish girls who had friends and seemingly carefree lives.

After we moved to Independence Drive, we began attending Wheat Ridge Presbyterian Church and our family became friends with the Elfelds. Finally, I had a new friend, Jean Elfeld, and then through her a second friend, Stephanie Poe. We were out of that crowded duplex, I had new friends and life was looking up! Although I had new friends, my time with them was strictly regulated by Mom. Housework and care for five year old Sarah and ten year old Tim came first and too much free time was frowned upon. For the first time I was allowed a sleep-over at a friend's house. Another first, and only because he went to our church, that summer I was allowed to have a date with a boy in a car. And what a date! We went to a drive-in and I pretended to be asleep because I was so ill at ease. He kissed me and I continued pretending to be asleep. There was only one date with him. To say I was a little young for my age would be an understatement.

Dad now had a sales territory that stretched from Montana to New Mexico and he was gone from two to six weeks at a time. One fall Friday night after we had moved into the new house, Dad was expected home after a particularly long trip. He didn't arrive and Mom was furious. The next day, when he finally arrived home, a fight ensued but eventually Mom realized that he wasn't making sense. After a visit to a doctor the next week, he was diagnosed with cancer. As was usual in our family then, that diagnosis belonged to the adults and we children were only told that he was sick.

About the same time as I walked the mile to school (yes, it really was a mile) Dennis Glenn stopped to give me a ride. That ride stretched into more rides and he became my first honest to goodness boyfriend. Through Dennis I met his buddies and some of their girlfriends, Sue Capron, Cynthia Chaney and Pat Glenski. Included in this group were guys with cars. This was an exciting group who seemed to have known each other forever. That previous summer I made three skirts and was allowed to buy sweaters to go with them. I now knew how to style my hair and apply makeup. I was in heaven. My life was getting better and better. However, without being fully aware of what I was doing, soon I had changed friends. A little late, but I apologize to Jean and Stephanie for my callous disregard for our friendships.

Dad's health declined over the months, although he still tried to work by scheduling short trips. He also took me to the motor vehicle department so that I could get my driver's license. Getting a license for a sixteen year old was a big deal. But, more importantly to me, was the rare event of being alone with Dad. Being only 18 months apart, my sister, Suzy, and I had usually been treated as a unit. It was so unusual for me to be alone with him that I felt awkward and unsure of myself. Praise from him for passing the driver's test made my heart almost burst with pride.

In March of my junior year he was hospitalized. Bits and pieces of that time remain in my memory. On one of my visits, he told Mom that he wanted Suzy, and I to have pretty dresses for the prom. Still I clung to a hope that it was just a matter of time before he recovered, particularly as an aunt, no doubt trying to be kind, told me that he would get better. Later, another aunt told me that because of the severity of an operation he would be better off dead. He died with all of his family around. Days later at the funeral I was proud to see many high school friends. Strangely, I hadn't cried yet, perhaps in a state of denial, but finally the tears rolled when my little sister, Sarah, who was sitting on my lap began to sob. Reality began sinking in.

Mom took Dad's body on a train back to Kentucky for burial and another service. I don't know why she didn't take us children. But, Suzy and I were encouraged to continue with plans to attend the Junior-Senior Prom. That week was full of such contradictory feelings, sadness at home and happiness at school sharing the prom buzz. After school, there were young, unhappy, siblings to care for. Church friends stopped by often with food and condolences. The evening of the Prom, a kindly woman from our church came to care for Tim and Sarah and took pictures of Suzy and me in our prom dresses. Those pictures all have flowers from the funeral in the background.

With the confidence that accompanied the happiness at the beginning of my junior year, I began to wonder about cheerleading tryouts. I was fairly athletic and limber and I could learn the cheers. But, was it possible that I could get enough votes to win one of the five positions in the contest as I didn't know many students, particularly of other classes? I decided that my strategy was to work hard at practice and get to know more fellow students. I began saying hello to strangers as I walked down the hall and before long we exchanged smiles. I did win one of the coveted five spots and won new friends as well.

My senior Year accentuated the split personality of my home and school lives. At home, Mom who hadn't had a job since marriage and couldn't drive continued on a downward emotional spiral. Left with little money, a partly furnished house, and four kids 16 and under, she became increasingly agitated. There were constant fights and constant threats to call the school and refuse permission for me to continue with any activities including cheerleading. For my little brother and sister the threats were of a future home in an orphanage. It was difficult to think about school once I was at home and studying was usually last of my priorities.

Although Mom disapproved of me dating a Catholic, strangely she didn't try to stop me from dating Dennis. We went to school activities and to the movies, often at the old Vogue Theater. Kindly, his parents sometimes included me for dinner or for dining out on the weekends. I had never met anyone like his Dad and was fascinated by a man who played recordings of Le Mans races and the gospel music of Mahalia Jackson. Being with a fun family was soothing to my soul.

Patti and I often talked on the telephone, went to school athletic events together and double-dated. Looking back it is probable that our conversations were cathartic as we whispered the ups and downs of our personal lives. She became a lifelong friend, and when after marriage and children we both moved back to the Wheat Ridge area once again, we rode to events together.

I called Suzy to check some of the events of this story. Almost fifty years later to the day that our Dad died, we found ourselves crying as we remembered the hurt of those years. We agreed that at the time it seemed that Dad's death was the death of our family. After his death, Mom's emotional health worsened, however, as an adult I was able to handle the suicide threats and feigned heart attacks. A special place in my heart is reserved for my wonderful Wheat Ridge High School friends. Perhaps, unaware of their influence at the time, they helped me keep my head above the swirling flood of confusion and despair.

"Tuba-man!"

By Roger Bennett

One interesting experience for me in high school was in band. I played the bottom chairs in the trumpet section and got a "C" in band my freshman year, probably only due to the fact I showed up. In my sophomore year our tuba player got kicked out of school and another trumpeter, Roger Bales, and I were asked by Mr. Shelton if we'd like to learn to play the tuba. We both agreed. It was my BIG break! Even though it involved changing from music written in the treble clef to the bass clef, it was easy for me since I also played the piano. Of course changing from a small trumpet mouthpiece to the tuba mouthpiece, which was at least four times larger, was quite a change and resulted in my not ever being able to play the trumpet again. This was no big loss to those who heard me play. Poor Mr. Shelton - the suicide rate amongst high school band directors must have been high. After making the switch, Roger and I got straight A's in band the rest of our high school years. In my case, that A meant Mr. Shelton never had to suffer my trumpet again.

I also became the base player with the tuba in our high school dance band because they couldn't find a string base player. One of our mothers made a cover for the tuba with our band's name on it. I don't remember the band's name, but I believe Frank Fishman, who was a gifted trumpet player is the one who created the band and gave it a name. It should have been, "Frank and the Frankophiles."

We played at several different school dances and even recorded some songs on an album. Regretfully, nothing ever came of that, no fame, no riches, but it was an interesting experience - how many high school kids have "cut an album?" I wish I had a copy of that album, but it probably got tossed out by my Mom who was tired of listening to it over and over again.

When I started playing the tuba, the school had two silver instruments. The next year the band got a brand new brass tuba and I was the one who got to play it. I really loved it. The bell put out a wonderful sound. Of course at football games the giant brass tuba was a great snow magnet and I became a moving target.

Now, every Christmas season on Larimer Square in downtown Denver, about 2-300 tuba players congregate to play Christmas songs. I go down to listen and each year I think I will rent a tuba and participate the next year - but never have. If you want to experience this event it is worth your time, and for us old "Tuba-men" – it gives us goose bumps!

Hard Rock
By Roger Bennett

One of my main interests after returning to Colorado in 1974 was rock-hounding. I joined a club and started going on mineral-collecting field trips. I really got into it, collecting in Utah, Nevada, California, Montana, Wyoming, South Dakota, Nebraska, Kansas, Oklahoma, New Mexico Missouri, Arkansas, Mexico, and of course Colorado. Over the years I have assembled a mineral collection from all over the world. My wife and I also owned a gold mine. The "Moose Mine" was located about four miles south of Central City CO. We spent several years prospecting it for specimens of Rhodochrosite, a rose-colored manganese carbonate which is the Colorado state mineral. We thought about mining it for gold, but after a year of exploration and test-drilling, we decided it wasn't worth the expense. I must admit it was fun to act like an old miner and dream of riches.

Several of my rock-hounding trips resulted in close calls with rock falls both above and below ground. I was lucky not to get seriously injured. My rock-hounding led to me becoming a "facetor" of gem stones as a hobby. If you ever need to be "faceted," I can do it. It is a true delight to take an ugly mineral specimen and turn it into a beautiful gemstone.

Probably our most interesting trip was to Mexico near Los Lamentos with two other couples. We were the first Anglos allowed to go into an underground netherworld in a newly discovered section of a mine that was full of huge Selenite crystals up to 20-30 ft. long. If you are into rocks and minerals, this was somewhat like Indiana Jones and the Raiders of the Lost Ark. We had to crawl through some very small openings where there were three huge caverns full of the crystals, all intertwined. It was like discovering King Tut's tomb. If you visit the Cave of the Swords exhibit at the Denver Museum of Nature and Science you will get a feel for what we saw. With permission I took a crystal about 2' long from this deposit. I also have pictures. Unfortunately, what I have is about all that's left of the mine because the owners didn't protect the find. It could have become a major tourist attraction, a fantastic place for people to visit and appreciate for years - sad.

One of the most meaningful experiences of my life came in 2002 when I created a nonprofit 501(c)3 tax exempt corporation for a scholarship fund designed to help a brilliant student who had a difficult life before graduating from high school and needed help. I realized most college students end up with large student loans, a tough way to start life – in debt. I wanted to put a face on one person and felt if enough people pitched-in it would be painless. It would also make all of us proud. My idea was to allow this student to work part-time and go to school full-time. Unfortunately, the donations didn't materialize as I had naively expected. We were able to pay for the student's books and fees each semester as well as buy her two computers over six years. However, she still had to work full-time and squeeze-in as many hours each semester as she could. As a result the student still has large loans in spite of the help we provided. She has maintained a 3.8 GPA and will graduate after six years as an RN with a BS degree from the University of Colorado School of Nursing. The fund will continue to help her as long as necessary and when she is able, we will pick another worthy student to help. Her plan is to help another student like she was helped. When I discussed my frustration about how disappointed I was we could not pay for everything, she said it wasn't how much she had been helped but that we tried. That was the most important and meaningful thing to her and she was going to try to extend the philanthropy by helping another person when she was able. I felt good – at least we tried and she is off into life with a college degree.

The Monkey Girl of Reed Street

By Karen Carson (Karen Tileston)

Many of my favorite memories of our home on Reed Street center on a giant cottonwood tree in our backyard. When we moved into the house, the tree was already over 20 years old and it stood prominently behind the house providing dense shade in the hot dusty summers of our childhood. It was our favorite place to play and I read hundreds of books while relaxing high in the air on its branches. My brother, Buddy, and I eventually built a treehouse from which we could see the cornfields reaching south to 38th Avenue on one side and the green alfalfa fields that stretched towards Wadsworth across the street to the west.

When we moved into the house, it came with three lots, a wooden front porch with a sagging screen door and a resident pig named, "Bertha." Bertha liked to take her frequent naps inside out of the sun and preferred the kitchen where there was always the possibility for a small snack. After a summer of chasing Bertha out of the kitchen, my folks made the inevitable decision and Bertha made the transition to ham, bacon and sausage.

Our animal family also included a few goats - the Houdinis of the animal world. They could get out of every cage we built and they would streak over to Mr. Maker's farm to visit their buddies. We had chickens, ducks and one very special goose as well, and of course, an endless supply of cats and kittens. Ours was truly, "Animal House," and I was "Karen Tileston, Pig Farmer and goat roper."

Our house had no inside plumbing and no heat, except for the wood stove in the kitchen, and a very dangerous old oil stove that we practically never used. Mom heated water on the wood stove and we got our baths in a tin tub in the kitchen, which was the only warm place in the whole house! After baths, we made a beeline for bed as soon as we had our pajamas on! Later, we got a natural gas floor furnace, and then, I would fill my nightgown up with hot air and run for bed.

The alfalfa fields belonged to the farmer, Mr. Maker, who was very kind to our family the first winter, when my Dad left to work for the railroad, and never came home again - pigs in the kitchen, no heat, no plumbing?- I wouldn't come home either. Mr. Maker brought my mom extra vegetables from his root cellar and wood for the kitchen stove. Mom went to work at Meinigers, the art supply store downtown, and we went to daycare at another nearby farm that was located where the Catholic Church sits today.

In the spring my brother and I caught crawdads and pollywogs in the irrigation ditches on Mr. Maker's farm. We brought home big bunches of wild asparagus and hunted for spring mushrooms after the afternoon rains. We put the pollywogs in a dish in the living room and watched them make the magic transition to become frogs. Then, they inevitably escaped from the dish, and my mom found them expired in the furniture cracks.

My mom was determined to make a life for us and hold on to the property. Wheat Ridge was growing and pigs and goats were fast becoming politically incorrect. She met and married my stepfather and he helped her modernize the house. I can remember the day he finished the inside plumbing as "the day of miracles." Over the years he built things we had never imagined - a kitchen, installed natural gas floor heat, and by the time my brother Buddy graduated from high school, he had actually been in his own room for more than a year.

As the years passed Wheat Ridge developed and more homes were built on Quay Street. They filled in between Kugler's old house and 38th Avenue. My brother and I were happy to have some new friends, Stan Hart, Pat and Alan Blanchard, and eventually with further development, Gene Magnuson, and Jerry Bowser. This core group became "the procurement team" for our plan to turn the cottonwood tree into a training ground for future circus performers. On a camping trip to the Loveland area we came upon a major treasure - hundreds of feet of discarded ski-tow rope.

With the help of the guys who had their Boy Scout knot-tying badges, we fastened ropes from the highest branches of the cottonwood tree and devised a point system for tricks that we improved over time. My brother was President of the "Monkey Club." All of us did our best to catch up with him, but we never did - to this day he is the unquestioned leader of the Monkey Club and I was the original "Monkey Woman!" One of our rites of passage was having the least skilled member swing out and then the others would jump on - one at a time - until the leap to the rope's back swing became an impossible distance and someone would have to chicken-out. One event nearly caused the end of the Club. We had five or six kids on the rope, when the branch broke, and we all landed in a heap in the dirt and the branch slammed down on Jerry Bowser's head! His Mom was pretty mad, but Jerry was back in a few days for more Monkey fun.

That same summer the procurement team came up with a set of wooden-spoked wagon wheels. This opened a whole new world of "wheeled opportunities." The most memorable use we found was to attach a 20 ft. 2 X 10 to make a huge teeter-totter that we used to launch some of the Monkey kids high into the cottonwood branches. That was a little dangerous, so my friend Katherine Donaldson and I came up with another novel idea - we discovered we could build up tremendous speed on the road using the wheels and the 20 ft. 2 X 10 to get down to her house on 48th - Spartacus! This activity came to a halt when we were stopped by a Colorado State Highway Patrolman and warned that we were not a legally licensed vehicle! I am sure he wanted to give us a ticket, but he let us off - probably had a tough time finding a traffic code for teeter-totters.

That summer my folks decided we kids had entirely too much time on our hands. Both Buddy and I got jobs - mine was at the old "farmer's market" on the corner of 44th and Wadsworth. I worked four hours every day sorting out pop bottles. My brother went to work with our stepfather as a painter's helper. We were now among the "rich and famous" - we now had real money to spend and we extended our horizons. We often rode our bikes to the Oriental Movie Theater for the Saturday show and serials. We got in for 10 cents and were allowed to stay all day as long as we were quiet. We spent our days off swimming in Berkeley Lake, and when we really had money, we went to Lakeside Amusement Park to ride the roller coaster and spend unlimited time in the "Fun House."

This was about the time of life when the boys started to want us girls to "get lost." We all joined a girls softball team. Our first year was pretty pathetic, and we won very few games. Our best player was Ann Morgan, who was the catcher, and who could actually throw the ball from home plate to second base! Katherine Donaldson and I alternated positions in the outfield. In the four years that followed we improved and finally won a league championship - at least that's the way I remember it and have told it that way ever since!

The Jefferson County Public School system bought Mr. Maker's farm to build the new Reed Street Elementary School. For a short time it became the world's biggest jungle gym. We loved to play on the enormous piles of dirt and climb on the construction when the workers went home for the day. One of the most frightening evenings of my life came when we were climbing up 20 ft. walls and running along the top. We came upon the dreaded Superintendent Stevens conducting a tour of prominent businessmen! We flattened ourselves like lizards along the top of the walls and the group passed directly beneath and never saw me! I thought we were going to be busted for sure! We were much more careful after that night but we still had a few more evenings of fun before the school was finally finished - just as I went into the 7th grade!

At about the same time the new football field was developed and with the installation of the lights I fell in love with fall football. In my opinion, there is no sporting event that is as exciting as high school football, when the stands are filled with parents, friends, admirers and relatives. The Super Bowl has never made me scream or jump up and down but I can remember the nights when I was sure that the stands would collapse from the enthusiasm of the crowd. The crisp Colorado air made the steaming hotdogs and rich hot chocolate better than any I have had since.

Who could resist the magic of a high school Homecoming? The mud-splattered football hero kisses the cutest girl in school, and the crowd loves them both! I can still see the big yellow chrysanthemums on the women in the crowd. I can hear the band and I can see our Pep Squad executing their precision marching drills.

My friends and I loved to help decorate the gym for all of the dances. We strung miles of twisted crepe paper and stretched it across to make a canopy, set up bandstands and even found one of those mirrored reflective balls for one event. The process never failed. By evening, when the lights came down and the music started, the gym turned into Roseland and everyone had a good time!

After more than 40 years, I remember some things clearly while other events have slipped away into the far corners of my mind. Happily, I remember the really good things about growing up in Wheat Ridge. My brother, Buddy and I were in a group of kids who went from the 1st through the 12th grade on the same campus located only four blocks from our home. When I started school, we went to the old red brick building that later became the junior high. The class of 1958 was the last to graduate from the old high school that has since been torn down.

Jefferson County has grown exponentially since 1958, and despite their affluence today's kids can never have the personal freedom that I enjoyed growing up. How many of today's kids will ever be able to claim they were a "pig farmer, goat roper and Monkey Girl?" Whenever I return to Colorado, I make it a point to drive by the old schools and am shocked to see that they are disappearing. I will not be surprised to see the buildings gone altogether on some future visit. If that happens, so be it. Such is the way of things - progress. I will still remember all the good times - Monkey Girl!

Domo Arigato

By Karen Carson (Karen Tileston)

1984 in Los Angeles was magical. President Reagan opened the Olympics to theme music composed by John Williams, the torch run was completed by decathlon winner, Rafer Johnson, and the world fell in love with the mascot, Sam, the Olympic Eagle.

With a recent promotion at AT&T I thought I had it all – great clients and a staff to keep me out of trouble. We were positioned to sell our services and equipment all over the world and AT&T prepared us for our international responsibilities with cross-cultural training. My market segment included a very large network component manufacturer based in Japan. AT&T printed bi-lingual business cards and we practiced the correct way to present ourselves to a Japanese businessman. We were told that it would be customary to bring a small gift to an initial meeting.

Our client's local executive staff invited us to make a presentation of one of our networking products. This was a challenge we were thrilled to take on – ours was the first female sales team invited to present to this very conservative Japanese client. Our excitement turned to terror when we were told that twelve executives were flying over from Japan for the meeting! My wonderful administrator Minnie and I practiced our card presentations and we purchased a Sam the Olympic Eagle lapel pin for each member of the client's team. These pins were very rare in LA and a hot trading item between the athletes, fans and corporate sponsors.

Our meeting room at the client's LA executive conference room was right out of central casting with an enormous black granite conference table, red leather chairs and real crystal water glasses. Minnie and I were alone in the room waiting for our client's team from Japan. When they arrived we presented our cards perfectly and gave each man a lapel pin, welcoming them to LA and our Olympic Games. During the presentation the client's team spoke perfect English but they conferred with each other in Japanese. We had no translator.

During the meeting it became clear that our objectives were in conflict. Our job was to sell our stuff and as it turned out their objective was to get the technical design and a sample component back to Japan. The client team was unfailingly polite, almost gentle in their questions, and I made every effort to avoid saying what I was thinking which was, "...are you guys delusional or what?" Their spokesman requested wiring plans, proprietary designs and actual equipment to take back to Japan for 'testing'. When I finally had no other option I gave them my best exit line, "I really wish we could do that but I am so sorry…"

Without another word the entire client team stood, bowed slightly to me and, as if on cue, each man sadly removed his Sam the Eagle pin, placed it gently on the granite conference table and filed out of the room. As my career flashed before my eyes I was amazed to see Minnie collecting all of the Sam the Eagle pins! Ever the pragmatist, she was not leaving those pins behind!

By the time we had gathered our materials and made it back to the car we were starting to giggle. The tension of that day had finally gotten the best of us – we were draped over the hood of my car laughing so hard that tears were streaming down our faces when the limos taking the client team back to their hotel drove past. Now we were sure that our careers were over, but, as it happened our client team sent a very nice letter to our boss complimenting us on our presentation!

This encounter and many subsequent meetings with this client taught me more about negotiation than a hundred western-based classes on the subject. They taught me to appreciate and enjoy the differences and that business, and life, is all about the process.

My Sports Career
By Daryl Hall

What follows is more of an evolutionary process and the circumstances and happenings that surrounded it. I am speaking of my illustrious sports career that began at Wheat Ridge Jr. High School:

Sports had always been an interest of mine even as a young boy in Nebraska prior to my fourth grade migration to Wheat Ridge. As a child in Nebraska, we played sandlot baseball and football with neighborhood kids of all ages. Once we arrived in Wheat Ridge in 1949, our family lived on Davis Brothers Florist property at 38th and Wadsworth. Our home was next door to the Methodist Church on the corner. There weren't very many kids in the immediate area to play sandlot ball, so most of the activities were at school. Sports seemed more organized in Wheat Ridge than in Nebraska. There was Jeff Co (Jefferson County) summer baseball and school yard play was more with kids from your own class. In Nebraska, kindergarten through eighth grade played together and it was usually a free-for-all.

Jr. High School was quite sophisticated to me. We even got uniforms and had referees. Having great confidence in my sports abilities, I looked forward to playing Jr. High sports. However, there was a slight problem beginning to appear - all of my peers were growing up faster than me. I was always a runt but determination seemed to overcome this until Jr. High.

Jr. High football proved interesting, since a few of the guys were growing into young men, while some of us were still boys. As a result, our wise coaches divided us into heavyweights and lightweights. Being fit for uniforms was an experience of its own. We were taken to be fit in old high school suits. Jersey and pants were OK, but there wasn't a helmet small enough to fit. If I turned my head quickly I could see out of the ear hole. Needless to say I took a trip to Dave Cook Sporting Goods on downtown 16th Street and bought my own. It was even gold with a blue stripe, our school colors.

Our lightweight division consisted of two teams. I was elected captain of my team and we were called the "Rams." Victor Bird was captain of the other team and under his influence the team was called, the "Flying Turtles". If my memory is correct, every other week we played each other, in uniforms, on the high school football field. Alternate weeks were heavy weight games.

Being able to run pretty fast, I thought I would be a good halfback in the old "T" formation. Cliff Selby was also in the backfield. Dick Brazzell was an end. I played halfback for the first game, but coach Hicks decided I should share quarterback duties with Dennis Shields. Not having enough players to make a defensive squad, we played both defense and offense. On defense I was a linebacker, partly responsible for any runners having broken through the line.

Victor Bird was a halfback for the "Turtles." Victor, even in grade school, was one of the fastest runners in the class. He would often win blue ribbons on Field Day. Not only was he fast, but stout for his size. The "Turtles" were on the 20-yard line headed for our goal. Victor was given the ball and broke through the line like a bowling ball. I was in his sights in the backfield. When he hit me, it felt like a small freight engine had been unleashed. He split my lip, which bled profusely, and knocked me flat. Somehow, I managed to catch a leg and he went down. His team went on to score while I was bleeding on the bench. Not only did the "Turtles" score but they went on to an undefeated season.

Undaunted by that experience, basketball was next. I had learned to dribble pretty well and had a good shot. Though I was short, I was quick and felt I could compete. Uniforms were again a problem. I would take two steps before my shorts would move, I looked more like a poor animated Disney cartoon character than a real person. Not to be discouraged, I persisted and played anyway. Not knowing too much about organized play and referees and rules on a full court, one of my first games provided a good laugh for the coaches.

The referees were high school athletes and not necessarily basketball players. Vaughn Justice was one of the high school athletes that refereed one of our first Jr. High games. I was driving for the basket and was fouled in the process. Justice took me to the wrong end of the court to shoot my free throws. Fortunately, I missed and didn't score for the other team. Totally humiliated, I glanced at the bench and everyone was having a good laugh, everyone but me. Oh well, it was truly a learning experience.

Moving into high school it was obvious to me my football years were over. Though I still felt confident of my abilities, I was also pragmatic. There was no such thing as heavyweights and lightweights. Still, weighing less than 95 pounds and less than five feet tall, I pictured myself like Wile Coyote being smashed with a huge rock off a cliff. If I was to play against guys like Dennis Glenn, Dick Weber, or Bill Stuerke the obvious problem was I wouldn't pop back into form after being flattened like the coyote in Road Runner cartoons.

Fearing bodily harm, I decided to wait for basketball. I was still small but still quick and could shoot, so I thought I might make the team. Sure enough, I survived the cuts and made the team.

Before the first game winter set in and ice was on the pond at 32nd and Estes. Many remember that a good percentage of the school, all ages, came there to skate. We were playing a game called, "Capture The Flag." I won't go into details, but I was making a break to get the flag at the opponents goal. I hit a rut in the ice and went feet in the air and landed on my left wrist to break the fall. The fall was broken and so was my arm. Basketball was over for the season for me.

Sophomore year brought another experience in my pursuit of being an athlete. We were now competing for "B-squad" varsity basketball. Again, I survived the cuts and was at least going to be a bench warmer. But, once again I met my fate.

Running one-on-one exercises in practice I leaped into the air in a futile attempt to block an opponent's shot. I came down, severely twisting my left ankle. After a late afternoon visit to Dr. Tilquists' office and two weeks on crutches, basketball was over for the season. I did return to practice but never saw a uniform.

In spite of the desire and determination I reassessed my future in sports. Again, being pragmatic, I thought my efforts could be better spent elsewhere. I still enjoyed cheering my former teammates on, but my sports career was over!

The Career Evolution
By Daryl Hall

After spending four years majoring in Horticulture at Colorado State University, my intentions were to work for what we considered our family business. Three generations of the Halls had worked for Marshall Nurseries in Nebraska and in Denver, Colorado. The nursery was a corporation. My dad had acquired the third largest block of stock when Mr. Marshall in Denver retired. Upon his retirement, Dad became general manager in 1967. In 1973 one of the Marshall family members sold to a minority stockholder. This man took possession of 51% controlling interest, and after 67 years of our family and 87 years of the Marshall family, the Halls and Marshalls were out of the organization. By 1979 the Denver and Omaha branches were closed and the ground sold.

Dad and I started our own business in spring of 1974 called Green Gallery Landscaping Inc., where I designed landscape plans and was involved in sales as well as bidding on commercial projects. We also had a small garden center. We continued this operation until Dad died in 1988. I moved on and went to work as a grower for a wholesale nursery in Denver. It was established in 1907 as Northern Nursery and later became James Nursery owned by the original owners' grandson.

The division that I managed was a 70-acre plot northeast of Brighton near Lochbuie, Colorado. After helping develop all 70 acres, we were supplying our home office with shade and ornamental trees as well as shipping to other nurseries in Colorado and Wyoming. On June 20, 2001 the nursery was hit by a devastating hailstorm that severely damaged the entire inventory. 85-90% of the stock was not sellable. The remainder of the summer was spent pulling all of the trees out of the ground and burning them. By Thanksgiving of 2001 the growing division was closed. After 46 years, having started in high school and having the third major interruption in my life, my nursery career ended.

My choice at the time, since I was not yet of retirement age, was to take early retirement and travel with my wife, Helen, a professional artist. Helen had been doing Colorado art shows and some out of state shows on her own. Helen and I felt we could sell more paintings by gaining more exposure for her work. We have traveled to shows in Kansas, Utah, California, Arizona, Texas, New Mexico and Wyoming, as well as the Colorado mountain shows. The Colorado shows were in Copper Mountain, Vail, Beaver Creek, Aspen, Castle Rock, and Denver.

Helen and I are still traveling to art shows around the country. Our next show is an auction in Albuquerque, New Mexico. Many artists from the southwest including Helen donate a piece of their art work for the auction. The proceeds are used to fund scholarships for underprivileged children who cannot afford to pay for education. It's a great event in which we are proud to be participants.

It has been quite a journey after leaving Wheat Ridge High School. There have been highs and lows, happiness and pain as probably many other classmates have experienced. Looking back, I consider myself a lucky man with a good family and great friends. Our daughter, Susan, is a math teacher and our son, Dean, runs three businesses. Our daughter, Susan, has two children, Tyler 16, and Annamarie 12. Tyler's interest lies in math and computers. Annamarie's interest is in competing with her horse in jumping classes. Dean is not married. All are happy and prosperous and it makes Helen and I feel proud, thankful, and blessed. I must say that Wheat Ridge schools and my classmates helped lay the foundation for a satisfying life. We were all lucky to have grown up in the Wheat Ridge community which provided a wholesome environment in which to grow and develop. This was a community of decent people, good schools with good teachers and classmates, many of whom have become high achievers. All have made the class of '58 who we are. I would offer this as we enter our "Golden Years:" I still have things I want to accomplish and places I want to go. So, let's keep on keeping on and enjoy each day and year as they come.

Snippets of Memory – My Years at WRHS

By Judy Crosby (Judy Luntey)

One of the most memorable days of my life was registration for school at WRHS – it was a FRIDAY, October 1952!!! Coming from a huge school in Denver to a relatively rural (at that time) school in Jefferson County (and they were known as "the Farmers," no less, Gasp!!!) none of my family was prepared for the rude "Welcome" we received from the Principal, Joy Clap.

Little did we know that FRIDAYS were sacred, set aside for FOOTBALL!! The whole school was out to the game and here I was trying to register to get an education. How humiliating!!!!

Things did not improve over the next few months. This was 7th grade. Folks were polite, I was accepted, but another shock awaited me when the first grading period came. I was passing only because the teacher(s) felt sorry for me. YIIIIKES!! I had been a good student for all of my years in the Denver school system and now I was failing at a rural school - not good news!!! I think I spent most of the rest of the year studying. Boy, did I struggle, but eventually made it to a comfortable C-level with some A's and B's to follow in time!!!

My next real memory is of Mr. Mars and his Geometry class in 10th grade. I liked math and did well in Algebra I. I wanted to take Mechanical Drawing but it was a "Boys Only" class. In those days Home Economics was the preferred choice for girls. So, I enlisted for Geometry. I did fairly well the first couple of weeks and then another shock: I could not understand anything the teacher was trying to get into my head. Boy, did I sweat it out for another few weeks and then to my amazement, I GOT IT!!! All of a sudden, one day, all the little pieces fell into place and I understood Geometry!!! What an experience. I was a genius!!! It was surreal. I have related this experience many times over the years, but I still wonder if the teacher noticed?

Typing class was wonderful. That was my forte. Shorthand was less than wonderful, but I did use it a time or two after graduation to get a job. There were about 6 girls in the class named "Judy." Evidently it was a popular name at the time.

Two years of Spanish cemented my bond and friendship with Darlene Nelson. We became close, dubbed by one teacher as "the Bobbsey Twins." By the end of 11ᵗʰ grade there were about 7-8 of us who were tight buddies. Those were comfortable years and Darlene and I have kept in touch over the years. It is nice to have a long-time friend to share memories at this stage of life.

Our World History class with Mr. McGaffey was one of the best. He taught in a way that excited us. He made those dark, musty times live. He was removed from the school because someone did not like the way he was teaching. It was sad. For the rest of the year we read the dry old books and were bored!

I was happy at Wheat Ridge High School. It was a good time of life. We were the last class to graduate from the old building on 38ᵗʰ Avenue. The new WRHS was moved way out west on 32d and modern steel, glass and computers have replaced the musty smell of old bricks, wood and chalk - a little sad. The past few years I have taken part in a class "chat" group through e-mail. It makes me feel part of a group of old friends with a common bond even though I don't know all of the players well. Despite the modern world, I guess our bond is – "Farmers Forever!!!"

Call of the Wild – 50 Years on an Uncharted Adventure

By Judy Crosby (Judy Luntey)

Ah, where to begin?

"There are strange things done in the midnight sun…"

In 1958 we graduated. Yes, I passed geometry and after a summer of water skiing, camping and working here and there, I decided a week before I was to enroll at Colorado State University (formerly Colorado A&M – perfect for a "Farmer") in Ft. Collins, that I was not going. I got a job in downtown Denver. Most of our class headed out-of-town for action, but I stayed. My learning experiences have been mostly through "the school of hard knocks." I never regretted my decision to not attend college.

"…by the men who moil for gold…:

In 1960 I married my high school sweetheart, Norm Crosby, who graduated in 1958 from Golden and we set out to build a memorable life together. We lived in and around Golden, Lakewood, Lookout Mountain and Arvada for 17 years. We had three kids, one boy, two girls, and have enjoyed a life close to family and friends.

"..the Arctic trails have their secret tales…"

A wonderful opportunity came our way in 1977 and we decided to move to Anchorage. My husband was in data processing and his company moved us and all our stuff NORTH TO ALASKA! We drove our 1972, ¾-ton Ford truck pulling a 19 ft. travel trailer up the unpaved ALCAN Highway (does Chevy Chase's European Vacation ring a bell?). The Alaskan Pipeline was just opening and housing was at a premium. We stayed in a rustic trailer park north of Anchorage at Eklutna for two months until we could find a house. THAT was an EXPERIENCE!!! (This isn't Kansas, Toto).

"...that would make your blood run cold."

We eventually bought a new home in Eagle River, AK, 20 minutes north of Anchorage. We had no phone, no refrigerator (we didn't need one, and for 6 months used an ice chest) and one car. I took Norman to work one day a week and did our shopping while he was at work. Alaska was a new lifestyle for us with different vegetation, seacoasts, wildlife. Wandering through our yard were bear and moose, and we had to learn a whole new language. The names of everything just sounded different. We lived there happily for 25 years.

"The Northern Lights have seen queer sights..."

I worked as a bank teller at for four years and then went to work for the Anchorage School District. It was a most rewarding time - so many, many wonderful people I can call "Friend." Our kids graduated, married, and now we have six grandchildren. They all lived close most of the time and we were blessed watching them grow up.

"...but the queerest they ever did see..."

As the century turned, in 2001, we decided to build a house in the Palmer area. It is 40 miles north of Anchorage in the Matanuska Valley. In the 1930's farm families were brought in and helped create the wonderful vegetable farms for which we are still famous. Norman had retired from his data processing job and was able to do most of the work building our house. I retired in 2002 from the school district. One daughter lives next door to us and our son lives about 80 miles north towards Mt. McKinley. Beaver Cleaver has nothing on us. Our other daughter lives in Fresno, CA.

"…was that night on the marge of Lake Lebarge"

We have thoroughly enjoyed being in Alaska. We own a small airplane, a Cessna 150, and have flown it all over the state. We have 4-wheelers, snow machines, cross country skis, fishing tackle, hunting rifles and a cabin 10 miles from the base of Mt. McKinley. The "Call of the Wild" grabbed us and we are truly Alaskans. Our families come to visit and they all understand why we love it here. We like to go "outside" (what you say when you leave the state) at least every other year. Driving through Canada is wonderful and we have thoroughly enjoyed exploring all the states west of the Mississippi from Louisiana (BK - before Katrina) and the Mexican border to Alaska - some day the eastern half of the U.S - maybe in the next 50 years.

"…with me and my family."

We hope to see you all in the "lower 48."

* Sections liberally adopted from *The Cremation of Sam McGee* by Robert W. Service

Died and Gone to Heaven – A High School Memory

By Cliff Miercort

One early spring night of my senior year started out special. Bill Walgren, Eddie Manor and I were driving around in my '54 Chevrolet looking for something to do. At the Frosted Scotchman we met my best "girl friend" along with two other girls from WRHS '58. We all ended up in my car and took off for no place in particular. Someone suggested that a little beer would be good, so Eddie got us a couple of quarts.

We drove around for awhile having a great time laughing with everybody talking at once. Eddie suggested we park and neck! I was way too shy to have suggested such a plan. Bill said nothing, but to our great surprise, the girls said they thought that would be great fun. We drove north of Arvada on Wadsworth over the big hill and found a place on the side of the road that was somewhat private.

Then the fun began. I thought I must have died and gone to Heaven. I started out with my girl and we kissed and kissed and had what I thought was a great time. Then as if someone rang a bell, everybody changed partners and started kissing again. Whoa! The logistics were difficult being that there were six in the car, but where there is a will especially for teenagers, there is a way. I could not believe my good fortune. There I was with three of the most beautiful girls in Wheat Ridge, and I actually got to kiss not one, but all three. I thought I must have died and gone to Heaven. I did not want that evening to ever end, and maybe it would not have, had it not been for the cop that came by, slowing ominously as he passed our parked car. Fortunately, the cop moved on down the road, but the moment of passion had passed.

After I moved on with my life, I sometimes found myself remembering that night and how much it had meant to an adolescent boy.

At one of our high school reunions, I believe the one in Vail, my wife, Barbara, Bill Walgren, my old girlfriend and I were having lunch. My old girlfriend brought up her memory of the Kissing Event (gulp!). I was about to jump in with my recollections when she said, "I don't remember who was there, but I do remember Eddie Manor. He was absolutely the best kisser in the world. What a guy." I was crushed that I had to remind her that I had been there as well.

Eddie, wherever you are, you were always the best-looking, and I think you'll be happy to know you earned the title as the best kisser as well! Congratulations.

How I Became the Boss – A Memory After High School

By Cliff Miercort

I got a fateful call at 1 pm one memorable Friday in September, 1987. The newly elected president ordered me to fire my entire staff but allowed as how I could keep my secretary. I was stunned. Two months earlier, it had been clear to everyone that he and I (the president of the Southwest Division) were in direct competition for the job he now held. He won the prize and now was demanding that the young division I headed, which held so much promise, was to be discarded. He used the excuse that the Board had told him he needed to trim overhead and cut back on exploration activities. He must have thought he could solve two problems at once: he could do what the Board wanted by cutting my staff, thereby effectively getting rid of me.

I let him talk, saying little. When I hung up, I composed a five page letter to the Chairman of the Board telling him what had just happened and outlining why I had no intention of complying with the directive. I related the successes of the Southwest Division, our plans for the future and said that what the new guy wanted would be a disastrous blow to the entire company's growth potential. I copied the new president on the letter, sent it and prepared for my execution.

First thing Monday morning, I had a call from my new boss, "Miercort you are fired! Get out!" he screamed.

My wife and I had anticipated he would come after me if he got the top job, so we were already in discussions to purchase a small oilfield equipment manufacturing company in Lubbock, Texas. I was on the phone with Barbara discussing what steps we should take next when my secretary came in saying that the Chief Financial Officer (CFO) of the company was on the line. He was a friend who had also had many run-ins with the new president. He did not elaborate, but told me to "get my butt up to Cleveland ASAP" because the Chairman wanted me in his office the next morning. Apparently news of my firing traveled fast.

When I arrived, the Chairman, my adversary and the CFO were waiting for me. The president was so angry he was practically foaming at the mouth. He said I had disobeyed his direct order, was insubordinate and deserved to be fired. I remained silent. When his tirade was over, the Chairman turned to him and said, "You can't fire Miercort. I am the only person in this company who can do that." He asked us to work out our differences.

The next two months were not the best in my life, but at least, I'd kept the division office intact. When the President invited me to Cleveland to discuss how the overhead of the company could be reduced, I feared that this was step two in "getting rid of Miercort." When I arrived in Cleveland the evening before our scheduled meeting, an urgent message to call the CFO was waiting for me. He said he wanted to meet me for dinner.

We had a drink, and then he laid it on me: my foe had been fired that afternoon, and the Board was meeting the next morning to promote me to president of the company.

As soon as I could break away from dinner, I went to my room to call Barbara. When I told her, she congratulated me, then asked with tears in her voice, "Does this mean we have to move back to Cleveland?" "No," I said, "here's the unbelievable news; the board has agreed to move the company headquarters to Dallas!"

I held that job for 17 years, adding CEO to my title along the way, until I retired two years ago. You may have seen my foe on television last summer after a mining tragedy. He was in front of the camera daily maintaining that an earthquake was to blame.

Early School Memories
By Phyllis Zailer (Phyllis Shepard)

Starting to attend Wheat Ridge High School was rather frightening for about seven of us who had attended all eight years of grade school (sorry folks, no Jr. High for us) in Prospect Valley Grade School (originally a 3-room schoolhouse) – we went from a graduating class of seven kids who stayed in one room all day to a Freshman class of over 200 and having to find our way around a high school campus!!! Those seven of us were myself, my cousin Beverly Davis, Nancy Dannenberg, Jill Daniels, Eileen Banzhaf, Wayne Neely and Eric Siverts. Most of us had to ride the school bus to Wheat Ridge, and these were all new experiences. In our 7th & 8th grades, we weren't considered Jr. Highers, we were just the oldest kids in the school. I think this way we avoided some of the problems that people think of now as being caused because you're a "Jr. Higher".

We soon adjusted and Bev and I made friends with five other girls who had hung around together through most of their growing up years – Judy Luntey, Maxine Thomas, Darlene Nelson, Marilyn Randall and Carroll Holt. We went to most events together and really became close friends during those years. None of us dated regularly, so we did most things together.

One event I remember is a Halloween when some of us went trick or treating in about the 7th or 8th grade – we would walk from one end of Prospect Valley to the other getting treats. My parents were gone on vacation and left me in the care at home of some cousins who lived behind us. My folks had sold off the back of our property at 38th & Oak Ave. to a builder of new homes. The builders had put up two large billboards which blocked quite a bit of the view from our house and

we'd heard my folks complain about that soooooo, several of us decided
we'd push over the signs and hope they wouldn't put them back up
– we pushed and pushed, but to no avail, so we gave up and went on
our way. The signs were still standing when I went to bed, but in the
morning, we looked out and they were both lying flat on the ground!!!!
I knew we weren't guilty, and to this day I don't know who did it. The
Sheriff's office stopped by our house and asked my cousin (who was
also a deputy) if they heard anything during the night and they said,
no. Later on they told me they knew what we had <u>tried</u> to do and we'd
better get our act together and stay out of trouble in the future. I'm sure
that had a big effect on me trying to stay out of trouble in future years.
Many years later, my folks told me they knew what had happened and
had just waited to see if I'd ever tell them about it. So many times in
our kids' lives they have told us information about things they thought
we knew at the time but didn't. Guess I'm still in for surprises at this
advanced age!!!

Unusual Hobby???
By Phyllis Zailer (Phyllis Shepard)

My husband, Chuck, has had an active interest in trains and railroad history ever since he was a child in Denver and I guess the virus has been catching because we now both have what most people consider an unusual hobby – Garden Railroading.

For my part I just went along with his interest and tried to encourage it occasionally, including building a model HO railway and collecting memorabilia, but the bug finally caught up with me too in December 1992 when he expressed interest in owning one of the Bachman G gauge sets sold at Costco at Christmas time. I bought him the set and then a copy of a Garden Railways magazine – what a mistake!! I was also fascinated with reading the articles and seeing the pictures and discovered that the National Garden Railways Convention was being held right there at the Santa Clara Convention Center in July of 1993. We both decided to take a day off work, register for the convention and take one of the bus tours where you get to go see other people's layouts (Los Altos, San Mateo, etc.) – WOW – what an eye opener. The next day we drove ourselves around to other areas to see more layouts. The Bay Area Garden Railway Society (BAGRS) was hosting the event that year (it moves around the US each year according to which clubs have opted to host it). By the end of those two days, we were both hooked. Not only was it bigger and easier for aging eyes and hands to handle, but you could move it all OUTSIDE. I must have taken several hundred pictures over that week of tours.

We slowly began to change our aging Santa Clara yard around to accommodate this. Chuck does all the track work which included bending his own rail, putting on the ties (which I helped with) and ballasting, building trestles and bridges, etc. My interest has always been selecting miniature plants to put in place of monster-sized regular plants, gluing together kit buildings and setting out scenes to have a town scattered around the yard.

Over the years we held several Open Houses and meetings of the club where others could view our efforts. We met hundreds of wonderful people and many of them are couples with whom we found life-long friendships. The Bay Area Club had over 500 member families during that time, so we didn't feel like this was very unusual.

When we moved from Santa Clara to Lincoln in March of 2000, we decided to bring most of the railroad with us. That involved packing lots of boxes and moving about 60 pots of plants and keeping them alive for over a year. Chuck had chosen our cul-de-sac lot with the railroad in mind and even though he was still working full-time (I had retired after working as a church secretary for over 25 years) we began building, raking and digging. All those rocks you see in the picture came out of this ground and I dug MOST of them! The name of our layout is the *Rock City and Pepper Central Garden Railway* – there are still many more rocks you can't see). Our goal was to have everything ready for July 2003 when our Sacramento Valley Club hosted the National Convention here. We did a dry-run in September 2002 for our Sun City community and had over 250 people come through the yard, and when we had the 2003 convention we had over 600 people, plus 3 bus loads come through. That's a lot of people in your back yard – thankfully, not all at once!

We're very proud of our efforts and most people up here know us as "Oh, you're the ones with the trains in your back yard." It has truly been a labor of love and if you're in the area, we'd love to have you visit us.

Ah, Memories...Girls' Revenge

By Kent Schroeder

I don't remember much about high school, but I do remember the future seemed so far away and now we are it. Ah, memories – everything seemed so poignant then, so important, and now only the funny things remain. Maybe that is a lesson for real life – remember less, laugh more:

I don't remember who was in the car in the summer of 1957, but we bought some of those powerful half-inch firecrackers with evil in mind. We were cruising down 38th Avenue, looking for girls. Our plan, of course, was to toss the firecrackers out the car window, explode them right at the girls' feet, then speed away as the girls screamed and yelled with fright. It was about as wicked as we got in those days.

One night I was in the passenger seat and we spied a tempting target, not a just girl, but a group of girls walking down the street. The thought that we might injure someone didn't enter our minds, the temptation was too great, the target too lucrative. I reached into our sack, pulled out the firecracker, lit it with the cigarette lighter and tossed it out the window. Uncoordinated dork that I was, I hit the window frame and the burning firecracker bounced back into our car. WOW! Does a half-inch firecracker ever make a lot of noise when it goes off inside a car! It also stunk – the smell of gunpowder or whatever they put into a firecracker is really bad. I never got invited to ride in that car again. If the girls were paying attention they are probably still wondering what that big flash was in the car passing by on a nice summer evening.

...and then, there was, "one ball": He was a fellow in the class ahead of us who claimed to be a quick-draw champion. He wore a pistol buckled to his side with a leather thong tied to the holster bottom just above the knee. He also wore a cowboy hat and looked the part. He was in a contest one weekend and as the story goes pulled the trigger before the pistol was out of the holster – he got the nickname, "one ball," and limped for the remainder of his high school career.

Well, at least my weapons were firecrackers and not pistols – funny what we remember about high school.

Later Life
By Kent Schroeder

The old Wheat Ridge High School had been built for about 500 students. By the time we were seniors, almost 800 kids were jammed into the building. There were temporary buildings outside, and the basement had been converted into many classrooms. The temporary buildings were cold in the winter. You wore a sweater or jacket, but your feet, hands and nose always seemed to be cold.

I remember those basement rooms. They were small, low-ceilinged and had hot water pipes wrapped with asbestos insulation, running along the ceiling. The cold water pipes were not covered. They just sweated and dripped. It wasn't bad if the drops hit your clothing, but if they hit your neck and ran down your shirt – well, there was little danger of us sleeping in class. If you were tall enough, and I was 5'10," you could hit your head. I don't know how we, or the teachers, stood it.

As bad and obvious as the over-crowding and conditions were, the voters repeatedly voted-down bond issues. Edward R. Murrow in a nationally-televised program called, "See It Now," focused on the need for new schools in expanding communities across America. He filmed and used the classrooms in the basement at WRHS. After that, we passed bonds for a new high school.

The "new" Wheat Ridge High School was finished in the spring of 1958 in time for our graduation. But, to avoid disruption the decision was made for our class to graduate from the old school. So, the class of 1958 was the last class to graduate from the old buildings. The old buildings were torn down and my mother, Pauline Schroeder, was the second-to-last "elected" Superintendent of Schools, serving from 1958-1962.

I guess I shouldn't be too hard on the old buildings. The most important event of my life occurred there: During my senior year I began to date a sophomore named, Sally Salter. In January 2008, we celebrated our 46th wedding anniversary.

After graduation, I attended the University of Denver Law School and was admitted to the bar in 1967. I later became a District Magistrate in Adams County, Judge Schroeder. Sally became a dental assistant and worked as a clinic manager at the Community College of Denver Dental Hygiene School at the old Lowry Air Force Base.

My wonderful wife, Sally, the most important person in my life, the best woman I have ever met, has contracted lung cancer - she never smoked – sometimes life is not fair.

My Heroes Have Always Been Cowboys

By Sheila Christy (Sheila Stoll)

...well, not really, not always, but it seems that way. I was born October 17, 1939 as "Sheila Jean Stoll" at St. Joseph's Hospital in Denver. Early-on I developed a keen interest in everything western – horses, cowboys, cattle, campfires, and of course cowboy music. The only thing missing while I was growing up was Willie Nelson.

My sister, Sharon, and I listened to the radio for entertainment. We had no TV in those days, not even black and white. Our favorite program was, "The Lone Ranger," a masked-man, no less, (how romantic could it be?) with an Indian sidekick named, "Tonto," who said cool things like, "You betchum, Kemo Sabe," which in Apache means "one who is white" (oh, be still my heart). He also had a white horse named, Silver, and he dropped silver bullets as calling cards. I guess he would be ticketed for "littering" today. The programs always ended with LR (I called him "LR" after I got to know him) bellowing, "Heigh-ho, Silver, AWAY!" At the sounds of galloping hooves, the William Tell Overture kicked-in, and I was hooked not only on cowboys, but classical music as well. After years of listening to the Lone Ranger, I was officially a cowgirl, if only in my dreams. I lacked three things: a horse, a place to keep one and the money to feed him.

Growing up, our family lived on West 32d Street in the city. I was ecstatic when I learned we would move way, way, way out into the "country," – Wheat Ridge – it even sounded western.

When we moved to Wheat Ridge, we got some "acreage." Now, at least, I had a place to keep a horse, just no horse and no money, and oh yes, there was that other thing called "school." We were truly a happy family and I imagined that I now lived in a place very similar to the setting on The Lone Ranger Show. I could almost feel it – "Heigh-ho, Sheila, Away!" Just give me a horse and I would start dropping silver bullets everywhere.

My parents worked hard and there wasn't much money to go around. Dad was the co-owner of a small upholstery business down on Speer Boulevard that made "winter-fronts" for the trucks of the Denver-Chicago Trucking Company, his major account. As most moms those days, Mother, was a "housewife."

One morning as my sister, Sharon, and I awoke, Mom and Dad told us to look out the window. Behind our house was an amazing sight – in a corral which Dad had fixed up was a beautiful bay mare, the most beautiful horse I had ever seen. We named her, "Ginger." She was a pony mare and later gave birth to a colt we named, "Misty, " after the misty morning on which she was born. We were now "cowgirls" and had two ponies, one for me and one for "Sis." When we were older, we graduated from the ponies to real horses.

"Real horses" took us to a riding club called, the "Lakewood Westernaires." The club performed drill team maneuvers on horseback but also taught western modeling, singing, trick roping, public speaking and citizenship. Our family became very active with the club. Mother became secretary-treasure of the group and Dad at his upholstery business made riding chaps and colored horse blankets. Over time we "city slickers" became very countrified and Dad, my favorite cowboy, hauled horses and kids to arenas from Texas and California to Canada.

One of the club faculty was, "Lefty" Carson who was locally well-known as a country singer. He had cut a few records in Nashville and was an outstanding roper and rider. Our club and Lefty were featured in many articles in the Denver Post, the Rocky Mountain News and the Western Horseman. Lefty and I became a team and we became known, at least in horse circles, all over the country. The Westernaire Vocalettes were asked to perform on radio and TV and Lefty and I sang on the

Grand Ole Opry when it came to Denver. I guess I was the first "TV star" in the WRHS class of '58?

My life growing up was idyllic – a young girl living her dreams supported by parents who sacrificed to give their kids the things they themselves never had – I know there must be a special place in heaven for such people.

...And Then There Was Real Life...

By Sheila Christy (Sheila Stoll)

Like most from our generation, I found that "real life" after graduation wasn't totally idyllic. My life growing up on horseback taught me many things: mucking out stalls and grooming were some of the price to be paid for the pleasures of riding. And of course, Mom and Dad had footed all the bills. Now, I was on my own – real life had begun.

And, starting with a bang it did – after graduation I quickly got engaged to, "Lefty," my horse-borne riding and singing sidekick from the Lakewood Westernaires. It was a true dream to be – a real cowboy couple, raising horses, having kids, riding, roping and singing – what could be more perfect? Alas, as most young loves, this one didn't last. I decided to attend C.S.U. to further my education and our romance rode off into the sunset...such is life.

While attending C.S.U. I was in the Kappa Delta Sorority and met, Nathan, a Phi Kappa Tau. I was later "pinned" at a Kappa Delta function. I dropped out of school and Nathan and I married. My dreams of a western life riding horses were put on hold. Life took over and things such as making a living took precedence. Nathan and I later divorced, but we had two wonderful sons. The older son, Steven, now lives in Orland Park IL and commutes to his 10th floor office in the CNA building in Chicago daily. He is married to, Ronda, from Grand Junction. They have two teenage daughters, Krista a beauty who attends Montana State University and Amy who is 16 in high school.

The younger son, Craig, lives in Steamboat and is a builder of hotels, homes and ski areas. He married, Jill, from Fruita. They have a daughter, Corbin, 11 and a son, Hunter, nine, both great kids. Craig built a beautiful home for their family.

After Nathan and I divorced, I married Tom Christy. Tom had a degree in medical technology and ran hematology tests for the doctors of Mesa County surrounding Grand Junction. Although we never pursued my early dreams with horses, Tom and I traveled all over the world. By the time we were married I had attended Mesa State College and earned a B.A. and later got a Master's degree at Western State College in Gunnison. I taught school in the winters and during the summers we traveled. I missed my earlier high school reunions because we were always in Europe, Scandinavia, or in the Mediterranean, in the Virgin Islands or somewhere exciting. We also went to Turkey and Russia. We enjoyed a wonderful life until Tom died unexpectedly of a heart condition in 1999.

After Tom's death, I moved to a home in a subdivision located on two lakes in Grand Junction. I walk daily, ride my bike and swim to stay in shape. I have returned to my love of music. The William Tell Overture from Lone Ranger days led to an enduring love of music in all forms (well, OK, not Rap). I practice on the piano several hours a day, sing in the church choir, and attend concerts. I love to read and I hike on the mountain trails on Grand Mesa near my home.

Life has taken over. I realize dreams are replaced by joys as well as disappointments. My dreams of horses have been replaced by a quiet love of music. I am well and happy living alone, but please come see me if you are near Grand Junction. Don and Rose Shepperd stopped by last summer and we had some good laughs about the old days – oh, yes, bring your horse – I still remember how to ride.

Almost Famous
By Gary Atkins

OK, that's a little overstated - "I" wasn't almost famous, but I was next to people who were, and few of my high school classmates ever knew it. It happened to me both early and late in life - I grew up in show business - almost. Let me explain:

My parents arrived in New York City in 1938 with their close friend, Lester Polfus, a.k.a. Les Paul - THE Les Paul. They had less than one dollar remaining, after making the down payment on an apartment in a building known as, "Electracourt." Dad took a job as an laborer firing switch engines in the Pennsylvania Railroad yards in New York City. Somehow, as did most people in the late depression era, they made ends meet.

Les Paul was "Uncle Red" to me and the Electracourt was a haven for "successful" (all starving) musicians. It was in Electracourt that Dad and Les created BBC, the Booger Brothers Broadcasting Network. With too much time on their hands Les and Dad created what they thought was a private intra-building-only broadcasting station. With so many musicians around and talent abounding they created a small studio in the basement and proceeded to broadcast live jam sessions and Les's recordings within the building, they thought. The "jam sessions" turned into a bad pun, when one evening during the festivities, the F.C.C., F.A.A. and F.B.I. came calling. It seems the intra-building broadcasting was jamming the navigational beacons at nearby LaGuardia Airport. And, so ended the short life of the BBC from Jackson Heights, Long Island.

I came along in 1940. By that time Dad and Les had landed a job with Fred Waring and the Pennsylvanians. Landing the job wasn't easy.

Their agent found out which elevator Mr. Waring used and encouraged Dad and Les to block the elevator exit with an impromptu performance. They were granted a formal audition and became the featured vocalists on the, "Chesterfield Hour," a nightly network radio program broadcast nationwide during W.W. II.   Dad's Group was know as, "The Les Paul Trio." They were supposed to be the, "Jimmy Atkins Trio," but Dad rejected celebrity status to his dying day and acquiesced to his partners' wishes.

This period of our lives was full of success. My parents made annual trips to east Tennessee and the hard scrabble dirt farm where Dad was raised. The trips were made to deliver care packages to my father's younger brothers, Lowell and Chester. Dad helped raise his brothers through a difficult, poverty-filled childhood. Mother and Dad delivered shoes and clothing making sure Lowell and Chester would be able to attend school decently dressed. My father's youngest brother would eventually eclipse Dad's own success, a fact that made my Dad very proud. Little brother, Chester, became the famous, "Chet Atkins," one of the world's greatest guitarists, and one of Nashville's most successful record producers of all time. Uncle Chet eventually retired from R.C.A. as Vice President of Recording and Director of Nashville Operations. My Uncle Lowell became a very successful small business operator specializing in the remanufacture of industrial electric motors, and a wonderful musician himself - it ran in the family. The success of Dad's brothers made him glow with familial pride.

My first memory is one of a music jam session. Mother insists it is impossible because I was under two years old, but I swear I remember it clearly to this day. I can still see myself strapped into a high chair near a window at one end of what is a very long kitchen. Mom is tending to some cooking on the stove and threatening to put me to bed or, "…in your crib if you don't behave." Dad, Les, and Ernie Newton, the bassist, were rehearsing for the evening show in the adjacent living room and I was complaining, desperately wanting to be on Dad's lap in the middle of his music.

I well remember some of Dad's pals from this era. His best friend was the orchestral bassist named, Lumpy Branum, who shared an interest in photography with Dad. Lumpy later became famous as, "Mr. Greenjeans" on Captain Kangaroo. About three years ago I was driving home from work, when I heard Lumpy's death announced on NPR. I had to pull over to the side of the road for a moment and wipe away a few tears . I had flashbacks remembering what a wonderful person Lumpy was and the experiences he and Dad shared.

From childhood I was a chronic asthmatic. I often stayed home with my illness, and since there was nothing else to do (this was before television), I learned to read well at an early age. My favorites were Swiss Family Robinson, Robinson Crusoe, and the Black Stallion - all great memories. I wonder what my life would have been like if I had stayed home with television, videotapes and the computer technology of today.

Our family was growing. We moved to a larger apartment, and I enrolled in Kindergarten in P.S. 69 of the New York City School system. My sister, Gale, came along three years after me and sister, Liegh, four years after Gale. That was in the midst of W.W. II and everything was scarce; housing, food, cars, gas. Ration stamps were required for everything. I remember those warm summer days before air conditioning. Dad had to practice for his program with the windows open. We had a garden-level apartment. I would sit hidden in "the fort" (boy's always built forts in those days) under the window and listen to Dad practice…strumming his guitar and singing the pop melodies of the day; "South of The Border…Some One To Watch Over Me," …timeless melodies still ringing clearly in my memories.

After the war, Dad left Fred Waring. The "Big Band Era" of pop music was fading fast. Uncle Red took off for the west coast, where he met Mary Ford, and as they say, the rest is history - "Les Paul and Mary Ford."

I recall many evenings, when just as we sat down for dinner, the telephone rang, and it was Uncle Red from California. My mother would be quite upset at the interruption because Les would keep Dad on the line for extended periods trying to convince him to pack up and move us to L.A. where he was experimenting with the new "multi-track sound recording." Les was convinced we could all become wealthy with the new commercial sounds he was creating. He was probably correct, who knows, but Dad was very happy with a recording contract he had with Coral Records and Decca. His daily job was a radio program broadcast live in New York City on WNEW. The show was named, "Calling all Girls." Mom didn't mind. Dad thought it was sort of silly, but it paid the bills.

We moved out of the city and Jackson Heights to Montvale, New Jersey, when I was in the third grade. Montvale was an idyllic, bucolic little town about 40 miles northwest of the George Washington Bridge, the gateway to New York City. Today, Montvale has been discovered and it is the home of several large corporations, including Sony Corp. of America. I still remember Montvale as my hometown. I was there during the intensely formative years of the fourth through seventh grade. The town and my friends are indelibly implanted in my memories.

Our Montvale neighbor was a successful self-made businessman, born and raised in Brooklyn. He gave me a pair of his prized homing pigeons and helped me build a coop. I had one prize cock that I carefully inserted in a shoebox and took to school. At noon recess all the gang gathered, and we released the poor pigeon. Wonder of wonders, when I arrived home in the afternoon, the pigeon would invariably be there, a whole half mile away - magic.

It was in Montvale that I became interested in all things electric. I spent several months allowance on wire and batteries trying to make a telegraph and connect it to my friend, Clifford's, house. It finally worked, after a fashion, with one serious impediment - neither of us knew Morse code. So, two clicks was, "Can you come out and play; answered by one click for, "Yes," and two clicks for, "No" - very inventive. You can imagine the confusion that generated. In those days you picked up the phone and said to the operator, "May I speak to one oh nine oh?" We generated lot's of work for the switchboard operators establishing whether or not the last reply was "one click, or two."

In 1951 my parents decided to move, a gut-wrenching decision for them and me. My asthma was becoming more acute and Dad was tiring of the music hassle. He had never done anything other than perform but he was determined to leave that world for new horizons. Johnny Ray's record, "Cry," had just become a national sensation. That offended Dad's artistic sensibility. He thought it was bad music and wanted out. At the same time my doctor recommended a high and dry climate to alleviate my chronic asthma.

The previous year we had taken a family vacation to Colorado and driven through Rocky Mountain National Park, and on up to Yellowstone. Dad had a longtime friend from the entertainment business, who was general manager of KOA radio station in Denver. They respected each other greatly, and Mr. Sereal offered Dad the position of Program Director at KOA. So, off we went to Colorado. We sold our beautiful home in Montvale and headed west into the unknown where I ended up at Wheat Ridge High School.

Few of my Wheat Ridge classmates ever knew of my "famous" family because I didn't talk about it. It is probably just as well. I might have been besieged with requests for autographs and free records. Also, my parents, especially Dad, always de -emphasized show business and I was too unsophisticated to understand the importance of what was happening with Uncle Chet Atkins in Nashville. My personal music skills at the time were meager. I played a little piano in high school, but poorly. I played some during our rehearsal for the Junior Class Play. Our director, Mr. Criche, must have wondered what gene pool that side of me came from!

Almost Elvis
By Gary Atkins

I picked up the guitar in college and damned near picked my way out of school - a serious love affair! I went to college in fits and starts, mostly fits! I didn't know what to study and wound up, quite naturally, as a music major at C.S.U. On weekends I used my electronic skills to repair television sets for Paul Dontje Radio & TV in Wheat Ridge. After one year of college, I was off to the Army, but not before a magic year in Nashville.

At the risk of being considered a name-dropper - during that year I met and became friends with Jim Reeves, Don Gibson, Skeeter Davis, Eddy Arnold, The Browns, Boots Randolf, Homer and Jethro, The Everly Brothers, Roy Orbison, Archie Campbell, Ralph Emery, Hank Snow, and others if I stop to think about it.

I was best friends with Gary Burton. Gary was only a year younger than me. He was spending the summer in Nashville working recording sessions before heading to College at Berkeley School of Music in Boston. I recently read that Gary was retiring as Director of Curriculum at Berkeley. The article mentioned his great career as a jazz musician, recording and playing with notables like George Shering.

While in Nashville I also "almost" met Elvis. When we were sophomores in high school Uncle Chet called his boss in New York City and told him to please get his rear on an airplane. They had an interview with a new talent that Uncle Chet really wanted to sign with RCA in Memphis that evening. Decca Records was also in hot pursuit and Chet was determined to sign Elvis with RCA. He did and produced Elvis' first huge hit record, "Heartbreak Hotel." I knew nothing about it! I learned that Chet was responsible later. When I was living in

Nashville, RCA cut the record, "Elvis is Back," upon his discharge from the Army. I was supposed to attend this middle of the night (for security reasons) recording session with my girlfriend. I was living in a boarding house across the street from the studio. Midnight came, and I was fast asleep with no phone and no way to contact me. I missed the whole damned deal, and that was my one and only chance to meet Elvis! And I "almost" did.

I came home from Nashville and it was the time of Vietnam and the draft. My Wheat Ridge classmate, Steve Trolander, and I decided it would be fun to get out of town and join the Army. We wound up in the Army Security Agency, an outfit that no longer exists, but which at the time was attached to the National Security Agency. I chased Vietcong through the jungles on the air waves as a, "High Speed Manual Morse Code Intercept Operator," - Morse Code in Vietnamese, no less - memories of my early electronic adventures came back - one click for, "Yes," two for, "No." Maybe it's perverse, but that was really fun. Steve did the same thing from Homestead Air Force Base in Florida, except he listened for Cuban traffic.

After Vietnam, I got out of the Army and started to work at a Boulder radio station. The station went broke before I could quit. I got a job teaching electronics at Emily Griffith Opportunity School in Denver and then, returned to C.S.U. I wasn't cutout for teaching and wound up in an engineering position for Telemation. I quit and formed my own business with the Senior V.P. of Sales from Telemation and later went to work as V.P. of Engineering for Wickerworks Video production in Denver. I was later promoted to Executive V.P., then became Regional Sales Manager for Microwave Associates, selling things to TV stations, like the helicopter news-gathering microwave relay devices. My asthma returned and I wound up in the intensive care ward with asthma. I then went to work for a friend in South Dakota developing a home satellite division for his company. Finally, I returned to C.S.U. as Senior Engineer in Television Services.

As for my music career - I play around C.S.U. where I have spent 17 years of my life. I have a steady job whenever I want playing for the cocktail hour on Thursday evenings in the University Faculty Club. I try to do that about once a month. Professors don't have ears any better than normal mortals! They can't hear my mistakes. For three years I played with the most popular jazz (early swing and Dixie) band in town. I learned a lot and had a ball.

I once had to make a speech to a group on campus, I had no idea what to say. I talked to Uncle Chet, and he said, "Just tell them your life story. It works every time." I thought, "... easy to say if you're Chet Atkins." Now, after a few years reflection, I realize he was right! Everyone's life story is interesting to others. You just have to learn not to become a bore. It's Ok to be "almost famous" as long as you don't talk about it.

How did this all end up? Well, my own dad died at age 64 in 1977. Uncle Chet Atkins filled in the void. We became very close over the last 20 years. He and I were in constant contact until recently. He is very ill and in a home. I plan to visit him this summer. I suspect it will be the last time.

There are three things that have been important in my life - a passion for electronics and music; my loving wife of 31 years, Lorene, and our two beautiful children, all grown up and on their own; and my memories of my wonderful family. I still play with a wonderful guitar given to me by Uncle Chet. Every time I play a tune I see his face. I hope to leave my children the same wonderful memories my family left me. I was "almost famous" and I "almost" met Elvis.

Does Timing Mean Anything?
By Elaine Miller (Elaine Obialero)

Having hatched out of my own little separate egg six minutes and two seconds after the remarkable birth from the first egg, two beings were born. I presume the minute the first shell cracked that the first born must have come from a brown egg as the individual that arrived had brown hair and brown eyes, and I entered the world with blond hair and green eyes from a white egg. Who knows for sure; only the attending doctor at St. Joseph's Hospital in Denver, Colorado could possibly postulate an answer and attest to such a rare event in those days 68 years ago.

Throughout my life I have often explored in my mind if that small difference of time, six minutes and two seconds, made for variances in my life. Being the younger of the two twins who were born on that cold, winter day in February put me in second place no matter how anyone viewed our existence. Could one's birth placement be an issue with fraternal twins?

The spelling of our names placed me first alphabetically as Elaine comes before Elinor. This was a factor on all lists which used alphabetical order, especially school rolls and seating charts. Then again, if only our initials were used, EBO and EDO, I would lose out because the B in my twin's middle name comes before the D in my name. The B in her name stands for Beltram and the D in mine translates to Dickey. Both middle names have family heritage attached to them. The hatching from the brown or white egg did not depend on the color of the egg, but rather on our genetic make up. Elinor, or Elle as she is called today, resembled our father's Italian, Beltramo side of the family, and I resembled our mother's Scotch,

Irish, and English inheritance. Meiosis and mitosis, genetic mixing, definitely favored two very distinct physical personas.

Practically every detail of the early days of our lives was illuminated through the lens of a camera. Portraits taken in the studio of Francois, candid black and white pictures stored in many shoe and department store boxes, and baby albums attest to the uniqueness and togetherness of our lives. Pictures of both parents holding each of the twins and pictures of us sleeping in the perambulator, as our exquisite baby carriage was called, were carefully packed away for safe-keeping. Each phase of our development, moving from carriage to cribs, wooden high chairs, and our wooden play pen, finds the twins happy, playful, and with a sense of bonding not found with most siblings that are not twins. Easter pictures, Christmas photos, pictures of "the twins" playing together in the yard, in sand, catching butterflies, monitoring ant piles, and smelling roses in the large rose garden, all reveal a specific quality that takes me back to a life with just Elinor.

The twins were always together riding the Denver Tramway Bus from 38th Avenue and Sheridan, which was the end of the line in Denver. Called, "Line #13," the bus was only two blocks from our home. We took bus rides to our grandmother's house on 6th and Gilpin, to our dance lessons on Tennyson Street, to downtown Denver for swimming lessons at the YWCA on Welton Street, to Public Service Cooking School on Champa Street, to lunch at Bauer's on a top floor in The Denver Dry Goods building, and to the health food store nearby for dates and other goodies. But most importantly, we rode the bus to our piano lessons every Saturday. After exiting the bus at Lowell and 38th Avenue, we would walk to the corner of 47th Place and Lowell. We would always remember where to turn because of a pillar of stone on the corner. I can't imagine as a second grader, taking a bus to piano lessons all by my self. What a treat it was to have a constant companion who agreed on each step of the way! Every time, as we descended upon the same path, we would automatically jump the cracks and joints in the cement to amuse ourselves during the long walk. It is interesting to note, as I think about it now, how we always walked on the same side of each other. We knew our place; there was never any talk of who was going to walk the inside or the street side. We were always in sync with one another like the metronome that keeps time and the beat during a piano lesson. At the sight of moving human forms in black and white vestments, we did not say a word to each other, but would cross the street to avoid these bodies that were walking on *our* side of the street. These figures were nuns from Saint Vincent's Orphanage on Lowell. Who had ever seen a nun in a habit? Being frightened, Elinor and I would keep our eyes focused straight ahead, and we quickly picked up our pace to get out of their way. Once safely past the nuns, we would cross back to *our* sidewalk and resume jumping the crack and joints. With a sigh of relief we reached 44th Avenue, knowing we were close to our destination.

As we ascended the steps into the little house of our piano teacher, we knew that Elinor would take the first lesson and I the second. While she took her lesson, I listened to the beautiful sounds as she gracefully pressed each key and afterwards, she in a like manner, kept a close ear to the melodies I was playing. Finally finished, we couldn't wait to begin the trek back to the bus. Our treat along the way was to stop at the Dolly Madison store near 44th Avenue for a delicious, double scoop ice cream cone. This same walk continued until we changed piano teachers in junior high school. I shake my head in disbelief that we never argued, fought, or had something unkind to say to each other. We truly enjoyed being a twin.

As we progressed through many piano books, Elinor became the better piano player, but I was right under her in level of skill. Our repertoire also included playing duets, with my sister playing the treble or upper stanzas, while I played the base or lower stanzas. We even learned to play on two pianos, and displayed our talent for the public at a large Denver cathedral. The caliber of our piano playing was awesome and very rewarding for us; however, little was ever said about the skill and dexterity in which our hands moved up and down the keyboard.

When we performed individually at our yearly piano recitals, we always dressed in long formal gowns. These recitals were held at the Women's Club in Denver and open for the public to hear. My twin played near the end of the program and I played just before her. There was never any rivalry as to who was the better or worse as we so enjoyed each other for what each of us could do.

Wheat Ridge Junior High School and Senior High School were over a mile, directly west of our home. We certainly knew how to walk to school having all too well learned the rigors of doing it in rain, snow, cold or heat. Walking was the avenue to new friendships at the junior high level. Students from another nearby elementary school, such as Shirley Eroddy, Gerry Heaston, and Devona Hubka would walk the same path to school as we did. These classmates, who came from Columbia Heights Elementary, became our friends. Marilyn Newton, from the corner of Chase Street and 38th Avenue would also be visible on the asphalt sidewalk. It was at this time that we began expanding our perspectives. We no longer dressed in the same style or colors of clothes. In the past from early childhood, I was always dressed in blue with my blond hair and my twin would be in either pink or red with her dark brown hair. During the fall season before entering junior high school, we shopped for our long wool winter coats at Daniels and Fisher. The coat only came in brown or grey. I bought the brown one and that left my twin with the grey one with the black and grey checked wool lining. She despised her coat and would have rather had the red coat with the black velvet collar. There was only one in the store and not two. After this incident, not only did we branch out in our appearances as individuals, but also in our friendships.

In high school my sister and I were constantly with different sets of male and female classmates during the day and into the night. The heterogeneity of our groups varied at parties, sleepovers, and school sponsored activities which let us diverge in different directions. However, the recession from each other did not affect the strong ties we had developed for one another. One area of this unique separateness, only experienced by twins, involved the opposite sex. My eyes opened to another world when thoughts and experiences with guys were now possible.

The 38th Avenue strip brought boys to my attention. The black pavement attracted young hot shot drivers showing off their highly polished autos. Their driving skills, when we girls were present, tended to be on the reckless side: skidding, screeching, popping sounds, slamming brakes, and blaring radios quickly turned the calm of each afternoon after school into a nightmare. Since most of these guys were very noisy, I was fortunate to become acquainted with one male individual who was a bit more unassuming and had a different modus operandi. He chose to take me for rides in his car singing to me all the way to my home. These casual "song rides" led to our further dating with his guitar always in the car. He strummed his guitar and sang while "parking," a phrase used for "making-out" in a car. His boyish face touched me as much as his singing, but he soon evaporated from my life. His name was Dean Reed (WRHS-1956) or the "Red Elvis", as he was called in press releases. In the Soviet Union he became more famous than Frank Sinatra and Elvis Presley. A quick "Google" of his name on the internet will reveal his accomplishments and early questionable drowning death while in the hands of the East Germans. Or, did he commit suicide, as some believe? At one point, his sudden departure alarmed me; however, I was lucky because there was never any real emotional involvement. His biography revealed four wives, and a host of not only major accomplishments, but serious questionable behaviors.

Another car ride home led me to become acquainted with several other students from the class of 1956. One of them owned a motorboat from which I did a lot of water skiing. He fell in love with me, but I suspect it was the red and white motorboat I was in love with and not him. We spent many weekends boating and sunning on Ward Reservoir in Arvada with many groups of classmates and other boating friends. We girls were especially careful not to burn our bodies while sunning ourselves from sun up to sun down on the warm sandy and slightly rocky beach.

As my twin and I advanced through our high school curricula semester by semester, our social paths continued to multiply. Our lives were more and more divergent and less predictable. It did not matter which egg cracked first or what color it was. It did not matter if there was six minutes and two seconds between our births. Our close bonding remained, but we had become individuals with our own unique sense of style and purpose. The twins were going to excel in whatever they undertook and I knew it.

After the Textbooks...
Fate Took Me Away...
By Elaine Miller (Elaine Obialero)

Life in the real world, away from the closely-knit, small community of Wheat Ridge, proved to be challenging. Knowing myself and what could be achieved marked the beginnings of new adventures derived from circumstances, acquaintances, and placement in different arenas. The avenues which I selected were numerous and varied, as I advanced with more knowledge, skill, expertise, and wisdom.

My years of university education and experiences in teaching prepared me for my first foray into the business world. This adventure looked good from the outside, but what was happening under the roof of the rented office space turned into a complete catastrophe. Inside the two story home close to downtown Denver, was my office dedicated to the helping of urban students in need of developing reading skills. After signing on the dotted line for a loan and forming a partnership with a professor on leave from the University of California, we were in business.

When the entire lower floor was completely redone, a big truck arrived with the newly purchased office furniture and was emptied from the parking place that I had marked off for clients. I can visually remember the excitement and thrill which radiated through my entire body as the move-in was taking place. As the final seven tall bookcases were carried through the door and carefully up-righted into position, our sign - The Reading Clinic - was hung on the front porch. Through some political moves and contracts, my business associate and I secured the right to teach the incorrigible students from Gilliam's Juvenile Hall. As slowly as it took to get the business established, its collapse became inevitable when I found money disappearing from the business account. When questioned about the incident of missing funds, I no longer had a partner to help with our clients. During the course of my investigation, I found pot in her office drawer and I rather suspected the money was used for drugs. Even more disturbing, when we spent some working hours together, was her making overt sexual moves on me. This was extremely frightening and degrading and I quickly ran away from the costly experience never once looking back.

The possibility of one of my daughters making a suggestion that I talk on the phone to a man I had never met was certainly remote. He happened to spend some time on the tennis courts at a local country club talking to her after the tragic death of his wife. Her summer job was teaching tennis and running the shop as an assistant to the tennis pro. My daughter, who closely resembles me, always helped with the afternoon and evening tennis functions. At one of the events he said to her, "I really like you, but…either you have to get a lot older or I have to get a lot younger!" She instantly replied to him, "I have just the right one for you, my mother." The pro, who was a friend of mine, assured him that her advice was right on target. His first call lasted forty-five minutes with the two of us in a full-fledged question and answer session. This was the beginning of a romance that led to my second marriage.

He was a talented and bright surgeon and Professor of Urology at the medical school. With him I had the opportunity to attend many medical meetings and conferences. These events gave me new insights to knowledge in a field which I had never studied while getting my advanced degrees. My skill at writing and making presentations helped him prepare his lectures and handouts for a tour of five medical schools in China. We easily and quickly worked together in whatever had to be undertaken and accomplished. One evening while out for a casual supper, he popped a question to me as he placed "the ring" on the top of a Corona Beer bottle. I accepted his proposal and we were married within the year.

Traveling the world turned me away from textbooks and into the real environment of history, adventure, culture, and the actual demographics of certain selected regions for weeks at a time. As I look back, I realize these trips gave me a balanced outlook not found in classroom texts, mathematical statistics, nor in the formulizations of a null hypothesis and conclusions all of which were necessary when I undertook the "project" of acquiring my Doctor of Philosophy.

One of my earlier adventures, after receiving my undergraduate degree, was a trip to Greece which was initiated while I studied ancient history at CU in Boulder. My professor, Dr. Robert Holfelder, asked me to join his group during summer recess while he researched the ancient ruins of civilizations off the shores of Greece. Underwater archaeology and maritime expeditions were his forte and such an offer was one I knew I could undertake. To this day I regret my decision to stay in the U.S., as a vast number of his projects, several books, and manuscripts have been published. Nevertheless, Greece became one of the special places I first visited to witness the many ancient ruins located near the Aegean Sea. In Athens the actual viewing of the Parthenon touched me emotionally as I explored the outside and inside of the huge structure with sensations of the crumbling stone beneath my sandals registering through my senses. Tears literally rolled down my cheeks as I stood gazing as its magnificence. Nearby I visited the tiny island, Aegina, off the Port of Piraeus, the big harbor of Athens. While there for three days, I was submerged in the Greek culture and constantly tried to avoid the passionate and handsome Greek men.

My numerous travels after my second marriage included yearly trips to Hawaii in January for R &R. and extended travels to Italy, Istanbul in Turkey, South Africa and Zimbabwe, France including Provence and the Riviera, Great Britain including the Cotswolds, and hiking the Swiss Alps. We often picked the same countries to visit year upon year, as we felt comfortable in these regions. We took many trips to Italy because of its special cuisine and fashion houses. I enjoyed hearing the language there, having heard it spoken daily while growing up and also listening to my step-daughter and her husband, who are fluent in the language. We were totally immersed in the Italian lifestyle when we visited with all of his (Franco) relatives who lived in a small hill town near Venice called Asolo. This was the home of the famous poet, Robert Browning. Italian speaking cousins of Franco picked us up from the train stop several miles away and took us to his town. Most of the relatives did not speak English including his mother, except for a couple of the younger ones. The festivities and eating binges were beyond belief; as was their constant concern, warmth, and total receptiveness. This experience closely paralleled the hospitality my younger sister received at sixteen years old when she visited my father's relatives in Torino which was recently the site of the Winter Olympics. It must be the Italian way of being sincerely gracious to other people.

During our many sojourns in Italy, when searching for the perfect restaurant for lunch or dinner, the smell of spices and cooking brought back memories of the Italian dishes prepared in my parent's kitchen. While we were in Tuscany, we even went to cooking school to acquire the skill of making fresh pasta, Italian sauces, and a special apple dessert. The recipes, which we learned to prepare there, are ones that I use to this day. The touring of the vineyards and wineries of Tuscany made me think of the wine-making in our family home with the wooden press which squeezed juices from our own grapes.

Sometimes while traveling, the foreign people you meet and converse with and possibly bond with produce an experience even more rewarding than the sites one visits. While staying at a hotel high on the Isle of Capri, we met a couple on their honeymoon. She was a beautiful slender young woman; he appeared slightly older and somewhat portly. They had just come from their wedding with more than 400 guests in a garden in the country of Jordan. He was the first cousin of King Abdullah. Mr. Faisal Abboud Salem, was in the Ministry of Water and Irrigation in Jordan, where water is one of the very important problems. He had a major role in completing the peace pact between Israel and Jordan. We knew quite a bit about this, making our communication with him easier. Much to our delight, we spent three afternoons around the hotel pool conversing with them and learning much about their part of the world first hand and not through media releases. Before they departed from Capri, he invited us to visit them in Jordan and said his father, who was head of the Air Force, would also fly us to Beirut, Lebanon. We made plans to go there the following fall when "all hell broke loose" in the region with the intifada between the Israelis and the Palestinians and with trouble in Lebanon. A week after Capri, while walking in a very busy square in Rome, we heard someone calling our names and it turned out to be the couple from Jordan. Unfortunately, this was our last personal contact with them. We have seen pictures of them in magazines and newspapers, together, alone, and with the king, and still hope to visit them in their country.

While in Rome, my early learning of Latin from Mrs. Knudtson (WRHS) and my ancient history courses at C.U. about the Romans awakened me. I was driven to see more of the archaeological sites, significant buildings and structures, and other attractions I had missed in past visits to the area. On my first tour of Italy I had viewed the body of an earlier Pope lying in state at the Vatican. I was one of many who passed his casket and I quickly snapped a picture of him lying in state in the dimly lit area. On a later trip we were lucky as our hotel was located close by and our guide arranged a quick tour of all the places to see and knew how to avoid the long tourist lines. We even entered the Vatican by going in the back way to save time. The long-term memories which I possess definitely added a patina to my travel experiences.

France, including Paris became a prime place to visit often, since our honeymoon was there some 22 years ago. Not only did we love the city for its fashion houses, shopping, and magnificent museums, but enjoyed the upbeat mood of those stylishly dressed individuals who crowded its sidewalks. To get away from the "hustle and bustle" of the city we returned numerous times to Southern France and the Riviera, renting a car in Nice to drive through Provence on its fantastic highways. While stopping along the way in several cities, our hedonistic pleasures included superb food, lavish sleeping accommodations, and pleasurable moments of sunning and swimming on the topless beaches of Cannes and St. Tropez. Upon our arrival in Provence, we always undertook a number of intellectual pursuits. One of these was to follow the pathway to some of the Roman ruins including the Arena in Arles, the Ponte du Guard in Nimes, and the Antique Theatre in Orange. In wanting to learn more about the Popes of the Vatican, we visited Avignon, the residence of seven popes from the early 14th century. Much to my dismay, once while trying to find our hotel for the night, I drove on the bricks of the entrance of the Palais des Papes, going in the wrong direction.

Another one of our educational experiences took us to the town of Grasse which is one of the homes of the perfume industry. We saw the various flowers which are used for fragrances, and the techniques used to make the final product. I kept many a note, as I had always done during my classroom studies. When returning to the States, I further engrossed myself in several books on the subject, having on hand the special bottles of the perfume which I had purchased from the companies we visited.

You wouldn't think that a small round edible would consume much of our time, but it did. One day, we went on a quest to discover the many varieties of this object--the olive, brought to Provence by the Greeks over 2,500 year ago. We drove from one small town to another, to see the different varieties of olive trees growing in the various regions, and arrived many miles away from our hotel finding an ultimate place for olive production near Nimes. It was interesting to see the huge olive press there, the pressing of the olives, and their production into olive oil. On subsequent days, we continued our interest in another round object--the grape. We spent time visiting the vineyards and wineries of the Rhone Valley, and another whole day in the area of Chateauneuf du Pape sampling the wines from one winery to the next. We left there giddy and happy, and fortunately returned safely to our bed.

The chiming of the bells and the sounds of the muezzin calling the faithful to prayer was the alarm awaking me from my bed not in France, but in Istanbul, Turkey. While staying here, we were not far from the Blue Mosque, the Haghia Sophia Church, and the Topkapi Palace, on a hilltop overlooking the Bosphorus and the Golden Horn. We enjoyed seeing the palaces related to the Ottoman Empire and we relearned something about that period in history. A special place for me was the Grand Bazaar with over 3,000 shops. I particularly enjoyed seeing the Turkish carpets displayed, as I had bought books about woven carpets before purchasing several for my home. At the Spice Market, also known as the Egyptian Bazaar, I was allowed to smell many of the interesting spices, oils, and essences. Being on the Bosporus Sea in such a different culture was gratifying beyond belief. We were told by some locals at our boating pier, that John F. Kennedy, Jr. and his wife, stayed in the same area not long before their death and we dined at the same special restaurant as they had which was reached by a boat ride across the sea. Memories of them had me thinking about how fragile life can be.

While studying at CU, I immersed myself not only in ancient history, but also in African history. The desire was always within me to experience countries on the African continent. This inclination was met on our longest trip, which was to South Africa for a month with a few extra days in Zimbabwe. We went with a Denver couple, who were born and raised there in what was then called Rhodesia. They returned there frequently because they were not allowed to take all of their money (rand) out when they emigrated to the United States, but could only spend it there. A few of their older relatives remained, and we visited and dined with them. The children of those relatives had emigrated to Australia, Israel, and the United States. The major reason for their exit was because of apartheid and their concerns about the future.

We started our journey in Cape Town, South Africa and saw the hospital where the first heart transplant in the world was performed. We then went to see the Cape of Good Hope where the Indian Ocean meets the Atlantic and sat on the tip of a rock conversing with English speaking tourists as the ocean breezes were gently felt. Driving there, we first stopped at a large fishery that had smoked the same delicious kind of fish we had enjoyed the previous evening. Besides the magnificent scenery on the way, we saw a number of baboons just off the roads and stopped to watch their behaviors.

We went to stay in a second hotel in Cape Town, when our time was up at the first. I asked for a room change, not liking the one they had reserved for us, and we ended up in the Presidential Suite for the same price. Our friends could not believe the opulence of our new quarters. We laughed at this move of mine because it had happened several times in such places as Paris, Lake Como, Avignon, and Wengen in Switzerland. I began to score my successes and was amazed how often my requests were always met with upgrades far outreaching my expectations. It almost became a game to play.

From Cape Town, we visited the wine country in Stellenbosch with its beautiful university and returned to our lovely suite later. Before leaving the city, we spent a wonderful evening in the penthouse apartment overlooking the Indian Ocean of a rabbi that my husband had brought to Denver as a young man. I had hardly met him when he quickly went to a shelf in his living room and pulled a book showing me an early photo of my husband with him. I learned that he had left Colorado over twenty year before and they had not seen each other since. In South Africa, he was a Professor of Philosophy at Cape Town University and had a congregation that turned out one thousand strong to pray and listen to him talk every Friday night. We toured his place of worship and as expected, I learned a lot about the Jews in South Africa.

One of the major activities we planned on this trip was playing golf. The container we shipped our two sets of clubs in looked like a coffin on wheels and caught the attention of many people, who suspected there was a body inside. We played golf in Cape Town, Durban, Sun City, Fancourt in George, and Johannesburg. South Africa happens to be one of the great places in the world for the game. The courses are beautiful and well manicured, the caddies cost only a few dollars a round, and many private clubs allowed us to play on their facilities. At the golf resort of Fancourt, the great and talented golf star, Ernie Els, owned a beautiful home. He had stayed in Colorado with our friend's son while playing in the International Tournament at Castle Pines. Upon learning we were going to Fancourt, he invited us to stay in his new dwelling. I was disappointed that Ernie was not going to be in town during our stay, as I had planned to discuss my passion for golf and my "swing" with him. We stayed two nights in his bedroom which had wallpaper with a unique motif of monkeys. Possibly, only in South Africa would you find decorations featuring monkeys.

We spent a few more days playing golf in Sun City, which is the Las Vegas of South Africa. Sun City has ostentatious hotels with gambling, exquisite shopping, and swimming facilities with man-made beaches and wave machines. At our hotel, we saw beautiful women prancing around in high heels, who we learned were contestants in the finals for the Miss World Pageant. They were rehearsing, and enjoying themselves while shopping. I was able to communicate with a number of them about their respective countries and only wished I was their age and still possessed their curves.

One of my inclinations, while studying about South Africa was a desire to go on a safari. While we were there, we spent three days and nights at a beautiful, private game reserve called Mala Mala. We would go out on an open Land Rover at 6:00 a.m. before breakfast and again in the evening to see the animals. This particular reserve had elephants, rhinos, buffalos, leopards, lions, as well as cheetahs, tigers, crocodiles, warthogs, gazelles, hyenas, zebras, and giraffes. We were told that the most dangerous to us were the elephants. One afternoon we walked away from our camp without our guide and unexpectedly encountered a large bull elephant. Fortunately, a guide had followed us with his large gun, and frightened the animal away by firing shots into the air. One of our spectacular sightings was a cheetah, the fastest of animals, tracking and killing a gazelle, and we followed her back as she brought it to feed her cubs. Needless to say, with our cameras and telephoto lenses, we took hundreds of pictures.

On the outskirts of Johannesburg, with a black guide also carrying a gun, we visited an infamous township called Soweto. He drove us in his black sedan with darkened windows. Obviously, whites were not too welcomed in black townships where severe poverty reigned associated with apartheid. It was an extremely frightening experience. When our guide felt it was safe to exit his car, we were amazed at the number of black children who ran up to see and touch us. The hundreds of flies around the meat hanging in the open market was nauseating, the smells were obnoxious, and the site of the tin roof shanties where the people existed was heart-rending. The day after our visit, the front pages of the local newspapers informed us that an American tourist had his eyes shot out while visiting Soweto.

We even had some fear in Johannesburg in the streets outside our hotel of being robbed of money or passports. When we arrived at the airport on our departure, at least a dozen men and boys came towards us to take our luggage. I wondered, "Who wanted to service us or who just wanted to steal from us?" Cautiously, we gave up all of our luggage and slipped a few of them large tips hoping to "insure" that everything would be safely placed with the airline. The irony of this was the fact that all of our belongings and possessions did arrive safely when we went through Customs in Miami, Florida. However, our bags and golf clubs were three days late arriving in Denver from Miami. Upon opening our bags, many items had been stolen and much of our purchases from Africa, except for an African wall hanging, were missing, presumably taken by our own U.S. handlers!

This is just a modicum of where I have been, what I have seen, and what I have done regarding my worldly travels which further enhanced and went beyond my classroom knowledge. My life has been very complex and has encompassed many more experiences in the business world in the field of health and with the advancements of the computer. Fortunately, I happened to be on the cutting edge of the computer revolution with my early studying and writing in the computer languages, Pascal and Fortran. I even taught special education children--gifted, behavioral, and those, deficit in skills--to do their own programming and word processing beginning at the first and second grade level and up. I gave presentations on the subjects and was able to pass my knowledge on to other educators, administrators, and boards of education in Denver and the suburbs during their visits to see my students in the classroom. My research indicated the value of the computer in schools as an aid for learning the basics: reading, writing, and math skills.

Tennis and golf lessons began for me in my early twenties, and I played with my children in conjunction with their lessons. I began lessons again in my forties and discovered, I had a real talent for golf and sincerely enjoyed it along with tennis. My skills improved in both as I continued playing in Denver, Vail, during our travels in Hawaii and abroad, and foremost in Rancho Mirage, California at our second home. I was on the golf team at our clubs in both Denver and Rancho Mirage, thus, having the privilege of playing at many different private clubs. In Rancho Mirage, I devoted myself to thirty team members as their captain for almost ten years and retired just this year. Since giving up skiing at our place in Vail for the warmth of the desert in the winter, my life has been somewhat altered with the addition of four toy poodles. I call them my musical poodles: Jazz, the black one, who is the alpha to three whites--Drummer, Cello, and Oboe. These four males bark for my attention while I am playing the piano just like my four children once solicited my attention.

We continued our travels to many of the same locations we came to love. On two different occasions while in France, we visited a patient and his wife from Denver, who had bought a home in St. Maxime which is on the gulf above St. Tropez. We went with them to the local outdoor markets, stores, cafes, and bistros which was reminiscent of Peter Mayle's book, "A Year in Provence". It was fun to immerse myself in the life of the locals and thought I might want to live either in Provence or in Italy for a prolonged period sometime in my life. Time goes by and I go forward with all my knowledge and "joie de vivre."

Once an Entrepreneur....
By William Perry Smith

This story begins before I was born. My grandfather operated a hog farm in Newberry, SC. He had a high school education followed by some college. When the hog farm went broke, he opened a hardware store. After the hardware store went broke, he became an insurance agent in Columbia, SC. This enterprise was successful until he died. He was an entrepreneur.

My father, William Perry Smith, Sr., obtained a high school diploma and attended some college. One of his early jobs was working for a Chrysler dealer in Columbia. He started as a shop foreman and later became general manager for the entire business. After W.W. II, he saw an opportunity to open a car dealership of his own. With the help of friends, who had some cash, he started up a Studebaker dealership in 1947. It proved to be a good decision due to the huge post-war demand for cars. Customers lined up to pay "above sticker price" because there were too few cars to meet demand. My dad was also an entrepreneur.

In 1950 my dad saw another opportunity - NASCAR. He entered his first car in the Darlington Labor Day race, the last race of the 1950 season. He did this for two reasons. First, he was a very good mechanic and enjoyed working on cars. Then, there was the prospect of promoting sales for his automobile business. In 1951 he put a Studebaker on the NASCAR circuit for the entire year. His driver was Frank Mundy, and his car placed fifth in the NASCAR point system that year. Among several accomplishments during the year, were winning four races and getting the pole position at Darlington's Labor Day race. The most exciting event that season was winning the 100-mile race at Columbia,

SC, his hometown, on a Saturday night. This was NASCAR's first night race. His business sold 27 cars the following Monday.

Unfortunately, my father was killed in a private plane crash December 8, 1951. It was his own plane, and he was trying to take a patient, who needed surgery, to Detroit. My mother continued to operate the business and was elected president of the SC Automobile Dealers Association. She sold the business in 1954. In 1955 she remarried a man that owned a Studebaker dealership in Denver, CO, and my Wheat Ridge adventure began.

...Always an Entrepreneur – It Runs in the Family

By William Perry Smith

I graduated from Wheat Ridge High School in 1958. In 1963 I received a diploma from the University of Colorado with a B.S. in Business Administration. It also was the year I returned to SC looking for a job. After my father's death, many adults advised me to work for a large company which had a good retirement plan and benefits. They also told me I should always give my employer 110 percent - go to work early, stay late and keep your nose to the grindstone. I did and I was the youngest supervisor promoted at a local nylon textile manufacturing plant. I received excellent ratings on my annual performance appraisals and was at the top of my pay scale. After fourteen years, the plant started laying off people because of economic changes in the textile industry. Supervisors were ranked according to performance and those at the bottom were laid off first. Then, came a stressful time in my life. The company started laying off supervision by seniority to avoid lawsuits about racial, ethnic and gender balance. No one could legally dispute seniority as a criteria for letting someone go. Being one of the youngest supervisors in manufacturing, I was number nine to be laid off. I was reduced to foreman and put back on a rotating shift schedule. A new hire with six months in accounting could keep his job while I was vulnerable if another layoff came. It didn't make much sense to me, and for the first time I began to think about working for myself.

As time passed it looked like there was not going to be any change in my situation. In fact, rumor had it the plant would shut down in 1985. After much thought, I decided my family had all worked for themselves, why not me? I researched what would be a good business with future growth potential that no one else operated in Greenwood, SC. In 1981 with one other investor, and another person who had computer knowledge, I opened a retail personal computer business. I was married with three children. The decision was not an easy one. I knew nothing about computers at the time but felt they had a promising future. To help the business survive, I worked part time without pay. It was a second job. My associate with computer knowledge worked for no pay as his investment. When we opened the computer store, I thought, "This is it. I will never work for anyone else again."

The business began to take off, and I became a full time employee. On my first day as a fulltimer, we won a bid for 32 Apple computers. Shortly after, I bought out the other two investors. They made a handsome profit.

1985 brought another change. We became a franchise of MicroAge Computers, Inc. This allowed us to sell both Apple and DOS-based computers, such as IBM. The business continued to grow until 1996. At one point we employed 12 people. During those 15 years we changed our marketing strategy about every four years due to changes in technology and public demand. By 1994 I saw an end coming to selling computers through retail stores. Direct sales by computer companies, such as Dell and Gateway and Internet direct marketing, made it nearly impossible to make a profit in a retail store. I almost bought a business in 1994, which installed siding on homes. The owner wanted to retire at age 50. A friend told me I was smart enough to learn a new business, but I should consider staying in computers, an area I knew something about. This led to another search for a new business with significant growth potential and which no one else operated in Greenwood. A customer, who was a friend, came up with an idea - being an Internet Service Provider (ISP). I had observed some early start-up ISPs and saw this as another business opportunity with great upside potential. Little did I know that ISPs would develop into something similar to the Industrial Revolution.

In 1995 I opened an ISP business with three employees. It grew so fast I could not give any attention to the retail computer business. My wonderful wife, Sue, operated the retail store until 1998, when we shut it down. Many of my friends kept trying to operate their retail stores and went deep in debt. I loaned money to some and recovered little.

The ISP business continues to grow and has been very successful. In 1998 I hired my middle son to learn the business. He is a Clemson University graduate with a sales background, including a hardware store that went south and left him in debt. At a young age he has already acquired a number of hard-earned entrepreneurial lessons. In a short time I saw in him the ability to successfully manage the business.

In 1998 I had my left and right knee replaced. While convalescing my wife and I considered semi-retiring to Pawleys Island, SC and letting our son, Scott, manage the business. When I hired him, I knew there could be problems between us because we are much alike; however, Scott continues to do very well, and I hope to turn the business over to him in the future. We have had a few disagreements but always resolved them amicably. I have tried to teach him, "Always keep an eye on the future while monitoring the cash flow," both essential lessons in business. I have also told him, "There were two thousand automobile manufacturers in the early days of the Industrial Revolution. Now there are only three big ones. There is an IMPORTANT lesson in that."

There are three thoughts that come from my adult life: First, if you become an entrepreneur you will be one in your heart as long as you live. Second, if you want to be a "successful" entrepreneur you must watch the future and maintain cash flow. Finally, just like firemen, policemen, Marines, "following in your father's footsteps," often happens in families. Once an entrepreneur always an entrepreneur - it started with my grandfather, and I guess it just runs in the family.

(*editor's note: our classmate, Perry Smith, passed away after writing this story. Perry was a character – always happy, always smiling. Although his father was killed in a plane crash, Perry was interested in flying. He held an FAA Commercial, Instrument-rated Pilot certificate and later owned a Piper Cherokee Six. He also ran for City Council as a Republican in a heavily Democratic district. He won by "16" votes and became known locally as, "Landslide Smith." Perry had several physical ailments, among them a severe heart problem. It was deemed he was not a candidate for transplant. The doctors told him he had five years to live. He and his wife, Sue, decided to spend those five years enjoying life to the fullest. They did, and the doctors were right almost to the day. Perry died on May 7, 2006. The story is published courtesy of Perry's widow, Sue Smith)

Polly Sue
By Kay Schoonmaker (Katherine Donaldson)

Fingernails bit into my arm. "Polly Sue and Kitty Lou..." A droning, eerie tune surrounded my ears and crept down my spine. Years dropped away as the image of a long-forgotten childhood friend began to form. Polly Sue had been one of my best friends before I moved across town to Wheat Ridge.

I turned slightly towards the woman at my side hoping her grip would loosen. "Polly Sue? What are you doing here?" My words sounded dumb.

"Why, I'm a patient here. Aren't you?" Wild eyes viewed me angrily from behind thick, horned rim glasses.

"Uh. . . well. . . no. I'm a nurse out here." My free hand fidgeted with the cigarette case in my pocket. "I work over in Cottage 1."

"I thought so! You're one of them! You and Susan and Pattie. You caused it all!" Short, untamed light brown curls surrounded her pudgy face. Her cheeks were flushed with anger. "I'm crazy, you know. . .I've been in Pueblo."

"I know you've been ill." Damn my arm hurt! "How are Susan and Pattie? Gee, its been a long time since we've all gotten together. Remember the fun we used to have as kids?"

"They never come to see me anymore." She hesitated, giving me a coy smirk as she let her nails dig a little deeper. "They know it's their fault!" Her large, violet-brown eyes traveled from my face to my toes, then riveted back on my face. I felt like a hotdog skewered on a stick.

"Have you been here long?" There must be common ground somewhere I thought to myself.

"No. Have you?" A saccharine smile made my spine react again.

"About a year, I guess. I think you'll like it better than Pueblo. Hey, do you remember the great ghost stories?" My mind went back to the big, fluffy four-poster bed at her house where we four girls would bunch up together in the dark and see who could tell the scariest story. "You always won, Polly Sue. Your stories were the greatest." She'd punctuate her stories with a laugh that rose from her toes, gaining volume in her belly, rising and falling like a witch's cackle at strategic points. Pulling the quilts over our heads like a pup tent with four humps, we'd giggle and story into the wee hours. We loved those slumber parties at her house. We couldn't get enough of her wonderful laugh. After I had moved to Wheat Ridge, I would call her and beg her to do her laugh into the phone so my friend, Ann could listen to her.

Polly Sue wasn't very physical. She sure wasn't an asset to our softball team. And, she could never come to our slumber parties because her mother said she was a little different and did best at home in her own bed. But, she was jolly and kind and definitely one of the gang. On Halloween she would dress as a gypsy and read our palms. At our backyard carnivals she would sit inside a sheet tent with her crystal ball. For ten cents she would tell our fortunes. On stormy days when Susan and Pattie were busy, Polly Sue and I would lock ourselves in her bedroom to cut out paper dolls and share our private thoughts.

"WELL! At least they haven't locked me up yet." I leaped out of my reverie. Her grip on my arm had loosened but, her eyes still had me in a hammerlock. She began to sing our names in rhyme again. Where had my childhood friend gone?

"Your Dad always sang our names like that." I had liked Polly Sue's father. She resembled him. He was short, stocky and friendly with lively, intelligent eyes. Though I hated my nickname, he always made me laugh when he put it to music. "How is your Dad?" I asked.

"He's dead, he's dead, he's dead," she chanted as she wandered off towards her cottage. The laugh began to rumble up from her toes through her body and chill the air. "He doesn't sing anymore."

Remembering Christopher
By Kay Schoonmaker (Katherine Donaldson)

"Mom, I wish I had a brother. We could play football."

"I wish you had one, too." A hazy, far away microdot lurched in my brain.

"I could teach him to be tough like me. Could we have a boy, Mom, please?" Soft blue eyes from behind freckled cheeks looked into mine.

After a long intake of breath I let out the words. Jon, you had a brother. . ."

"I did?" His eyes grew wide. The room was silent.

"Yes, Honey, you did, but he died when he was born. . ."

Jon nibbled his sandwich in silent thought. His unruly light brown hair caught a breeze from the open kitchen window.

I smiled fondly at my children as they intermittently ate and played with their food. Slowly, that terrible night of anguish crept to the forefront of my mind. And, oh, the dreadful months that followed as my spirit tried to mend. The sight of rounded bellies and little children had been like simultaneous jolts of pain and anger.

"Was he older than me, Mom?"

"Yes, two years older."

"What did he look like?"

"Well, Honey, I never got to see him." The lifeless little bundle had been whisked quickly out of sight.

"You don't want to see him, do you?" The doctor's sad, tired expression pleaded with me.

Stunned by the night's sudden turn from joy to grief, I acquiesced. And ever since, I, too had wondered what my infant son had looked like. Why hadn't I taken just a peek?

"Wow, I have a big brother. . . Awesome. . ." Jon voiced his thoughts out loud.

Each month had been a searing reminder of the emptiness, the loneliness and the longing. Instead of feeling better as more time elapsed, panic began to overtake the grief. The sudden fits of weeping and bursts of intense anger were subsiding, but a despairing fear that I would never have another child possessed me.

"Mom. . .? Mom. . .?" There was a gentle tugging on my sleeve. "What was his name?"

"Hmm. . .? Oh, it was, Christopher." I was remembering the small headstone that read only Baby Boy Schoonmaker. With no family nearby, my husband had made the necessary arrangements by himself. His mother would be flying out from New York in a few days. My Mother was just reeling from the death of my father and was emotionally unavailable. Sometimes that whole hazy fragment of time seemed like just a bad dream.

"Chris, Chris Schoonmaker." Jon rolled the name over on his tongue several times. "Me and him would have been real good friends, Mom."

I smiled and hugged the impish cherub at my side. I had not felt completely healed until I had given birth to Jon and a nurse had placed him alive and wiggling in my arms. Now, nine years later he had given rebirth to the memory of my firstborn son.

What Happened to Them
...After Wheat Ridge

<u>Don Shepperd</u> joined the Air Force at age 17 with the fourth class of the United States Air Force Academy. He became a pilot, went to Vietnam and flew 247 fighter combat missions. He retired from the Pentagon in 1998 as a Major General, after almost 40 years in uniform. He married Rose Driskill, who attended WRHS for one semester in their junior year. They have one son and three grandchildren. He has his own consulting firm, serves on several boards, is a Military Analyst for CNN, a speaker and author and writes from his home in Tucson, AZ.

<u>Robin Gilbert (Marie West)</u> attended C.S.U., Presbyterian Hospital School of Nursing, and The Real Estate Institute - C.U., married, taught drama, directed a few musicals, managed a ski lodge in Winter Park, CO. and just retired from a 30 year career as a real estate broker. She has two daughters and one granddaughter, who share her love of the mountains, rivers, and nature in general. She splits her time between her home in Arvada, CO. and her cabin near Tabernash. Since retiring in 2000, she has become an artist and writer and spends much time camping and traveling.

<u>Dennis Shields</u> attended the University of Colorado, where he majored in ancient history and philosophy. After a wide ranging career in the restaurant industry, at the age of 42 he entered law school and graduated, Magna Cum Laude, from Thomas Jefferson School of Law in 1986. He enjoys a civil litigation practice as a trial lawyer, and is an adjunct professor at San Diego State University. His only child, Sharon, graduated with honors from U.C. Davis School of Veterinary Medicine, and is in her residency for Board Certification

as a surgeon. Dennis resides in Ocean Beach, California, two blocks from the Pacific, revels in his Corvette, and lives with his cat, "Squid."

Gale Newell (Gale Taylor) graduated from University of Puget Sound and taught art and leadership for 30 years in secondary schools. A counselor, and later director of one of Washington's high school leadership camps, she has spent 15 years facilitating at Ropes Courses, and now is a partner in a women-owned business, called Team Designs, developing portable teambuilding challenges for various groups. Gale is now taking time for her own art work, as well as, illustrating several children's books, to be enjoyed by her four grandchildren who live in Scotland with one of her sons. Gale's second son is a practicing attorney for a firm in Colorado. Gale and her husband, Gregg, enjoy playing with their two dogs on Washington beaches. (Sadly, Gale's husband, Gregg, passed away during the publication of this book).

Mike White married Betty Fatzinger, also from the class of '58. He went to the University of Colorado, got a masters degree in Chinese History and did doctoral work in education at the University of Northern Colorado. He became a teacher and administrator in the American Community Schools, teaching overseas. Betty attended D.U., got an ABA degree and worked in the same schools. Mike has taught all over the world including Iran before the fall of the Shah and in Taiwan. Mike and Betty have four children and five grandchildren. They are retired on a golf course in Houston, TX.

Lois Kropp (Lois Andrews) attended Baylor University and C.U. followed by clinical training at Mayo Clinic. She worked 35 years as a physical therapist, adopted 2 children, a boy and a girl, and has one grandchild. She owned and operated a restaurant for five years with her son in Fairplay, CO. She was divorced, remarried and lives in Arvada, CO.

<u>Victor Bird</u> graduated from C.S.U. and was commissioned in the U.S. Army. He retired after 24 years as a combat infantry officer and served overseas in Korea, Vietnam , and Germany. He was awarded a masters degree from Texas A&M. Victor taught biology and marine science in the public school system where he retired a second time. Living in Port Aransas, Texas on a barrier island, he is married and has two children and four grandchildren. Victor presently is a cat nanny for his wife's four cats.

<u>Pat Wilkinson (Pat Stephens)</u> married in 1960 and celebrated her 40th anniversary in 2000. She lived in Colorado Springs for several years, moved to Kersey, CO. (farm country) to raise two sons and one daughter. She has three grandchildren. Her oldest son died in 1984. She was a grocery store checker and stay at home wife and mom. She has lived in Las Vegas, NV. for 20 years.

<u>Doug Rhinehart</u> attended Colorado State University where he received his Bachelor's degree and teaching credentials. He taught one year in Center, CO. and ten years in Aspen. He primarily taught literature classes. He is currently an adjunct faculty member of Colorado Mountain College teaching photography. He is also a fine-art photographer whose black and white work is in many private and corporate collections. He has exhibited throughout the west and in New York City.

<u>Nancy Keyes (Nancy Winslow)</u> graduated from C.U., moved to New York City and became a reporter for Life Magazine. She married, had two children, attained a Master's Degree from Ohio State University and became a college professor teaching English as a Second language at Mt. Holyoke College. She has traveled and taught all over the world including Japan, Kyrgyzstan, Poland and a Fulbright year in Sarajevo, Yugoslavia. She currently lives in Massachusetts but frequents Yampa, Colorado in the summer to pursue Rocky Mountain trout.

Dave Sutcliffe attended Colorado Sate University where he received his bachelors degrees in teaching. He participated in Air Force ROTC and after graduation became an Air Force pilot flying transports during the Vietnam War. He later became a high school teacher in Minnesota and died of cancer.

Elle Raeder (Elinor Obialero) graduated from the University of Colorado Health Science Center as valedictorian with a B.S. in Nursing. After one year as a psychiatric nurse, the rest of her career was in pediatrics. The past 25 years she has been in the furniture manufacturing and retail store business with her husband where she utilized her education in design. They have three sons and nine grandchildren with triplets just added to the family. They live in Greenwood Village, CO.

Bob Walden attended the University of Colorado and the University of Denver for pre-Med. He graduated from Indiana University as a dentist and went into private practice in Denver for three years. He then moved his practice back home to Wheat Ridge. He sold his practice in the 1990s and he and Leslie became medical missionaries, spending a year in Romania. Later, he resumed practice and has since spent a month helping the Kosovo refugees in Albania. He continues to focus on medical missions to help people of the world in Jesus' name. He and his wife, Leslie, live in Lakewood, CO.

Stephanie Moore (Stephanie Poe) earned her bachelor's degree from C.U., and her Master of Fine Arts degree from UCLA. Her produced screenplay aired on ABC, and Disney hired her to write the sequel. She continues to write screenplays, and teaches screenwriting online for UCLA. In fall 2007 she retired from her position as Coordinator of Professional Programs at UCLA School of Theater, Film and Television. She has four children from her first marriage, and eight grandchildren. She remarried, David Persoff, in 2006, and they retired to North Carolina in 2007, where she's busy writing, teaching, and trying to develop a Southern accent.

<u>Gary Taylor</u> attended the University of Colorado for pre-med and Northwestern University Dental School. He became an Air Force dentist. After leaving the Air Force, he moved back to Denver and established his private practice in Lakewood. He was married and had three children and six grandchildren. He knew three of his grandchildren before he died in 1994.

<u>Cindy Carroll (Cynthia Chaney)</u> moved to California in 1961 where she received a B.S. degree from San Jose State University and an MBA from the University of Santa Clara. In 2000 she retired from IBM where she had held positions in finance, business planning management and business strategy. She and her husband moved to central Vermont in 2002 where she currently lives with her dog, Trixie, and horse, Casey. She enjoys the many outdoor activities available in Vermont and is active in her community through a variety of volunteer positions. Since her walk for breast cancer, she has participated in other walks to raise money for cancer research while living in Vermont. In total, friends and relatives have contributed over $20,000 towards cancer research as a result of her walking. Unfortunately, her husband, Joe, passed away in 2007 after a 5 year battle with renal cancer.

<u>Duane Burtis</u> attended C.S.U. He was active duty at a naval air station in Brooklyn N.Y., worked thirty-one years for United States Welding in Denver as a route sales truck driver, salesman, manager of the Price, UT branch, and purchasing manager for the eastern half of the company. He moved to Seattle, WA, joined Central Welding Supply Co. as a salesman and retired August 31, 2007. He lives with his soulmate/artist wife, Sandy, and Jack Russell terrier and terror, Leroy. He is currently packing up the household to move back to Colorado to be nearer his son, Dean, who is with a Denver engineering firm, and daughter, Cheryl, who gave up her career to be a stay at home mother, her husband, John, who is with Seagate Technology, and grandchildren, Luke and Grace.

Dixie Jones (Dixie Savio) went to the University of Arizona. She moved back to Colorado and worked for the Colorado Cattleman's Association and later the Governor. She then became an executive for Samsonite and retired after 25 years. She lives with her artist husband, Bob Jones, in Castle Pines, CO.

Jerry Jensen attended BYU on a track scholarship graduating with honors in 1962 followed by Harvard Law School. He became a Special Asst. to Senator Frank E. Moss (D.Utah), joined the Army Reserve and later transferred to the Navy Reserve. He practiced law in Denver from 1968-77, had a son and daughter and was divorced. He married Colleen Carroll in 1979. They had two sons. He was the chief executive in several companies. He is now the owner of a real estate development company and Jenex Petroleum Corp. He is seeking to form a micro-finance company to lend money to women in under-developed countries to establish their own businesses

Phyllis Anderson (Phyllis Findley) married and had two daughters. Her youngest daughter was 15, when Phyllis had a surprise baby. The baby is now 22 and in the Marine Corps. Phyllis then divorced. She spent 38 years raising children, then married her soul mate. Between Phyllis and her husband they have 13 grandchildren. She has spent the last few years traveling the U.S. She lives in southeast Texas in a small town named, Warren, 30 miles from the Louisiana border and two hours from the Gulf of Mexico. Phyllis spends as much time as possible fishing, while her husband stays in an air conditioned travel trailer encouraging her to catch dinner.

Patti Knipp (Patti Glenski) attended C.S.U. She was a Flight Attendant for United Airlines based in New York and married in 1962 after her husband graduated from the Air Force Academy. After 12 years in the military, her husband joined Continental Airlines and they eventually moved back to Lakewood. After 23 years of marriage, two children and two grandchildren, she was divorced and went back to work at the

Rocky Flats nuclear plant for nine years. She then worked for Coors Brewing in the Sales Dept. for six years. After retiring from Coors, she does volunteer work at the Democratic Headquarters. She is working on her degree at Regis U., hikes in the mountains and plans the WR class of '58 reunions. Movies, a book club and bridge club occupy her time.

<u>Phil Nichols</u> attended Yakima Valley Junior College and then joined the USMC in July of 1960. He enlisted for a three-year tour, then decided to extend his tour for another three years to become a Marine Security Guard at our Embassies overseas. Upon returning to the U.S. he finished his enlistment and joined the U.S. State Department while attending American University in Washington, D.C. He later opted to go to George Mason College of the University of Virginia where he received a BA degree in Business and Public Administration. He continued his career with the Department of State retiring in 1999. Phil married twice. His first marriage resulted in a divorce and mutual agreement to his custody of their two children, a girl and boy. Seven years later he married Joyce Yutzey, and they are happily married with a son, Marc, who is graduating from the U.S. Air Force Academy in May 2008. Philip and Joyce live in Vienna, VA. They have two grandchildren and no dogs or cats.

<u>Beth Dougherty (Beth Barbich)</u> attended C.S.U. She met her husband, Raymond, at the Wheat Ridge Bowling Alley. It took - they have been married 48 years and focused on family life. They live in Arvada and have two children, four grandchildren and two great grandchildren. Beth has specialized in tax preparation and still works part time as an accountant.

<u>Bill Weiss</u> attended C.U. forever, decided to get married, transferred to Western State College where he graduated in the summer of 1965. Nancy Flora married him in October and they bounced around the domestic oilfields while raising two girls and a boy (they lost Linda to

the Mettawee River in upstate NY in 2004). They lived in Evansville IN, Denver, Pittsburgh, Dallas, and Abilene TX before moving to Socorro, NM in 1985 where Bill worked for 20 years at the Petroleum Recovery Research Center at New Mexico Tech. While at NMT he presented his research groups findings throughout the US as well as Italy, Portugal, Croatia, and India. He is retired but continues to pursue his research interests through Correlations Company. The five man company does contract R&D working with various university research groups if laboratory investigations are required.

Devona Spykstra (Devona Hubka) had two careers: professional model for 16 ½ years and owner of Gold Spike Printing for 28 years with her husband, Joe, who graduated from Lakewood High. Joe is an eight-year cancer survivor and they retired in 2000. They enjoy hosting family reunions and entertaining friends and family with jet-skiing, water-skiing, windsurfing and fishing from their home on Horseshoe Lake in Loveland. They garden and support their grandchildren competing in sports year around – life is good.

Dale Sprinkle served four years in the Marines. Thereafter, he had a career with the L.A. Police Department. Assignments ranged from uniformed patrol, undercover vice, and finally administration. During this time, on a part time basis, Dale went through college and subsequently graduated from law school. After retiring, he farmed a vineyard (for raisin production) in the Fresno area for six years. Thereafter he had a second career as a real estate appraiser for the State of California. From a prior marriage Dale has two boys and three granddaughters. He is married to Ann Kelley and they reside on a narrow peninsula between two bays in "downeast" Maine.

Carol Greenwood (Carol Combs) has moved 31 times since graduating from WRHS. During those years she was a weekend ski instructor, full time mom, legal secretary, an investments broker, a rehabber and a developer. She is divorced, has two children, two grandchildren and in her fifties entered into the frustrating world of foster parenthood. She is an avid reader and movie buff. The last move brought her back to God's country where she is semi-retired and living with a significant other in Evergreen. After an 18 years absence, she is becoming reacquainted with beautiful Colorado.

Roger Bennett) graduated from C.U. with a major in geography that he never used. He married Janie, who also graduated from C.U. with a B.S. in Nursing, in 1963. Roger joined the federal government and retired in Denver after 32 years with the Bureau of Census. He and Janie have two sons, Scott and Brad. His C.U. "minor" in geology led to an interest in rock-hounding. He has traveled widely in the U.S. and outside in search of minerals. He even owned a gold mine. He never struck it rich but is willing. He and Janie enjoy family and traveling and still hope to find The Lost Dutchman.

Karen Carson (Karen Tileston) went to work out of high school attending college classes as needed to advance her career with the Public Service Company in Denver, Pacific Telephone and AT&T in Southern California and Seattle. She took time out to have her daughter, teach dancing and become a Reserve Deputy Sheriff for L.A. County. She retired from AT&T after 27 years and moved to Alaska where she is now a Real Estate Broker. She still enjoys the outdoors and helped organize a local art group, "Artists Without Borders." She loves her friends and her cantankerous cat, Hank. She is having too much fun to retire anytime soon.

Daryl Hall attended C.S.U., majoring in horticulture to continue his family's longtime tradition in landscape nurseries. He started a business, Green Gallery Landscaping, Inc. with his dad in 1974. He later went to work for a large wholesale nursery near Brighton. When a hailstorm wiped out the nursery stock, Daryl retired to travel with his artist wife, Helen. They have two children, a daughter, Susan, who is a math teacher and a son, Dean, who runs three businesses, and two grandchildren.

They travel to shows throughout the western states marketing Helen's works, enjoying life, their Wheat Ridge memories and the "Golden Years."

Judy Crosby (Judy Luntey) married and had three children. She has six grand children, two graduating from high school in May of 2008. She and her husband lived in Jefferson County for 19 years, then moved to Anchorage, Alaska. She worked as a bank teller and then 22 years for the Anchorage School District as an Administrative Assistant. She and husband, Norm, built a home and now live in Palmer, 40 miles north of Anchorage. They are both retired, but enjoy travel, gardening, photography, reading, and life as it comes.

Cliff Miercort attended the University of Colorado majoring in Architectural Engineering, then took a year off for an adventure in Alaska. He worked as a roughneck in the Kenai Peninsula, as a salmon fisherman and built a homesteader's home. He returned to C.U. for a B.S. degree in 1964 and married, Barbara Dolan. He received a Masters in Structural Engineering from the University of Illinois and worked for Shell Oil in New Orleans designing and constructing oil platforms in the Gulf of Mexico. He had a son and daughter and moved to Denver, then to Houston. He was hired by the North American Coal Corporation and after a brief stint in Cleveland, moved to Dallas to head the Southwest Division. He went to the Harvard Business School Advanced Management Program, was made company president and moved the headquarters to Dallas. After 18 years as President and CEO, he retired in 2006. Barbara retired from teaching creative writing at SMU. Cliff is on several boards. He and Barbara have been married 44 years in 2008 and have two granddaughters who live in Dallas.

Phyllis Zailer (Phyllis Shepard) attended one year of college in Salem, W.VA, came home and worked as a legal secretary for 4 years. She married Chuck Zailer in 1962 and had one daughter while living in Denver and loved being a stay-at-home mom. They moved to Scottsdale

AZ for 2-1/2 years where their son was born and then moved to the San Francisco Bay Area in 1967. While the kids were in grade school, she fell into a job at their church as a church secretary and worked at a couple of churches for a total of 25 years and loved the jobs (most of the time!). They have one grandson 17 and a granddaughter 3 (one from each child). They lived in Santa Clara, CA for 28 years until 2000 when they moved to Lincoln Hills Sun City in Lincoln, CA (Sacramento area) and have both retired. They both volunteer at the California State Railroad Museum. She helps in the office occasionally and Chuck is a docent and helps on the excursion railroad. They live close enough to the Bay Area to still see their families as often as they can.

Kent Schroeder married Sally Salter from WRHS in 1962, graduated from C.U. in 1963 and University of Denver Law School in 1967. He went into private practice and later became a Public Defender and then an Adams County Attorney. He became a judge-appointed Magistrate from 1988-2000 covering domestic relations and juveniles. Ken and Sally are retired and have a daughter, Lisa Fay and a son, David both of whom live in Colorado.

Sheila Christy (Sheila Stoll) attended CSU, married and had two sons, Steve, who lives in Chicago and Tom, who lives in Steamboat Springs. She was later divorced and received a Masters degree from Webster State College in Gunnison. She remarried Tom Christy in 1999 and they traveled the world before Tom passed away. She still enjoys travel and music and living in Grand Junction.

Gary Atkins attended CSU, then went into the Army and to Vietnam where he was a radio-intercept operator for the"Agency." He worked for Denver Public Schools, then for Telemation as a salesman. He then returned to CSU as a Senior Engineer for TV Services. He is married to the former Lorene McIrvin of Cope, CO. They have one daughter, one son, two grandchildren and are retired in Ft. Collin CO.

<u>Elaine Miller (Elaine Obialero)</u> received a PhD (Doctor of Philosophy) from the University of Denver, where her dissertation on word productivity using computers was published in English and translated into other languages, and included a Communication Cognate. Her prior studies comprised an undergraduate and Master's Degree from the University of Colorado and Business Administration from the University of Denver. She has four children and lived with them in Denver CO, Lido/Long Beach NY on the ocean, and had a condo in Copper Mountain, CO. She resides with her second husband in Rancho Mirage, CA for the winter and Littleton, CO during the summer. Her interests include travel, reading, photography, theatre, hiking, skiing, golf, tennis and attending spectator sports. Her early piano playing and hearing Italian opera at home provided interests in music, including opera and the symphony. She enjoys riding her black Vespa in California. She has six grandchildren and four toy poodles.

<u>William Perry Smith</u> graduated from the University of Colorado in 1963 with a B.S. in Business Administration. He moved to SC and worked for Monsanto for 17 years as a supervisor in the textile industry. He opened his own computer retail store, Greenwood Computers, Inc. in 1981. In 1985 he joined the MicroAge Group and also served on their dealer advisory board. In 1995 he foresaw the importance of Internet Service Providers and started Emerald Internet Services, a very successful ISP business. Perry and his wife, Sue, had three sons: Todd, a retired U.S. Navy Chief Petty officer, Scott and Bryan. He was a pilot, owned his own airplane and was a great golfer. He retired and moved to Pawleys Island SC where he passed away in 2006.

<u>Kay Schoonmaker (Katherine Donaldson)</u> graduated from the University of Colorado School of Nursing in 1964. Her first RN job was at Ft. Logan Mental Health Center in Englewood, CO where she unexpectedly bumped into her childhood friend, Polly Sue, the subject of her first story. In 1967 for fun and adventure she moved to Los Angeles, CA with a friend. She worked first as a psychiatric nurse

and then as a public health nurse. In L.A. she met her husband, Gary, who worked for Oscar Mayer Foods. In 1973 they were transferred to Madison, WI where they have lived ever since. They have three grown children and three grand children. In WI Kay has worked mainly in public health with a primary focus on geriatrics. Aside from the grandchildren, her interests are traveling, creative writing, bridge, and reading. Skiing and softball were included in those interests when she was younger.

The Way We Were

1949-1953

4th - 8th Grades

4ᵗʰ Grade

5th Grade

6th Grade

7th Grade

8ᵗʰ Grade

The Way We Are
from
The Reunions

20, 25, 30, 40, 45th

WheatRidge High School
Class of 1958
20th Year Reunion
Aug. 12, 1978

20th Reunion
Rolling Hills Country Club
1978
Photo by F.W. "Bill" Worthen

25th Reunion
Rolling Hills Country Club
1983
photo by Joyce Cook (now Joyce Jay)
Legends J Photo LLC –
Wheat Ridge, CO

30th Reunion
Winter Park, Colorado
1988
photo by Joyce Cook (now Joyce Jay)
Legends J Photo LLC –
Wheat Ridge, CO

**40th Reunion
Vail, Colorado
1998**
photo by Wayne Barbich

45th Reunion
Estes Park, Colorado
2003
photo by Wayne Barbich

Fifty Years Later
By Daryl Hall

It's hard to believe it's been 50 years
Since we left old Wheat Ridge High
With hopes and dreams of life to come
Of conquering all we tried

Some things we conquered sometimes we failed
To reach our lofty goals
But up we jumped and dusted off
Becoming weathered souls

We thought adults had all the answers
But finding we were wrong
We re-accessed our bumpy ride
And found we could be strong

We found the more we learned in life
The less we really knew
Mom and Dad didn't know all of life
But were there to help us through

Now we have kids and they have kids
And they look to you and me
For support in their same journey
To be all that they can be

But little do they know of us
While some hopes have grown cold
There still are many things to do
Before we all grow old!

Acknowledgements

The Class of '58 owes its undying thanks to Patti Glenski Knipp and Beth Barbich Dougherty whose unceasing efforts over the years have kept our class contacts and reunions going. The efforts to maintain constantly changing rosters of names, addresses, emails, births, deaths and marriages most often go unnoticed but not unappreciated. Others have helped, but these two good women have kept us together.

We also thank the photographers who captured our changing features over the years: A.C. Martin from grade school days, our photographer from the 20th reunion F.W. "Bill" Worthen could not be located, but then Joyce Cook (now Joyce Jay) of Legends J Photo LLC in Wheat Ridge took our 25th and 30th. Wayne Barbich, brother of Beth, captured our 40th and 45th and will be there for our 50th, God-willing and the creeks don't rise. We also thank Mr. Doug Granbery, teacher, Wheat Ridge High School and Advisor for "The Agrarian," the new WRHS yearbook, for coordinating permission for us to print pages and photos from our 1958 yearbook, The Remraf, (Framer spelled backwards).

40 of our classmates chose to write two stories for this book about school days and later life. Writing comes easy to some, arduous to most. We thank the authors for their efforts to share their travel through life's hills and valleys and for their photos. For those who chose not to write: thanks for being our friends and family. You produced the memories that made these stories possible.

To our teachers, coaches, mentors and schoolmates in other classes: thanks for giving us the skills, tools, examples, perspectives, advice and contacts that launched us into life and thanks for teaching us to laugh.

To our 29 deceased classmates: we miss you very much.

To my sometimes understanding wife and former classmate, Rose, who offered her proof-reading skills for free: thank you. Now you can stop yelling, "Get off that damned computer!"

The Editor

Postscript

"The sun cut itself on the Rocky Mountains to the west
and bled memories onto the plains below…"

…the class of 1958, Wheat Ridge High School

Printed in the United States
122954LV00002B/161/P